The Next Big Thing

The Next Big Thing

Spotting and forecasting consumer trends for profit

William Higham

**KOGAN
PAGE**

London and Philadelphia

Publisher's note

Every possible effort has been made to ensure that the information contained in this book is accurate at the time of going to press, and the publishers and authors cannot accept responsibility for any errors or omissions, however caused. No responsibility for loss or damage occasioned to any person acting, or refraining from action, as a result of the material in this publication can be accepted by the editor, the publisher or any of the authors.

First published in Great Britain and the United States in 2009 by Kogan Page Limited

120 Pentonville Road
London N1 9JN
United Kingdom
www.koganpage.com

525 South 4th Street, #241
Philadelphia PA 19147
USA

© William Higham, 2009

ISBN 978 0 7494 5450 0

British Library Cataloguing-in-Publication Data

A CIP record for this book is available from the British Library.

Library of Congress Cataloging-in-Publication Data

Higham, William.
    The next big thing : spotting and forecasting consumer trends for profit / William Higham.
        p. cm.
    Includes bibliographical references and index.
    ISBN 978-0-7494-5450-0 (alk. paper)
 1. Consumer behavior--Forecasting. 2. New products. 3. Sales forecasting. I. Title.
    HF5415.32.H54 2009
    658.8'342--dc22
                            2009017056

Typeset by Saxon Graphics Ltd, Derby
Printed and bound in India by Replika Press Pvt Ltd   448 0716

To my family and all the friends who supported or put up with me while I wrote. And to all those who have dedicated their lives to spotting trends.

Contents

Acknowledgements

This book was made possible by the actions and assistance of a huge number of people. My family (Jean, Norman and Kathy), friends (too many to name) and colleagues (Jo Peters, Pippa Chandler, Sean Pillot de Chenecey, Jo Rigby *et al*) have given their continued support through a life of trends. Those who were of particular help during the writing process were: Laura James, Louise Donald, Louise Voss, Richard Milner, Becky Fincham and especially my patient editor Jon Finch. Many from across the globe agreed to be interviewed for the book, contributing not just their time but their knowledge and experience too: P T Black, Mark Broughton, Sheila Byfield, Dave Capper, Hanna Chalmers, Stephen Dalton, Denise Drummond-Dunn, Sue Elms, Gavin Emsden, Ewan Adams, Annie Freel, Wayne Garvie, Michele Giles, Phil Guest, Rod Henwood, Alison Hughes, Amanda Meers, Bruno Montejorge, Alex Owens, Tom Pickles, Liisa Puolakka, Tim Richards, Jo Rigby, Andy Routley, Andy Shaw, Steve Simpson, Craig Thayer, Helene Venge, Camilla Vickerage and Brechje Vissers. And all my clients over the years have allowed me to spend my time studying trends and gave me the experience and financial stability to get here today. Thanks. It's been a great ride so far.

Introduction: Predicting success

It is hard to escape the word 'trends' today. We are constantly told that A is 'in' but B is 'out', that X is 'cool' or Y is 'hot'. Fashion magazines regale us with the latest catwalk trends. Colours next year will be vibrant or monochromatic, hemlines high or low. Newspapers provide us with the latest house market, parenting and even Christmas toy trends. Technology magazines predict new product trends from electronic books to intelligent fridges. The word is increasingly heard in commercial circles too. Business publications explain how the latest media and purchase trends may kill off television advertising or bricks-and-mortar retail. Conferences are scheduled on trends in marketing or online practices. Insight directors are asked to explain trends among teens, tweens and early adopters. But little is said about how to actively use trends on a practical level, where to look for them, how to predict which industry they will affect next, and how they can be spotted and then utilized within the business process.

Identifying trends can provide enormous benefits for companies across a range of sectors. And it is increasingly important in today's rapidly changing world. Yet the process of utilizing trends in the marketing process is still hugely under-explored. The exploitation of trends today is, even in otherwise far-sighted companies, often an *ad hoc* process. Companies that want to use trend data typically have to navigate their own course through the process by trial and error. There is little agreement within the marketing or research community on how to determine which trends will grow or last, and the best way to exploit them. I believe strongly that this should not be the case. Consumer trends are far too important for their inclusion and utilization to be left to chance. The confusing and often secret world of trends should be opened up. Recognized, formal methodologies should be developed to enable effective exploitation of trends.

I have been professionally identifying, interpreting and implementing trends on behalf of my clients for almost 10 years. But I have had a passion for trends for as long as I can remember. Growing up in the cultural melting pot of the 1970s, I was fascinated with how one fashion style, film or music genre could flourish and then disappear, to be swiftly replaced by another. I spent my formative working years working for record companies and learned there how trends in music consumption could make or break an artist. At concerts I would often spend more time studying trends among the audience than I did looking at the bands! Since then I have spent years working with clients to help them better exploit potential changes in their markets. I have helped companies expand their markets, create successful new products, adopt more cost-effective marketing and distribution channels and even extricate themselves from unsuitable sectors. I have studied and advised on trends from banking to beer drinking, luxury to low-cost and tweens to Greys.

My aim in writing this book is twofold. I want to use my experience and knowledge of trends to strip away the ambiguity and mystery that surround them, to provide a straightforward introduction to the topic, to clarify meanings and to debunk myths. I also want to offer some suggestions for a standardized trend analysis and implementation process that I call 'trend marketing', and to show how it can be learned, practised and incorporated into everyday business practice.

For this reason I have divided the book into two sections: 'Trends' and 'Trend marketing'. In the former, I consider what trends are and why they are important, how they start, how they can affect every industry sector and every customer segmentation, and how understanding and anticipating them can help you target customers more effectively, expand current markets or establish new ones, and develop more desirable products and communications campaigns. I give examples of companies and sectors that have profited from trends and others that have missed them, and provide practical tips on how to approach trends: from avoiding fads to running a trends team.

In the second section I offer a suggested framework for the trend marketing process. I look at how to identify trends before they reach the mainstream: how to discover them in nightclubs and government reports, focus groups and online forums; how to predict the way a trend will develop; how to determine if and when trends will affect your industry and your customers, and how long they will last; what the most effective ways are to respond to trends and use them to power your business; how to exploit positive trends, avoid negative ones, take up opportunities and halt threats; what the ways are to convince others of the importance of a trend and how to integrate it into company policy; and how to use trends to create more effective strategy across all 4 Ps of the marketing process.

Effective trend analysis is a collaborative process. While researching the book I interviewed dozens of professionals about their dealings with trends. They ranged from marketing directors and brand managers to global media agency insight directors and independent research consultants. They are employed across a variety of sectors: from FMCGs, telecoms and finance to toys, film and fashion. And they are located across the globe, from Chicago to Beijing, Sao Paolo to Amsterdam. They represent the varied professionals who are at the coalface of trends, regularly scanning, sifting and sorting them to try to determine what is going to happen tomorrow, and how to turn that to their company's advantage. Their practical knowledge further informed my understanding of the process, and my own comments in the book are regularly prefaced by theirs.

I have a passion for and belief in the commercial power of trends. By the end of this book I hope you will share them both. On the way I hope you will also gain vital, practical information about where trends come from, how they spread, what impact they can have, and how they can make you and your company a great deal of money.

Section 1

TRENDS

Part 1

The value of trends

1

The importance of trends

THE MEANING OF CONSUMERS

My mantra has always been that you need to know what the consumer is doing. There are lots of matrices that seek to explain how the world is changing, but consumer insight is by far the most effective.

Wayne Garvie, Director of Production and Content, BBC

Marketing is about meeting consumer needs. To do this successfully, you need to first understand what consumers' needs are.

Amanda Meers, Group Account Director, Jigsaw Strategic Research
(Australia)

Consumers are incredibly powerful. Their behaviours have a massive impact on society and business alike. What consumers do, how they behave and how they think affect not just business but society as a whole. This is as true in the leisure industry as it is in food manufacturing. It is as true in India as it is in the United States. No matter what territory or sector a company is working in, consumer attitudes and behaviours are of the utmost importance. Consumers drive consumption and purchase behaviours. They are the basis of commerce itself. Without anyone to buy, there is no point in selling. As marketing guru Peter Drucker said: 'There is one valid definition of business purpose: to create a customer.'[1]

Consumers also drive innovation. Companies are constantly trying to 'second-guess' consumer tastes. To keep up with changing consumer demand, manufacturers launch huge numbers of new products. Twenty thousand new products per month are recorded by Mintel's New Product Database.[2] But nothing new can thrive unless consumers are willing to accept it. Huge numbers of innovations fail. In one study, only 56 per cent of 11,000 new products launched by 77 different companies were still on the market five years later.[3] In another a full 83 per cent of new products failed to meet their marketing objectives.[4] Some products and services fail because they are poorly designed, others because they are poorly marketed or underfinanced. But the vast majority fail because consumers simply do not want the product. It might not fulfil a current need. Consumers may not yet be ready to accept it. Or conversely it may seem too old-fashioned for them. This is true for marketing too. A campaign will succeed only if it appeals to current consumer attitudes and behaviours. Its tone must resonate with consumers. It must be on a platform that the market frequents.

To avoid marketing and NPD failure requires an understanding not just of current consumer needs but of how those needs are changing. Companies can drastically reduce failure rates for new products, services or marketing campaigns if they know when they are planned how consumers will be thinking and behaving when they launch. Correctly predicting consumer attitudes and behaviours is a way of 'future-proofing' business strategy. It enables companies to better determine consumer response rates and potential demand.

THE MEANING OF CHANGE

Understanding how consumers are changing is absolutely critical. If you haven't a razor-sharp consumer insight at the very beginning you've got problems. It's integral to the marketing process.

Andy Routley, International Brand Marketing Director, Miller, SAB Miller

Understanding change should be at the centre of what any company does. I can't think of a brand or a company that wouldn't need to know the ways in which their consumers are changing.

Helene Venge, Global Director, Business Development, Lego Group (Denmark)

Marketers need to understand the behaviours and attitudes of their customers. That is a basic marketing principle. And it would be a relatively easy task if they remained the same. But they do not. Consumers change. When they do, it can affect many different facets of their life. It changes consumption patterns and drivers. It can affect what they want, how they want it presented, and when and where they want to get it. Companies need to recognize these changes. When your customers change, it can affect what and how they buy from you. If a significant enough number change, it may force you to revise your entire marketing and development strategy. If you do not, you could lose their custom. And even if you do so, but do it more slowly than your competitors, you could lose market share.

Consumer change has always been an important social and economic driver. It has had an effect on every sector and in every nation. It has made an enormous impact on the profits, strategies and structure of brands, products and even whole industries. On a micro level, consumer change has driven design and fashion styles for centuries: from beards, ruffs and tapestries in medieval times to long hair, jeans and posters in the 1960s. But on a global scale it has been responsible for stopping wars and starting religions, toppling governments and creating new markets. Modifications to consumers' circumstances and environments can radically change their attitudes and behaviours, which in turn drives political and commercial change. The Swinging Sixties, the student protests of 1968 and the inward focus of the 1970s Me Generation were all catalysed by fluctuations in birth rates and income levels. Changes in attitudes among the Russian people encouraged reformist policies (*perestroika*, *glasnost*) that ultimately led to an ending of the Cold War. Shifting consumer attitudes to global warming are today forcing governments and industries alike to alter their environmental policies.

Ask bond traders and they will tell you that a lot can happen in a day. But a lot more can happen in a week, a year or a decade. Remarkable change can occur in just a few years. It took only four years from President Roosevelt asking scientists to build atomic bombs to their initial manufacture. The moon landings took place just eight years after Kennedy first asked NASA to put a man on the moon.

Compare consumer behaviours today to those of 10 or 20 years ago. Even in the single field of personal technology usage, change rates have been remarkable. In 1989, computers were a minority interest. Just 15 per cent of US households owned a computer,[5] and the average household spent less than $300 per year on home computer products.[6] Amiga, Commodore, Atari, Amstrad and Sinclair computers were still popular, and floppy disks still standard. Mouse-driven computers such as the Apple Macintosh had been introduced just five years before. The CD ROM had just been launched but was yet to become an industry standard. It would be six years before the first mass-market web browsers were launched and mainstream consumers introduced to the internet. Some executives owned cellular telephones, but they were impractical and unreliable and typically so large and heavy they could only be installed as car phones. The first commercial GSM network would not be available for two years. VHS had just won the format battle with Betamax. Consumers would not start using

DVDs for another 10 years. The CD was just five years old, made up less than a third of all recorded music sales[7] and could not yet be used for recording. Digital cameras would not be available commercially for another two years, and MP3 players for another 10.

By 1999, technology usage had changed radically. The internet had revolutionized computer use. Approximately half of US households now owned a computer.[8] Windows 95 and 98 had enabled mainstream consumers to access the web easily. The cell phone market too had grown enormously. With commercial text services just two years old, Britons were already sending 5 million text messages a month. The DVD format had been launched in the United States just two years before and just a year before in Europe, but already DVDs were being purchased more than VHS. In the music industry, CD sales now dominated, constituting almost 90 per cent of all recorded music sales.[9] The first hard-disk MP3 player was launched, but was seen by consumers as little more than a novelty. Walkmans and Discmans still dominated. But there was still room for growth. Although Google and eBay had just been launched, they were still known only to a few consumers. And sites such as MySpace, Facebook and YouTube were all years away. Consumers still did not have access to ringtones, camera and music phones or the 3G network. They had begun to use PDAs, but these typically had less than 500 kB of memory.

Fast-forward to today and usage patterns are barely recognizable. A billion consumers own personal computers worldwide. About 180 million are likely to *replace* their PCs this year alone.[10] Three billion consumers now use a cell phone. That represents over half of the entire global population.[11] Between them, cell phone users send 2 trillion text messages per year.[12] The once-novel CD is losing its dominance to the new MP3 format. Legal sales of the latter now make up 12 per cent of all recorded music sales, with millions more each year downloaded free. MP3 players are no longer a novelty: they have become ubiquitous. Over 163 million consumers own iPods,[13] and 50 million own Sony Ericsson Walkman phones.[14]

The effect of all these changes in technology use has been enormous. Digitization and the ubiquity of computer and cell phone use has altered not just the way consumers behave but the way they think. And change has driven commerce. As consumers have adopted some products and not others, they have driven development strategies. Their choices have encouraged the growth of some industries and helped bring down others. Personal technology purchase is no longer limited to young early adopters, but has spread to the very oldest members of society. New purchase drivers, from portability to convergence, have come to dominate commerce.

Such radical change has not been limited to technology use. It is true of finance too. Twenty-five years ago, chequebooks were commonplace.

Consumers were still getting used to credit. The first American Express credit card had launched just two years before and the Discover card only a year before that. But today, there are over 170 million credit cards in the United States.[15] Over half of all US consumers have two or more credit cards, and the average citizen has four.[16] The average US household owes almost $10,000 in credit card debt.[17] And many retailers no longer accept cheques. As with technology use, this has affected behaviours and attitudes that have in turn affected sales and strategy.

Even a sector such as health and fitness has seen a wealth of change in recent decades. In the 1970s when consumers felt ill they consulted their doctor. Apart from that they did not typically consider their health. There was little public concern over the detrimental effects of fat, salt or nicotine. Those consumers who were interested in healthy or organic food were considered 'faddish'. Only sportspeople exercised regularly. But in the 1980s consumers began to show a greater interest in their health. There was an enormous growth in personal fitness regimes like aerobics. Weight and heart disease started to become of more concern. By the 1990s many consumers had become interested in the concept of holistic health and well-being. They began to explore alternative remedies and fitness regimes, from organic food to yoga. Gym memberships rocketed. Sales of cigarettes and fatty foods started to decline. Today personal health has become a key life priority and food purchase driver for millions of consumers. Smoking is banned in public places across dozens of territories. There is a trend away from gyms to the 'natural fitness' of walking, running and cycling. Again, behavioural change has had a massive impact both on consumer purchase patterns and on commercial strategies.

When consumers alter their behaviours and attitudes, it has an enormous impact on society and commerce alike. Today's changing consumer behaviours are forcing companies to rethink strategies and revenue models across all sectors: from food to cars, financial services to personal technology. It is these changing consumer patterns that researchers refer to when they talk about 'trends'.

THE MEANING OF TRENDS

A trend is something that's going to happen that's really going to strike a chord amongst the 'Joe Bloggs', the people of our everyday society: something that we need to be aware of because it's going to be impactful.

Alison Hughes, UK Agent, Carlin International

The term 'trend' can be confusing. It means different things to different people and in different contexts. To scientists it typically means the direction of a curve. To the fashion industry, it means the latest styles. To traditionalists, it is a pejorative term meaning something ephemeral. To a media planner it might mean new media consumption patterns. Running an online search for the word 'trends' produces some diverse examples:

- 'A recent history of trends in vegetation greenness and large-scale ecosystem disturbances in Eurasia...'
- 'A history of trends in punishment from the end of the 18th century to the present...'
- 'Trends in intake of trans-fatty acids...'
- 'Trends in disk drive technology...'

The term clearly requires a tighter definition for marketing purposes. The word 'trend' was first used in the 16th century as a verb meaning 'to run or bend in a certain direction'. It is a derivation of the Old English 'trendan', which meant 'to roll about, turn or revolve'. It was first used as a noun in the 18th century, meaning 'the way something bends'. Its application was initially limited to science, particularly as related to natural phenomena such as a coastline or a mountain range. The term began to be used more generally in the 19th century to refer to the way in which anything changed. The textile industry, for instance, began to use the term to refer to changes in design styles.

But usage was still typically limited to the scientific and commercial world until the 1960s. It was at this point that media and public alike began to use the term. This was no coincidence. The 1960s was an era when the idea of 'newness' itself began to be celebrated. Politicians and the media championed the idea of the new. President Kennedy accepted his party's nomination for presidential candidate with the following words: 'Today our concern must be with that future. For the world is changing. The old era is ending. The old ways will not do.' Taking his cue from the White House, British prime minister Harold Wilson talked excitedly about submitting industry to the 'white heat of technological change'. Fashion, film and music were celebrated for the very speed of their adaptation. Musical artists like the Beatles, designers like Mary Quant, models such as Twiggy and photographers like David Bailey were celebrated for the rapidity of their rise to fame. The word 'trend' was used to refer to these cultural and stylistic changes. The terms 'trendsetter' and 'trendy' were coined in 1960 and 1962 respectively.

Today the social and scientific meanings coexist. A trend is defined as 'A line of general direction or movement... a prevailing tendency or inclination… the general movement over time of a statistically detectable change… [or] a current style or preference'.[18]

CONSUMER TRENDS

The trends that matter are the trends that show how consumers are changing.

Wayne Garvie, Director of Production and Content, BBC

Such a definition is too broad for the purposes of marketing. The only directions and styles marketers need be concerned with are the ones that directly affect them. And when it comes to marketing, it is the consumer who matters. What a marketer needs to predict is *consumer* trends. These are the trends that will drive strategy and make the difference between profit and loss.

Non-consumer trends are important for marketers only in so far as they drive consumer behaviours. What is happening to products, industries or the economy might help drive that change. But what is important is the effect it will have on consumers. The job of trend forecasters is to try to predict what their customers are going to think or do tomorrow, and find ways to utilize that in company strategy. Just knowing what products are being launched cannot explain that. Product trends are like a menu. A customer is not necessarily going to order something just because it is on the menu. Ask those restaurateurs who have tried to sell kangaroo steaks or reindeer pâté. Financial trends too have no immediate benefit. Just knowing the direction house prices are moving in does not in itself dictate what consumers are going to do. Product and financial trends are useful only as offering clues as to how consumers will behave. Knowing what products are available to a consumer helps predict what products they might use. And if a major manufacturer is developing a particular type of product, this suggests the manufacturer has evidence of strong consumer demand for it. Financial trends also offer clues as to how consumers might behave. Consumers concerned that their house value is falling are typically more wary of borrowing and spending money, and more likely to do home improvements. In a marketing context therefore a trend is: 'a change that occurs among consumers'.

But what is it that is changing? To understand consumers, marketers need to know how their behaviours are changing. Are they watching television less? Are they shopping online more? But marketers also need to know the way consumers' attitudes are changing too. Are consumers more concerned today with the environmental impact or provenance of a product? Has the economic downturn affected their attitude to value? Consequently, a trend should be defined as: 'a change in consumer *attitudes and behaviours*'.

It is also important to set a time frame for trends. Small cohorts of consumers can change their behaviours for a short period of time. But this is not a trend. It is just a fad (see Chapter 12). Knowing about such minor changes might perhaps be of use in short-term, tactical marketing campaigns. But it cannot help effectively in determining marketing strategy. The changes in consumer behaviour that matter to marketers are the ones that deepen and last. So for marketing purposes a trend needs to be defined as: 'a *long-term* change in consumer attitudes and behaviours'.

Finally, a trend is of interest to a marketer only if it provides a return. Changes that cannot be exploited for profit should be discounted. In marketing terms, therefore, a trend is best defined as: 'a long-term change in consumer attitudes and behaviours that offers *marketing opportunities*'.

NOTES

1. Peter Drucker, *The Practice of Management*, Harper & Row, 1954
2. Mintel, 2008
3. Kuczmarski & Associates, 1993
4. Group EFO Ltd Marketing News, 1993
5. Bureau of the Census, 1991
6. Research Alert, March 2002
7. RIAA, 2008
8. US Department of Commerce, 2000
9. RIAA, 2008
10. Gartner, June 2008
11. International Telecommunication Union, February 2008
12. Strategy Analytics, 2007
13. Apple, 2008
14. Sony, 2008
15. US Census Bureau, 2006
16. Experian, 2007
17. Gfk Roper, 2007
18. *Merriam Webster Dictionary*, 2008

2

The relevance of trends

TRENDS TODAY

I find it difficult to see how you can be in marketing today and ignore trends. Unless you pick up on change you're running to catch up. You can't do anything without knowing about trends.

Annie Freel, Head of Knowledge, McCain Foods

Trends have always been important, but knowledge of consumer trends is more vital than ever today. The commercial world is being influenced in ways that make it more and more important to understand how its customers are changing. The speed of consumer and product change, the blurring of traditional demographic boundaries, the growing power of the consumer and the nature of globalism are all making trend determination a necessity. Trends can help companies make sense of their market in time of change. They can help companies navigate through the enormous number of changes that are taking place across the world today. Systematic analysis of change patterns and cultural dynamics can help companies avoid retreating markets, adapt marketing to changing attitudes, and even identify and target whole new markets.

ACCELERATED CHANGE

When I talk to my kids, they look at me in disbelief and say 'I don't know why you're making a fuss, Dad. Yes, we've got this big TV and, yes, we've got computers in every room in the house. But so what?' That's all they've known growing up. They don't know any other way.

Phil Guest, Managing Director Western Europe, Sulake

Previously you could do things in the traditional way and you'd be OK. But not any more. I think people are more open to insights now that traditional advertising opportunities are no longer enough.

Sue Elms, EVP Global Media Practice, Millward Brown

The relative importance of trends to business practices fluctuates. In periods of behavioural and attitudinal stability, trends have less impact on the marketing mix. At such times companies can rely much more on best practice in traditional marketing. If their customers' attitudes and behaviours remain constant, companies can focus on the best ways to exploit current needs, rather than having to continuously identify and then exploit new ones. But in a period of change, traditional consumer markets can no longer be relied upon. Innovation is key, and survival increasingly rests on the whim of the consumer. Companies that continue to target the same market in the same way can find sales falling away, as that market develops new behaviours or new attitudes. Customers may decide they no longer need a product. Or they may want to purchase it in a different form or on a different platform or via a different channel. Alternatively, consumers who previously had no interest in a product may become a potential market, so need to be targeted. The more markets change, the more important it is to pick up on trends.

This makes trends particularly important now, because today's world is far from stable. Trends have affected governments and businesses alike for centuries, but increasing rates of consumer change are making trends more important than ever now. One of the most common concerns I hear from clients today is how hard it is to keep up with changing consumer patterns. This is as true for directors of marketing or new product development (NPD) as for insight directors.

Change rates today are faster than ever. New products are being introduced more and more often. One hundred and eighty-two thousand new products were introduced globally in 2006: a 17 per cent increase on 2005 figures and more than double the growth rate seen between 2004 and 2005.[1] The speed of product and behaviour turnovers is increasing. Americans change their cell phone every 18 months[2] and Koreans even more frequently.[3] Consumers are becoming accustomed to change. More than two-thirds of cell phone users expect that music phones will replace portable music devices.[4] Almost half of all Britons believe that today's traditional TV schedules will be 'a thing of the past' in 10 years' time. Over half of British under-24-year-olds believe the CD will die out within five years.[5] Consumers are becoming more acclimatized too to multi-platform and multi-sector brands, products and services. It is considered perfectly acceptable today for a company like Apple to manufacture computers,

MP3 players *and* phones, or for Ferrari, Jaguar and now even Humvee to manufacture men's scents as well as cars. Consumers are increasingly platform and brand promiscuous. They are increasingly less afraid of trialling upmarket or unusual products, and crave novelty.

BOUNDARY BLURRING

The scope of change is greater too today. Many things we have taken for granted for decades are changing. Several of our longest-lasting traditions are open to adaptation. Trends are impacting across an increasing number of sectors, markets and demographics. Change is taking place among young and old, male and female, rich and poor alike. Consumer segmentations, life stages, opinions and behaviours are all evolving. Traditional platforms and channels are being bypassed and new ones utilized.

We are seeing a blurring of accepted boundaries and a breaking down of established barriers across an enormous number of sectors and demographics. Today few if any of our traditional consumer segmentations can be taken for granted. Traditional segmentations are changing, across age, gender and social grade. What constitutes key markets is changing. For instance, in the 1960s and 1970s populations across Europe were relatively young, but today this is no longer true. Grey (55-plus years) and Greying (45–54 years) markets are becoming increasingly important. Throughout the European Union the proportion of people aged over 50 is rising dramatically. Half of the population of Italy, for instance, will be over 50 by 2030.[6] And it is not just about weight of numbers: it is about financial influence too. Today's typically healthy and home-owning 50-plus age group looks set to be tomorrow's most affluent and highest-spending consumer segment. If relative amounts spent on leisure by under- and over-50s remain constant, we will see the proportion of all leisure spending accounted for by the 50-plus rise from 40 per cent today to 50 per cent in 2050.[7]

Meanwhile, even what constitutes old and young is changing. Today's 'New Old' grew up in the 1960s so have very different expectations to their parents. Today's young people are increasingly 'adult' in their approach to life. Gender and class boundaries too are increasingly blurred. Female and male interests, behaviours and purchase habits are merging. Women buy as many cars and personal technology products today as men, while men are the fastest-growing target demographic in the skincare market. High and low social grades are purchasing across similar categories. Limousines, flat-screen TVs and champagne are no longer limited to high net worth individuals (HNWIs).

Even the 'fourth wall' between consumers and producers – what constitutes a producer as opposed to a consumer, or a writer compared to a reader – is becoming less and less clear. Many of those who were once happy simply being viewers or readers are now creating their own content. They are no longer satisfied just to view or read their favourite media. They increasingly want to contribute to it too: uploading their *own* content as well as downloading someone else's. There are almost 80 million blogs today globally: up from 8 million in 2005.[8] Increasing numbers of consumers are even merging their real and fantasy worlds by taking part in massive online games. Their virtual selves or 'avatars' have lifestyles their real selves could never achieve. Still biggest in Asia Pacific, these games are proving increasingly popular with US and European consumers too. One single game, World of Warcraft, has 9 million players globally.

CONSUMER IS KING

You have to listen more to your consumers today in terms of what they think the brand stands for, what it means to them. They expect to have something to say in how the brand should develop or what it should say. And they have become much more proactive in terms of finding the information they want. This means you have to know a lot more about them.

Helene Venge, Global Director, Business Development,
Lego Group (Denmark)

Trends are more important now. It's harder to reach everyone at one time, so you need to understand trends within individual groups or tribes. And with the rise in word of mouth, trends can give you data on the right places to start having a dialogue with consumers.

Liisa Puolakka, Head of Brand Identity, Nokia

The power that consumers have over commercial decision making is also changing. The individual is becoming more powerful. New consumer behaviours are altering the way brands do business. Factors such as technology, brand development and economics still have a key role to play. But consumers are increasingly driving communications and marketing behaviours. This too is making the need for trend information even greater.

A few decades ago, successful mass-marketing campaigns were customary. Changes among particular consumer segments were of less importance. What mattered was how the vast majority behaved. Today cost-effective mass marketing is harder and harder to achieve. Traditional marketing channels have diversified. New channels are appearing.

Consumers are utilizing different media and environments for different behaviours. Targeted marketing is proving increasingly important. In such an environment, changes in consumer behaviours have a much greater impact on sales.

Customers are becoming more confident, more demanding and less loyal. Today's more affluent consumers are able to pick and choose from a broader range of products, so expect greater quality and service from their brands. In the mobile sector, customers can choose from a huge range of handset brands, carriers, tariffs, fascias and bolt-ons from cameras to MP3 players. The web is massively increasing the amount of products consumers have to choose from. Netflix offers tens of thousands of movies, Amazon hundreds of thousands of books, iTunes millions of songs and eBay tens of millions of sellers. The average French citizen receives over 50 commercial messages on the TV each day.[9] There are 1,500 newspapers[10] and 8,500 magazines[11] currently published in the UK alone. The total amount of digital information sent in 2007 alone would have filled over 160 billion iPod Shuffles.[12]

Many customers are also relying more on their own judgements and opinions. As trust levels fall and personal access to data grows, consumers are typically becoming more self-reliant. They are increasingly turning to the internet in search of information and advice. Technology has encouraged the trend, with review and comparison websites allowing easier correlation of products' quality and price. A wealth of information on various conditions and ailments has led to the growth of the self-diagnosing, and often self-treating, patient. The number of medical searches across most EU regions has risen in the last two years. In Britain, 60 per cent of adults have gone online in search of health information,[13] and sales of self-diagnostic kits have increased by almost 30 per cent in the last five years alone.[14] The global e-health industry is now estimated to be worth around €11 billion.[15] Consumers are also increasingly trusting the judgements of *other* consumers too. Word of mouth is having a greater influence on purchase decisions. 'Friends and relatives' are a more popular source of information for consumers than television in two-thirds of European countries. Seventy-five per cent of people over 40 in Spain and 60 per cent in Italy are influenced by friends', family's or colleagues' opinions when deciding what film to watch.[16]

Formal and informal peer-to-peer (P2P) recommendation opportunities are growing: from the aggregated 'reader reviews' on Amazon or Metacritic, to pure P2P recommendation sites such as communal travel recommender IGoUGo. And as brand influence declines and consumers become more aware of their own power, they are starting to flex their collective muscles. We are seeing more consumer protests and boycotts and other forms of user-generated *dis*content. Today's technology allows the rapid dissemination of anti-brand information. Disaffected consumers can no longer be ignored.

The more choice consumers have and the more they dictate their own decisions, the more commercial power they have. The more power they have, the more important it is to identify and predict changes in attitudes and behaviours before they adversely affect your business.

GLOBALISM

Trends are increasingly global because of the speed that information travels at. Today you can be friendly with the person next to you or the person round the other side of the world. A 16-year-old in Moscow has more in common with a 16-year-old in London now than they do with a 21-year-old in Moscow.

Sheila Byfield, Leader, Business Planning, Mindshare

Another reason consumer trend knowledge is increasingly important today is the growth of global communication. Our world is more open to the impact of trends. In previous centuries, countries and communities were more isolated. Societal structures restricted our ability and our desire to change. Slower-moving communications structures limited the speed of trend uptake. Up until the 19th century, the average community in Western nations was small and relatively self-contained. What mattered was what our neighbours and local political, religious or economic dignitaries did or said. What we did influenced only our own peers and family. Our actions were typically disconnected from other communities.

Today things are very different. The way the world is structured now is encouraging a faster and broader trend influence. Today, news can spread in hours rather than days. And trends can spread in months rather than years. Consumers in every country are part of a gigantic global media, marketing and communications ecosystem. If one market or one industry is affected by a trend, others can quickly become affected too. Socio-economic influences spread increasingly fast in this connected world. And that makes their trend impact grow more widely and more quickly than ever. In previous decades, the reduction in consumer spending, the default-ing of loans that caused the Credit Crunch and a subsequent economic downturn seen in the United States in 2007 might have affected just a few other territories. But in today's connected world, the effects were global. Economies from Iceland to Japan were hugely affected by what was happening. Similar patterns have developed with health issues such as SARS or AIDS. Today's increased travel rates and communications links encourage not only the spread of global diseases but also fears about them. And these fears then affect consumer attitudes and behaviours.

NOTES

1. Mintel, 2007
2. CTIA – The Wireless Association, 2008
3. Korea Consumer Protection Board, 2004
4. Nokia, 2006
5. Hutchinson 3/Dubit, 2006
6. Future Foundation, 2007
7. Eurostat, 2007
8. Technorati, 2007
9. Future Foundation, 2007
10. Newspaper Society, 2006
11. Audit Bureau of Circulations, 2007
12. Apple, 2008
13. Economic and Social Research Council, 2007
14. Mintel, 2007
15. Future Foundation, 2007
16. Vision, 2007

The impact of trends

MARKETING IMPACT

Trends are absolutely essential to consumer marketing. It's the best way of predicting the future and how things are going to change, so that we can make sure our products and innovations are produced at the right time and in line with consumers' needs.

Michele Giles, Head of Insight, Premier Foods

Trends can help you to develop new products. They help to identify the territories you could and should be playing in and how to develop an offer within them. In marketing they help you understand what you should say to motivate consumers, how you should say it and through which mediums you should get your message out to them. They can give you new ideas for how to connect with your target. Tapping into a current trend can give your marketing activity much more cut-through and resonance.

Amanda Meers, Group Account Director,
Jigsaw Strategic Research (Australia)

Changing consumer trends can have a dramatic effect on business strategy. Customers may have behaved the same way for many years, yet in a time of change they cannot be relied upon to behave that way in future. They may no longer purchase in those environments you are strongest in. They may be driven by different needs. They may no longer respond positively to the same advertising messages. This will necessitate strategic shifts. In recent years changing consumer trends have forced many companies to radically adapt their strategies across all marketing functions. The influence of new purchase drivers, changing communication, media and retail behaviours and new product and service needs have required companies to find new marketing approaches. There are examples to be found across a range of industries.

PURCHASE DRIVERS

Trends can help you determine what the emotional hooks are that drive people to respond to your advertising, and what your future communications message should look like.

Mark Broughton, Research Insights and Knowledge Manager, Global Product Development, Alliance Boots

If you find a trend that's relevant to your product, you can use that benefit as the marketing message. It almost writes your copy for you. It's like 'You have this problem; we're here to help.'

Sheila Byfield, Leader, Business Planning, Mindshare

History has shown that it is cheaper to sell more products to the same consumer than it is to find new consumers. To succeed, companies need to maintain the loyalty of their consumer base. But markets are dynamic entities. They are composed of constantly changing individuals. In times of flux such as we are living through today, the continued loyalty of such individuals cannot be guaranteed. Customers buy a company's products for a reason. They do so because they believe the products are cheaper or more convenient, because they trust or relate to the brand, and so on. If consumers continue to consider those same factors important, then they will continue to buy from that company. But in times of change, their attitudes too may change. They may begin to value other factors. Many of the consumers a company traditionally relied upon to buy their products or services may not need or want them in future. Even those who do still want them may not react as favourably to traditional marketing methodologies. A company could lose their custom, unless it identifies potential changes early enough and is able to adapt its offering to the new attitudes. The only effective way to do this is by correctly identifying and analysing changing consumer drivers, as part of the trend analysis process. As they see purchase drivers changing, smart marketers will adapt their brand message.

A single additional purchase driver can have an enormous impact across industries. One important recent new driver is heritage. As part of the Traditionalizing trend, consumers are caring more where their products are made and what their history is. Provenance and authenticity are becoming stronger sales drivers, especially in the luxury sector. The key consumption driver in Japan is now 'brand history'.[1] The trend has encouraged many companies to take a more and more heritage-focused approach. Provenance is proving a narrative and emotional fast track. Luxury brands such as Chanel, Lacoste, Du Pont and even cutting-edge Dior have run campaigns based around their founders and their history. Once-forgotten luggage company Goyard, whose reputation rests more on its heritage than its contemporary style, now produces one of today's 'must have' handbags of the season. FMCG manufacturers from Heinz to Premier Foods are utilizing traditional ingredients, recipes, packaging and advertising creatives. High-end car manufacturers are already beginning to utilize experiential heritage marketing to build and sustain brand loyalty, via interactive brand museums. Volkswagen was the first to do so. Its Autostadt in Wolfsburg has brought in well over 10 million visitors so far. Next was Mercedes, which opened a museum in Stuttgart that aims for a million visitors per year. The trend looks set to continue: Porsche and BMW have both now commissioned architects to design museums for them. Manufacturers are using a similar approach when it comes to building export markets. Richemont used an exhibition on watches in Shanghai to launch the brand in China, and Cartier ran an exhibition on its own brand in Moscow's Kremlin Museum. Even those companies that might not have a long history of their own to promote are utilizing the concept of heritage for their experiential marketing campaigns. Innocent sponsors the annual Innocent Garden Fete in London's Regent's Park, which re-creates the mood of a traditional day out. Hendrick's Gin sponsors the Hendrick's Chap Olympics. In this popular tongue-in-cheek event, leading-edge Londoners are encouraged to dress in tweed suits and take part in races such as the 'Hop, Skip and G&T'!

COMMUNICATIONS

The way in which you have to connect with and target young consumers is not the same as it was even five years ago.

Andy Routley, International Brand Marketing Director, Miller, SAB Miller

Just in the course of the seven years I was at Levi's, so much happened in terms of the consumer environment. We went from targeting just a few TV channels or a few web pages, to millions of different contact points.

Helene Venge, Global Director, Business Development, Lego Group (Denmark) (ex-Head of Digital Marketing, Levi's Europe)

The Boundary Blurring trend is seeing consumers spend their days on a broader range of digital platforms and media environments. And brands are having to amend their marketing communications accordingly. As consumers migrate across a range of channels and platforms, marketers increasingly need to target them in non-traditional environments. McDonald's now devotes less than a third of its US marketing budget to television, compared to two-thirds just five years ago, and is spending more than ever on experiential marketing. Heineken moved its entire £6.5 million UK advertising budget from television to sports sponsorship in 2007. Brands are using non-traditional methods such as in-game ads and product placement. They are having to investigate how to add advertising messages to the music and video consumed on portable devices. They are also studying how to exploit the smaller space offered by the handheld, and considering the implications for communications as consumers start purchasing more products using their mobiles.

Another trend affecting marketing communications is Wising Up, in which increasingly knowledgeable consumers are reacting against the 'dumbing down' of culture. As consumers become more sophisticated, brands are having to entice them with entertainment-based marketing, creating teaser ads and sending out virals to excite customers. Cultural sponsorship is becoming more important, from major concerts to local sports leagues, Oktoberfest to Benicassim. So too is cultural association, such as Louis Vuitton Paris's in-store art exhibitions. Austrian Airlines offers passengers free entry to cultural institutions in Vienna with their boarding card: valid for five museums for up to 10 days after the flight arrival date.

Consumers are also enjoying marketing that challenges. Brands are using puzzles and teasers, and advertising via stories that move from one touch point to the next. They have started using alternate reality games (ARGs) as viral marketing for new products: interactive narratives in which players work together analysing storylines and coordinating real-life and online activities, to try to solve plot-based challenges and puzzles. An ARG was used to publicize Warner Brothers' film *Batman: The Dark Knight*, contributing to its massive box-office success. Geographically specific clues were hidden across the United States, from 'leaked' police documents to phone numbers linked to fictional answer phones. Players were asked to send in photos of themselves dressed as clowns in key locations, which were then reproduced in fake newspapers, which other players distributed around city centres. To promote the launch of Windows Vista, Microsoft used an ARG called 'Vanishing Point' based around a fictional Microsoft employee called Loki, ornate puzzle boxes and other cross-platform clues. Nine Inch Nails' *Year Zero* album was promoted with Morse code clues, and visuals hidden in music videos and songs hidden on memory sticks in concert hall washrooms across Europe!

Meanwhile the Are You Experienced trend for interactivity and physical exposure is driving consumer demand for unique, rich and differentiated experiences whenever they consume or purchase brands. Experiential marketing is proving both popular and effective. Toilet tissue manufacturer Charmin now builds a temporary, branded 20-stall restroom in the heart of New York's Times Square for the Thanksgiving and Christmas holiday seasons. It was visited by over half a million people from 100 countries in the first two years it was open. US toy manufacturer VTech places its games in family rooms in Wyndham Hotels to help parents amuse their children. Turkish nappy brand Evy Baby places branded changing rooms in shopping malls. Zanussi-Electrolux offers free laundry services at Slovenian music festival Rock Otočec.

DISTRIBUTION

Boundary blurring is affecting distribution and retail strategies too. As consumer retail behaviours change, companies are increasingly having to look outside traditional distribution channels. The growth of e-commerce is the most obvious recent example. Brands have had to adapt to selling online or have suffered sales losses, as e-commerce has proven a more and more popular form of product purchase. US retail e-commerce sales for the third quarter of 2008 rose 6 per cent to over $30 billion.[2] In the UK, sales are growing at an even faster rate. E-commerce sales totalled approximately £60 billion in 2008: a year-on-year rise of almost 30 per cent.[3] The internet has consequently become a bigger and bigger part of marketing and sales strategies. The European online advertising market grew to €11.2 billion in 2007: up from just €7.2 billion the previous year. Online now makes up approximately 20 per cent of all UK ad spend and is predicted to outgrow television by 2010.[4] The amount of money spent on online advertising in Bulgaria actually rose by 60 per cent from 2006 to 2007.[5] And the proportion of advertising money spent on the internet in Japan doubled in the two years before that.[6]

Consumer demand for ambient and on-the-go retail too is growing. Innovative new robotic store vending machines are already offering consumers convenient 24/7 salespoints outside the traditional retail environment: Docomo machines offer prepaid cell phones, Sony machines offer their own-brand electronics, Zoom Shops sell mobile technology such as PSPs and iPods, and McDonald's-owned Redbox machines rent DVDs. Multiples are increasingly finding it necessary to target 'grab and go' shoppers: providing front-of-store counters selling more diverse food ranges such as cooked vegetables and side dishes, or offering separate short-term parking and separate checkouts for those who have phoned orders ahead.

Retail is also being affected by the Hectic Eclectic trend, in which a greater confidence has combined with the greater incidence of product choice to encourage consumers to trial more products and services across a range of sectors. Companies are trying different ways to adapt. Many high street fashion retailers have adopted the swifter turnover of 'fast fashion'. The product range of German retailer Tchibo changes every week, providing what it calls 'Each Week Another World'. 'Guerrilla' or 'pop-up' stores are retail sites open for a very limited period only, to create PR and tap into initial sales demand. Comme des Garçons has opened 27 since 2004, from Reykjavik to Athens, even opening one in East Beirut, Lebanon.

NEW MARKETS

We're increasingly looking for opportunities in new markets – new demographic markets, new cultural markets – so we have to be aware of any cultural or demographic shifts.

Hanna Chalmers, Head of Research and Insight, Universal Music Group

Changes in consumer attitudes and behaviours can shrink a market. But understanding new consumer trends can also provide opportunities to target whole new ones. A cohort that was previously uninterested in a brand or sector may change in such a way that its attitude to it changes. It may begin to look favourably on it, creating a whole new market. Alternatively a market cohort that is small today might grow as attitudes or behaviours change, making a positive impact on the bottom line.

In recent years there has been a trend for what I call Gender Blending. This is the blurring of traditional gender roles and behaviours. This trend alone has offered brands enormous opportunities to expand their markets. It has enabled them to move from single-gender products and markets into bi-gender or gender-neutral ones. Traditionally male products can increasingly be sold to female markets and vice versa.

Across many markets, women are now happily purchasing in traditionally 'male' sectors. Today women globally spend more than men on personal technology.[7] Despite clichés about the 'Sex and the City' generation, 35 per cent of British women would rather do without fashionable shoes, lipstick or a diary than live without a mobile phone, and are now spending £478 on consumer technology a year compared to just £74 on shoes.[8] Gaming, traditionally a male-oriented market, is becoming increasingly female. There has been heavy sales growth in music- and lifestyle-related games such as

'SingStar' and 'Nintendogs', and female-targeted consoles such as the DS and the Wii. There are many other examples, spread across industries. In the United States, Tomboy Tools manufactures DIY tools for women, using 'tool parties' inspired by the Tupperware parties of the 1960s. Austria's car navigation systems manufacturer Garmin has produced a version targeted at the female car owner. The Danish lottery Danske Spil has launched online bingo to attract the new female gambler.

At the same time men have become a key new market for the previously female-focused cosmetics industry. Global male usage of personal care products rose from \$26.3 billion to \$29.7 billion in just five years.[9] US men spend as much as US\$2.3 billion on skincare each year[10] and account for a third of all spa visits.[11] Forty per cent of men in France use high-end skincare products. In Italy, 'For Men' cosmetics sales grew by 3 per cent in 2005.[12] Men are also now being targeted by other traditionally 'female' sectors. Hair removal brand Veet is now targeting Australian and UK male markets with gel cream and wax strips. Dietary products too are being marketed to men. Walkers Crisps and Coca-Cola, aware that even weight-conscious males are wary of words such as 'diet' and 'low calorie', launched 'non-diet' diet brands for the male market. Coke Zero provided one of the company's first long-term new product successes in recent years. After two years, it was still growing, with 2007 sales volumes up 34 per cent year on year.

NEW PRODUCTS

Understanding trends can give you the confidence to launch something you might not necessarily have launched.

Sue Elms, EVP Global Media Practice, Millward Brown

Identifying trends is vitally important when working on innovation. You need to anticipate the future.

Bruno Montejorge, Senior Brand Manager, Kraft (Brazil)

Trends can help companies to determine new product development strategies, diffusion strategies and product portfolio diversification. The soft drinks sector offers a strong example. The market is worth billions of dollars globally. It is home to some of the world's most famous brands: from Coca-Cola and Pepsi to Britvic and Evian. It might not at first appear to be a trends-driven industry, yet consumer trends have had a massive impact. In fact a single trend, Healthy Living, was strong enough recently to shift the balance of products in the market and inspire a multitude of new product launches and portfolio diversification.

In the early 2000s consumers were becoming more concerned over health issues, and in particular the number of calories and non-natural ingredients they were putting in their own or their children's mouths. In the soft drinks sector, fruit juice started to be seen as a healthy alternative to carbonated soft drinks. The chilled fruit juice category grew heavily. By 2005 in the UK alone it accounted for £688 million sales and a 22 per cent volume share of all 1-litre soft drink sales.[13] By that stage, over half of the adult population was regularly consuming fruit or vegetable juice. Britons were consuming 2.2 billion litres of juice drinks per year: approximately 36 litres per person.[14] This was not due to marketing or a seasonal fad. The biggest sales growth in juice was in the healthier sub-sectors like the not-from-concentrate juice and nectar sectors.[15] It was clearly consumer health concerns that were driving juice sales.

At the same time, other health-related drinks began to see sales growth too. Fruit smoothies were increasingly seen as healthy snack replacements or a boost to a busy lifestyle or poor diet. By 2007 smoothies had become the fastest-growing soft drinks category in the UK, with consumption reaching 75 million litres.[16] The market, worth £282 million in 2008, is expected to grow to £304 million by 2010.[17] Functional liquid food sales also grew, and the trend was not confined to manufacturers. A trend for juice bars began in Australia. Boost Juice Bars launched in 2000 and has since grown exponentially. In 2004, it added 24 new stores to its portfolio. By 2005 it had over 150 stores across Australia and New Zealand, and its branded products, such as its TD4 yoghurt, were available in supermarkets. Several juice bar chains have since spread across the United States, such as Jamba Juice, Planet Smoothie and Smoothie King.

Those who picked up early on the trend found huge amounts of success manufacturing healthier soft drinks. The trend inspired the launch of several companies. One was smoothie brand Innocent. Launched in 1998, by 2006 it had sales that were growing 165 per cent year on year.[18] By 2007, it had gained a massive 66 per cent share of the UK smoothies market.[19] Danone too benefited from the trend. In 2005 it launched new functional yoghurt drink Activia. Sales rose by almost 70 per cent the next year. In 2007 there was a further 26 per cent sales rise to £123.4 million, placing the brand at number two in the UK yoghurts and desserts category and contributing 45 per cent of category growth.

One of the biggest health trend-led success stories was Pepsi. At the same time as sales of juices and smoothies were rising, cola and flavoured carbonate sales were in decline. Cola and flavoured carbonate sales fell 3 per cent year on year in 2005.[20] The Healthy Living trend was a potential threat to cola brands. Pepsi spotted this, and an understanding of the trend has helped drive its acquisitions and NPD strategy since. It bought juice manufacturer Tropicana from Seagram in 1998 and bought out PJ Smoothies in 2005 (since consolidated into the Tropicana brand). By 2006, Tropicana had become the UK's leading juice brand, with a 24 per cent market share and a growth of 88.5 per cent over the previous five years.[21] It is now three times the size of its nearest rival in the chilled juice category and the fourth biggest soft drinks brand in the UK. Meanwhile PJ Smoothies had obtained a 12 per cent share of the UK smoothies market by 2007, with year-on-year sales up almost 7 per cent.[22] In 2006, Pepsi signed a deal to bottle and distribute Ocean Spray. It has since also found huge success in the functional drinks category. It acquired Ardea Beverage, makers of Nutrisoda, in 2006, and in 2007 launched Fuelosophy and Tava. The success of its health-based product portfolio has boosted not just Pepsi's bottom line but its market value too, which actually rose above Coca-Cola's for the first time in over a hundred years.[23]

All of this was the effect of a single trend. Clearly trends can have a huge effect on company profits.

NOTES

1. Louis Vuitton, 2005
2. US Department of Commerce, 2008
3. eMarketer, 2008
4. Internet Advertising Bureau, 2008
5. Investor.bg, 2008
6. Dentsu, 2007
7. Consumer Electronics Association, 2005
8. Sony Ericsson, 2004
9. Datamonitor, 2006
10. Datamonitor, 2006
11. PricewaterhouseCoopers, 2006
12. Unipro, 2005
13. ACNielsen ScanTrack, 2005
14. Mintel, 2005
15. Euromonitor, 2005
16. British Soft Drinks Association, 2008
17. Mintel, 2008
18. ACNielsen, 2006
19. *Marketing Week*, 2008
20. GlaxoSmithKline, 2005
21. ACNielsen, 2007
22. *Marketing Week*, 2008
23. *Beverage Daily*, 2006

4

The benefit of trends

TREND AS OPPORTUNITY

Knowing about consumer trends is fundamental. You must keep aware of what's going on in the marketplace to ensure your business remains relevant and vital. Trends give you direction to evolve your business in a way that keeps you in sync with what people are looking for.

Tom Pickles, Senior Director, Global Menu Solutions, McDonald's (USA)

Trend data is absolutely core. It's business critical. It can be used at every level of the business, from marketing to A&R. A trend like the growing importance to entertainment of the older market can affect everything from single choice to video to marketing strategy.

Hanna Chalmers, Head of Research and Insight, Universal Music Group

Change is occurring faster, more radically and across more markets than ever. Consumers are having an increasing influence on commerce and strategy. Change is affecting businesses in every sector. But change does not have to be a negative factor. If approached correctly, it can be a positive. Trends can offer great opportunities. Exploiting a new trend can have a hugely beneficial effect on a company's sales, market share and profits. Companies that identify, analyse and utilize trends correctly can gain massively increased sales and a major competitive advantage. Trends can enable new companies and even whole new industries to launch and thrive. And even potential threats can be diffused if change is identified early enough.

There are many examples of industries and companies that have identified and exploited a trend to great advantage. Trends such as Trading Up,

Come Together and Gender Blending have provided many opportunities for profitable growth.

The Trading Up trend, which has seen consumers across social grades buying more premium products, has given brands an opportunity to broaden their market by 'branding up' their own offering via diffusion lines. Mass-market brands have created premium lines. H&M employed designers such as Karl Lagerfeld and Roberto Cavalli to create ranges for it. Carlsberg branded up its beer with the limited-edition launch of the Carlsberg 900 range. Brands such as Hermès, Bally and Bulgari have been able to enter the luxury stationery market previously dominated by the likes of Smythson, offering items such as embossed leather notebooks and leather-clad pencils. Cartier has produced 18-carat-gold-nib fountain pens. Ferrari has teamed up with Montegrappa, the Italian pen manufacturer, to create a series of desk accessories. High-profile designers are creating luxury lines for babies and young children: from Tiffany's silver spoons and nappy bags made by Gucci, Kate Spade and Louis Vuitton, to Hermès cashmere baby blankets and BMW pedal cars. Even the most 'everyday' products can be branded up. Swarovski and Philips launched Active Crystals: a range of crystal-embossed USB earphones and USB sticks costing €100 and €150 respectively. And Portuguese paper products company Renova now sells 'the first fashionable toilet paper', priced at over €2 per roll!

The Come Together trend, a trend for greater communality, has driven the growth in social networking, which has actually created an enormous new industry in just a few years. Total global revenues from the social networking industry are now estimated at approximately $6.5 billion. MySpace has over 100 million members globally, with 250,000 joining daily. Bebo, founded less than three years ago, now has over 40 million members worldwide. Facebook has 550,000 registered members in Finland alone, including almost half of all 20- to 40-year-olds in the country. In Italy the service has 450,000 unique users,[1] while MySpace there has a massive 931,000 registered users, with over 2,000 joining every day.[2] Seventy per cent of Irish consumers under the age of 18 use sites such as Bebo and Facebook regularly.

The Gender Blending trend has provided cosmetics brands with the opportunity to expand their markets. As noted above, skincare products for men now account for more than 30 per cent of the cosmetic market as a whole. Global companies such as Nivea and L'Oréal have successfully sold products to the new male market. National companies too have benefited. The Croatian skincare manufacturer Adrience now features male cosmetics as well in its Adrience Seapower range, as does the Finnish Lumene brand. In Austria, Reiersdorf has introduced a summer look product for men: a self-bronzer and moisturizer in one. The trend is affecting emerging nations too. Sales of men's cosmetics there are rising at 20–30 per cent per year. Chinese males can now buy not just basic cleansing and skincare products and fragrances, but scrubs, moisturizers, plant-based gels, non-alkaline cleansing gels and other high-end products too. Since 2003, men's beauty salons have sprung up in several Chinese cities. Men accounted for 30 per cent of all last year's cosmetic surgery operations in China. Half of urban Chinese males now approve of cosmetic treatments for men.

The On The Go trend for increased mobility has proved hugely profitable for technology companies. Mobile audio has become a $40 billion global market.[3] Apple has sold over 100 million units of its iPod and almost a million of its music-playing iPhones. Sony Ericsson sold 27 million Walkman phones in the first two years of production. In total 120 million portable digital music players were sold globally in 2006 alone. This was a rise of almost 50 per cent year on year.[4] Mobile gaming device sales too are soaring. The market is now worth over $7 billion. The next step looks set to be video. It is being predicted that by 2010 over 200 million people around the world will be watching TV on mobile devices, with 95 million mobile TV subscribers in Asia alone by 2011.[5] Other sectors have seen huge trend-based successes too. The spa industry has grown from a specialist market to a mainstream one. There are now over 150 million active spa-goers worldwide,[6] with experts predicting annual growth of 16 per cent.[7] In television, US sports channel ESPN has picked up on the Traditionalizing trend and launched the hugely successful ESPN Classic channel, which transmits exclusively *old* sporting events. Examples are endless.

TREND AS THREAT

But trends also offer threats as well as opportunities. A single behaviour change can decimate industries. When consumers began using digital cameras in the early 2000s, it devastated the market for film, film cameras and film developing. And it did so remarkably quickly. Although the average digital SLR camera was still costing over $1,000 in 2002, by 2003 US digital camera sales had surpassed film camera sales.[8] Sales fell approximately 30 per cent year on year from 2002 to 2006. Just 204 million rolls of film were sold in 2006: a quarter of what was sold in 1999.[9] The cost of changing to digital production and the lower profit margins offered by the format hit camera manufacturers hard. Olympus cut 30 per cent of its global workforce in 2005. Kodak cut over 20,000 jobs from 2004 to 2006. Polaroid, which had over 20,000 employees in the late 1970s, was down to just 150 employees by 2008.

The trend for downloading music free online had a massive detrimental effect on the music business. It led to a huge drop in recorded music sales, and massive restructuring and job losses throughout the music industry. Album sales today are the lowest, and retail sales have fallen at their fastest rates, since records began in 1969.[10] In the United States over 5,000 record company employees were laid off from 2000 to 2007,[11] and almost 3,000 record stores closed down in the four years up to 2007.[12] Meanwhile, as consumers rely more on their cell phones, fixed-line telephony companies too have seen revenues drop. In France, for instance, though 90 per cent of people in 2000 had a fixed-line phone at home and just 47 per cent had a mobile, by 2005 a mighty 70 per cent owned a mobile and just 83 per cent a fixed phone.[13] It is predicted that before the decade is over a third of Europeans will have abandoned standard phone lines in favour of wireless and broadband.[14] A new trend can also take money away from previously favoured products. Teenage spending on cell phones displaced $500 billion of their spend on other products from 1995 to 2005. The trend among young people to use their cell phones to tell the time or to provide an alarm is threatening the watch and clock market.

Attitudinal trends can appear that make consumers less interested in a product. The Conscious Consumption trend, for consumers to consider the ecological and social impact of their spending patterns, has reduced consumer demand for larger cars and houses. New attitudes or demands can also make a product appear less attractive than its competitors. A trend-friendly product can even succeed against a technically superior product. The greater number of film titles available on the VHS format enabled it to defeat the challenge of the highly advanced Betamax format. The simplicity and strong design of the iPod enabled it to dominate the MP3 player market. The playfulness and family orientation of Nintendo's Wii console helped it surpass the sales of high-definition consoles such as the Xbox 360 and PlayStation 3.

MISSING TRENDS

Identifying and exploiting a trend can benefit industries and companies enormously. Yet failing to identify a trend can have an equal impact and be much less beneficial. On one level, failing to exploit a positive trend in a market means missing out on a potentially highly profitable opportunity for growth. This could be the opening up of new markets or the chance to develop successful new products. But missing a trend can mean more than just missing an opportunity. While identifying a negative trend early enough can provide companies with the time and opportunity to limit its impact, failing to do so can mean suffering its full impact. Profits can fall. Market share can be lost.

For those not skilled in the art of trend analysis, it is all too easy to miss a trend. History is full of companies or individuals who have done so, often with catastrophic results. Many trends that have been missed are ones that today, with hindsight, seem obvious. The quotes below, although amusing today, meant loss of revenue for the companies involved:

- 'We don't like their sound, and guitar music is on the way out' (Decca Recording Company rejecting the Beatles, 1962).
- 'Who the hell wants to hear actors talk?' (Harry M Warner, founder, Warner Bros, questioning the trend for 'talking pictures', 1927).
- 'This "telephone" has too many shortcomings to be seriously considered as a means of communication. The device is inherently of no value to us' (internal memo, Western Union, rejecting the telephone, 1878).
- 'The world potential market for copying machines is 5,000 at most' (IBM, turning down a deal with the founders of Xerox, 1959).

Industry reaction to one of the biggest trends of the late 20th century, the growth of personal computer use, shows how even the most successful companies can miss out on a trend:

- 'There is a total world market for maybe five computers' (Thomas Watson, chairman, IBM, 1943).
- 'I have travelled the length and breadth of this country and talked with the best people, and I can assure you that data processing is a fad that won't last out the year' (business editor, Prentice Hall, 1957).
- 'There is no reason anyone would want a computer in their home' (Ken Olson, president, computer manufacturers DEC, 1977).

Companies can fail to identify consumer trends for a number of different reasons (Figure 4.1). Most of these are based around incorrect assumptions. Some companies assume that what has traditionally happened in their market will continue to happen. They believe that no trends can affect them, because their industry or their company is immune to change. But trends affect all types of consumers. Customers in one industry are as open to change as those in any other. Other companies assume their own industry will not be affected by a particular trend. For some this is because they consider themselves too large or powerful to be affected. For others, it is because they have not analysed the trend enough to realize its potential. Any such assumptions can be dangerous commercially. All too often they are wrong. And by the time the company in question realizes, it has lost advantage to its competitors.

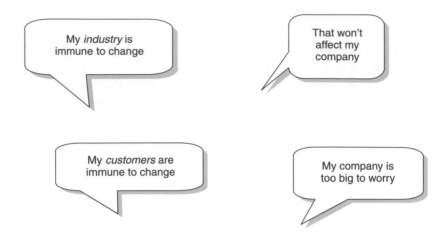

Figure 4.1 How companies miss trends

CATCHING TRENDS

Picking up on trends can be hugely beneficial. Missing out on them can be highly detrimental. But trends do not just appear in companies' in-trays. They need to be identified. And then they need to be successfully incorporated into policy.

Some companies are lucky. They stumble across trends passively via a form of commercial osmosis. This can happen if they themselves or senior members of their management team happen to be part of an emergent trend or share enough qualities with their target market to sense changes automatically. This is perhaps one reason why individuals like Bill Gates at Microsoft and Steve Jobs at Apple picked up on new trends in computing before large corporations did.

But such examples are rare. Unless your company is lucky enough to be linked into an emergent trend, the only way to identify and exploit trends successfully is to research them actively. To exploit new consumer trends successfully, companies need to engage in a formalized trends process. This can involve a single dedicated trends analyst, a full trends team or an outsourced consultancy. It can be run as an ongoing procedure or as a series of one-off studies. Yet to succeed it will need to include not just the identification of trends but their interpretation and implementation too. And the culture and organization of the company will need to be altered to accommodate the process.

NOTES

1. NNR/Facebook, 2007
2. Luglio, 2007
3. Informa Telecoms, 2006
4. Understanding & Solutions, 2007
5. iResearch Consulting, 2007
6. International Spa Association, 2007
7. SpaFinder, 2006
8. Infotrends Research Group, 2003
9. Photo Marketing Association, 2007
10. Nielsen SoundScan, 2007
11. *Rolling Stone*, 2007
12. Almighty Institute of Music Retail, 2007
13. nVision, 2007
14. Gartner, 2006

Summary: Part 1

- Consumer behaviour is at the heart of global commerce.
- Changes in consumer behaviour drive changes in commercial strategy.
- Long-term consumer changes are known as trends.
- The rate and scope of change today make trend knowledge more important.
- Strong consumers and globalism mean trends have more commercial impact.
- Consumer trends are driving change across all marketing functions.
- Trends can be an opportunity or a threat.
- Picking up on a trend can be profitable.
- Missing a trend can prove disastrous.
- Trends need to be actively researched.

Part 2

Beginning with trends

Part 2

Beginning with
trends

5

The three Is

WHAT TREND MARKETING IS

Looking forward

The utilization of consumer trend data can prove hugely beneficial to a company. But identifying and exploiting a trend successfully require a formalized trends process. Many companies today agree that consumer trends can be a vital tool for marketers and NPD departments alike. Most companies use trends at one or more points in the business process, but this is rarely formalized. In the course of writing this book, I have interviewed executives from across a range of sectors and functions, all of whom consider knowledge of consumer trends invaluable. The vast majority have found their best results when using a more formal approach. But the approach taken and practices used differ from company to company. There is still no single established practice for the process of identifying and analysing trends. There are no formal studies of the practice. There are no trend qualifications available outside the fashion sector. There is not even a single recognized term for the process. One reason is that the study of trends is still a relatively new discipline.

Looking back

What will happen in the future has fascinated people for millennia. Since the earliest days, people have tried a variety of means to predict the future. Over 5,000 years ago, Assyrian kings employed soothsayers. In Ancient Greece predictors cast lots, in Rome they picked at animal entrails and in

Polynesia they spun coconuts. Since then others have used beans, coins, knucklebones, stars, numbers, palms and even the flight of birds. But a commercial study of the future did not begin until very recently.

The only industry to study trends before the middle of the twentieth century was fashion. Even there, there was little analysis of trends to begin with. Initially fashion companies simply accepted that what the 'fashionable' people wore was by its very nature fashionable. But in the mid-19th century fashion magazines began including inspirational photographs and illustrations of the latest styles, and became more influential in spreading trends. Retailers began to feature the latest Paris trends. By the start of the twentieth century, fashion trends had begun moving in a yearly cycle, and the practice of fashion forecasting started to become more formalized. The first ever fashion trend consultancy, Tobe Associates, launched in 1927. In 1928, a number of different fashion designers got together to form the Fashion Group, which began issuing regular fashion trend reports. These gave advice to several different fashion houses at the same time, so many designers used the same trend. Fashion houses saw that using such trends increased sales, so the practice grew. As the decades wore on, fashion became more mass-market. There was an increase in the rate and change of directions. Dressmakers gave way to fashion conglomerates, distancing manufacturers from consumers. Because of this, being able to predict consumer demand accurately became more important. But it was not until the late 1950s and early 1960s that the fashion industry settled into the trend-led format we know today. It was then that high street fashions adopted a more seasonal direction. By this point department store fashion buyers were expected to know about trends and disseminate that information through the company. Trade fairs and industry exhibitions such as the German Interstoff began to take off, and global forecasting companies such as Informa and Promostyl were launched.

Outside fashion, commercial trend analysis has had a short but varied history. The first non-fashion-led trend forecasting actually took place during the Second World War. The US Air Force used an early form of scenario planning to try to determine what the Axis powers might do in the future. After the war, the government set up institutions like RAND to explore new methods of long-range military planning. Herman Kahn, who had been involved in planning during the war, helped create future planning practices there. When he left, he developed these for use in the commercial sphere. Self-styled 'futurists' such as Bertrand de Jouvenel, Dennis Gabor and Alvin Toffler developed further predictive theories for educational and business use. In the 1970s Pierre Wack, a planner in the London offices of oil company Shell, developed a formal predictive practice around scenario planning. This was picked up first by other oil companies and then by other sectors. Around the same time, advertising agencies began to introduce a new discipline into the mix: account planning. This was developed by individuals such as Stephen King of JWT, Stanley Pollitt of BMP and later Jay Chiat of Chiat Day. It brought the study of changing consumer behaviour into the advertising process, and has since become a key part of most advertising and media agencies. It was not until the 1990s that trend forecasting consultancies began to spring up. Faith Popcorn published *The Popcorn Report* (HarperCollins) in 1992. By the late 1990s, the research and insight departments of several major brands and media agencies were utilizing trend forecasting practices.

Naming names

Perhaps because of its brief and multifaceted history, the process of trend analysis has yet to gain an agreed name. As trends became more important, different names were used to describe the process of analysing them. One early term was 'futurology'. It was coined by German professor Ossip Flechtheim in the mid-1940s to describe a new science of probability and was used as a descriptor by many of the pioneers of trend analysis. Later several early adopter industries used the term 'cool hunting'. This referred specifically to the identification of style-focused trends, but strong media coverage enabled it to gain mainstream traction in the 1990s. The most common terms today are based around the word 'trend', such as 'trend spotting', 'trend forecasting' or 'trend prediction'. Pharmacy chain Boots calls the trend analysis process 'creatology'. The word 'trending' too is starting to find favour in the United States. But there is still no agreement on a definitive term.

Equally difficult to pin down is the word for a practitioner of trend studies. I have seen a wide spread of terms utilized in my years in the profession. These range from 'policy analysts' and 'prediction market developers' to 'foresight consultants', 'visionaries' and even 'trendmeisters'. Media-friendly forecasters are often referred to as 'trend gurus'. Lisa Suttora, CEO of WhatDoISell.com, for instance, is described online as 'a noted trendologist and Product Trending Editor'. Faith Popcorn's company refers to itself as 'a strategic trend based marketing consultancy'. When introducing me at conferences or company meetings, clients call me by a variety of different titles, and journalists or broadcasters use a range of terms when explaining what it is that I do for a living. I have at different times been described as 'a futurologist', 'a trend forecaster' and 'a trends analyst'.

To help create a greater standardization and subsequent formality within the trend analysis process, and to build credence for it, I think it is important to establish a single acceptable term. This should encapsulate the process and can be applicable across sectors. The term I personally use is 'trend marketing'. I believe it is important that the term include the word 'trend', despite the concerns some people have about it. It is a good short-hand term for changes in consumer behaviours or attitudes. But adding the word 'marketing' does two things. It grounds the discipline within a specific part of the business process. And it shows that the process is not just 'icing on the cake' but actually has a distinct commercial purpose.

WHAT TREND MARKETING IS NOT

Understanding trends is critical. It's crucial that there's an understanding of how the world and consumer behaviours will change, and what the trends are that you need to respond to. It means you can prepare your company for the future in time.

Liisa Puolakka, Head of Brand Identity, Nokia

Trends enable you to anticipate how people will react. They offer a much better view into how people are behaving, why they're behaving that way and the context they're behaving in than traditional research does.

Craig Thayer, Managing Editor, Mintel Inspire,
Mintel International Group (USA)

The ambivalence about what term to use echoes a general ambivalence about the business use of trends. Part of the reason the trends sector has yet to be formalized is the level of scepticism that exists around the practice. Some marketers I have spoken to almost feel a sense of embarrassment about the term 'trends' and the practice of trends analysis. To some the word evokes fast-moving fashion styles and fads that have little to do with 'serious' business practice. To others the predictive nature of trend analysis has echoes of guesswork or even fortune telling. Because of this, before I try to define what the process actually entails, I want to explain what it does not.

Many individuals have a negative attitude towards trends that is actually based upon incorrect assumptions about what the process entails or delivers. There are still too many marketers who see it as a pseudo-science or management fad or as 'nice to know' not 'need to know'. To some extent this attitude is understandable. As noted above, the discipline is relatively new. There are as yet no specific qualifications that can be gained in it. And its practitioners do not subscribe to a single agreed process. But such factors should not put people off. The process is now both systematized and effective. Most of the negative attitudes to trends are based on myths.

Cool hunting

There is a lot of scepticism about trends. One problem is that the word 'trend' is too close to the word 'trendy'. And 'cool hunting' is the ultimate toxic term. It suggests someone who just sits there waiting for someone cool to walk by, or just looks at skateboarders all day. But actually studying trends is so much more than that. Analysing trends correctly can actually provide information on major shifts in consumer behaviour. And there are countless examples of brands who have benefited hugely financially from that.

P T Black, Partner, Jigsaw International (China)

Trend marketing is not the same as 'cool hunting'. The process is not actually particularly concerned with 'cool'. Trend marketers will take an interest in what is fashionable, because it can sometimes provide clues as to more substantive behavioural changes. But they do not care passionately about whether, say, stripes and short hemlines will be filling the catwalks next season. Outside the fashion industry, few companies can usefully exploit such information in ways that have a positive impact on their bottom line. Trend forecasters therefore do not spend the bulk of their time studying training shoes or jeans styles in Williamsburg, Shoreditch or Harajuku. In fact, they probably spend as much time in front of a computer as they do on the street.

Unfortunately, many marketers still equate trend forecasting with cool hunting, to the detriment of the former. When I began in the industry at the end of the 1990s, it was the era of cool hunting. The focus within trend forecasting was on the identification of 'hot' new trends. But non-fashion companies found it hard to gain practical benefits from such information. Eventually, companies began to realize that the cool hunting process, while perhaps useful for short-term marketing tactics, was a red herring when it came to any form of strategic thinking or mass marketing. But when cool hunting became tarnished, trend forecasting as a whole did too. Many companies that had been using trend analysis companies and processes dropped them. Fortunately those brands that understood the nature of trend forecasting were not put off. They understood that cool hunting was simply one tiny piece of the process, and simply adapted their forecasting processes accordingly to include more rigour. Since then there has, correctly, been a greater emphasis placed on the interpretation and analysis of trends, not just on the identification of them. Today companies understand that it is not enough to identify what early adopters are doing. For the process to be worthwhile financially, it needs to deliver insights or foresight that will actively benefit a company's bottom-line sales. Increasingly today I find that what my clients are looking for is the intelligent, relevant analysis of trends.

Pseudo-science

The analysis of trends is not a 'pseudo-science'. Like any branch of research, true trend analysis utilizes a formal, rigorous process. It takes a positivist approach. Laws are determined and theories affirmed through the utilization of rigorous empirical techniques. Successful trend forecasting follows a logical pattern. It combines a variety of robust methodologies in a regulated combination.

Nor is it true that trend analysts can somehow create trends. Micro trends and fads can sometimes be encouraged by global marketing strategies and product launches. But trends are changes that typically occur across thousands and even millions of consumers. They are created by changes in political, economic, socio-cultural or technological environments. They occur because of a complex combination of circumstances. They are not just due to the actions of one individual or commercial concern.

The study of consumer trends is not the study of sector innovation or competitor benchmarking. Its purpose is not to tell marketers what new products or services are available in the marketplace. It might be able to offer some insights in this direction, but that is not its role. Nor is it there to report on what developments other companies are making in a sector. These are current insights that should be identified by insight teams or perhaps proactive sales teams. The trend forecaster's role is to study the attitudes and behaviours of *customers*, not products or competitors. Marketers should not ignore current product, economic and design trends, of course. They can be vital trend tools. But they are a means to an end, not the end in itself.

The objective of analysing trends is not simply to provide information on *current* trends. That is the purpose of traditional research techniques. Some consultants who provide information on what consumers are doing now claim that this is trend forecasting. It is not. Detailing current trends in social networking, for instance, is very different from predicting how they will develop in the future. What makes trend marketing so valuable is its ability to predict future behaviours, not simply catalogue current ones. In order to provide data that will improve tomorrow's bottom line, a trend marketer needs to determine how a current trend is going to develop, and what other trends will consequently occur in the future.

THE TREND MARKETING PROCESS

Three-stage process

> *There's no point knowing what the trends are if you're not sure how to apply them to your business. Interpretation and implementation are perhaps even more important than identification.*

> Amanda Meers, Group Account Director,
> Jigsaw Strategic Research (Australia)

> *There is so much trend information out there, but it's not always clear what to do with it. People want help to pick out the parts that are most relevant to them, to aid them in product development or their marketing.*

> Alison Hughes, UK Agent, Carlin International

So what exactly *is* trend marketing? It is more than simply spotting trends. That is just the start of the process. The identification of trends is a useful initial step, but on its own it is not enough. The reason to identify consumer trends is to improve marketing performance. My belief, based upon years of helping brands exploit trends for profit, is that the most effective way to do this is by including a strong generic and operational analysis element within the process. This is backed up by the experiences of many corporate trend experts. To do this I employ a three-stage process using the three Is. These are identification, interpretation and implementation (Figure 5.1).

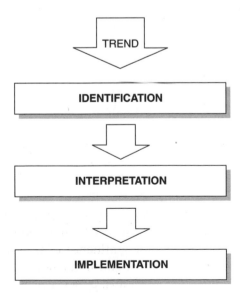

Figure 5.1 Trend marketing (the three Is)

Identification

Identification is the process of observing change and spotting trends. It is a necessary first step in the trend marketing process. It can be conducted using a wide variety of different methods. Primary observation, the study of consumer change at first hand, can be done informally by spending time observing or interrogating consumers in the field. This can involve distance observation, immersion, ethnography, depth interviews, vox pops and photography. Formal observation techniques bring a greater rigour and systematization to the process. They include the use of focus groups, listening posts and street polling. Secondary research, the study of other people's research data, can be obtained by scanning available polling data or media outlets. All trend marketers will use a different combination of these methods to obtain their data. I explore this process in more depth in Part 4.

Interpretation

Once a trend has been identified, the next step is to analyse or judge it, in order to predict how it will develop. This is becoming an increasingly important part of the process. If you have spotted a trend but not analysed it, you might perhaps be able to use that information in the creative execution or delivery platform of a very short-term marketing campaign. But you will not be able to use the trend strategically or for a wider market unless you can also predict how big it will become, whom it will affect, and the ways in which it is likely to evolve. A drinks manufacturer might hear of a trend for greater whisky consumption among young cutting-edge males. But it will need to analyse such data first, before it can confidently use the data to inform marketing or NPD. For instance, is it just a fad that will remain siloed among the cutting edge or will it cross over into the mainstream? Is it just about whisky or might it encompass all brown drinks? Will it affect consumption rates among older or female consumers too?

Effective trend interpretation is a systematic process. It is based around causal analysis: analysing why the trend happened and how it will develop. Although an experienced forecaster can utilize 'gut feel' in the interpretation of a trend, it is essential to employ a strong element of rigour. Trend interpretation requires some understanding of marketing theory and the social sciences. To predict trend developments, forecasters need to map any trend they identify against a series of social criteria in order to understand the strength, longevity and potential influence of the trend. These criteria include trend attributes; traditional consumer needs; and environmental factors, divided into the 4 Cs: constants, cycles, calculables and chaotics. I describe this process in Part 5.

The interpretation of a trend takes place only after it has been observed. But it does not mark the end of the observation process. A trend should continue to be monitored once interpretation has established that it is likely to develop. The longer it is monitored, the more evidence that can be obtained, and the more certainty there can be about the potential impact of the trend in the marketplace.

Implementation

The final step is ultimately the most vital, yet it is too often overlooked. Identifying and analysing trends are important. But the ultimate purpose of trend marketing is to help companies decide on their most effective strategies for the future. The final implementation stage deals with impact analysis: the effects that the trend might have upon an individual sector or business. In this phase, forecasters take an identified and interpreted trend and find ways to build it advantageously into company strategy. To do this, they have to establish which trends are most relevant to their particular situation and then determine how they can exploit them most effectively. Imagine if a sportswear manufacturer identified the trend for Natural Fitness, in which consumers are moving away from gyms and organized sports to 'natural' fitness regimes such as running and cycling. First it would analyse the trend to determine the general implications. Will it encourage a spectator interest as well as a participatory one in sports such as cycling or running at the expense of football or basketball? If so, will this be limited to older consumers? Moving to the implementation stage, it will try to determine what effect the trend might have on its industry and its brands. Will it reduce or diversify sportswear purchase? It then needs to understand how it might exploit the trend. Should it continue to focus on football and basketball clothing but limit itself to the younger market? Or should it expand into cycling and running gear? I will explore best practice in implementation in Part 6.

Employing a three-way process helps marketers get the most out of consumer trends. Describing it in practical terms will take up the second section of this book. But before a company can begin the trend marketing process, it must be properly prepared. It needs a culture of openness and innovation. It needs to be free from bias, informality and traditionalism. And it needs an infrastructure that allows the efficient input and implementation of trend data. That is the next step.

6

Preparation

FOCUS ON THE FUTURE

I will only recruit people who have an obvious passion for people and an inquisitive mind, those who really want to know what makes people tick.

Sheila Byfield, Leader, Business Planning, Mindshare

You need to be passionate about understanding where the consumer is going, not just where they are today.

Denise Drummond-Dunn, Vice President Consumer Excellence, Nestlé (Switzerland)

Consumer focused	✓
Future focused	✓
Free from personal bias	✓
Free from assumptive bias	✓
Free from reported bias	✓
Open to different interests	✓
Open to different sectors	✓
Open to different ideas	✓
Systematic	✓
Innovative	✓

Figure 6.1 Trend qualifications

Trend marketing is a unique discipline that requires a non-traditional approach from both individuals and organizations. Before embarking on the process, marketers need to prepare themselves and their companies. This requires the attainment of certain attitudes and skills (see Figure 6.1). Some of these a company or individual may already have. Others they will need to learn. Those who work in statistics or sales, for instance, may need to become more people focused. Traditional market researchers will already be people focused, but may have to become more future focused. Cool hunters may be future focused but need to become more systematic. A company that has spent many years in a single sector may need to open itself up to ideas and developments in other sectors, and one that has a strong sales culture may need to develop a greater innovation culture.

Consumers should be the focus of any marketing activity. This is particularly true of trend marketing. The most important qualities a trend marketer can have are an interest in and understanding of consumers' behaviours and motivations. An interest in people is typically innate. Most people either have an interest or they do not. But an understanding of behaviour and motivation can to some extent be learned. Behaviour patterns are regularly explored in marketing and research training, and there are hundreds of books that cover the topic.

This is an essential quality for anyone involved in the market research sector. But what differentiates traditional market researchers and trend researchers is that the former focus on the present and the latter on the future. When market researchers look at someone they will typically ask 'Why are they doing that?' Trend forecasters will ask the same, but are likely to add '... and what will they do next?' Successful trend marketers need therefore to train themselves always to think about the future implications of any data they obtain. They will also typically need to make more intuitive leaps and deductions than traditional researchers.

AVOID BIAS

Personal bias

One of the first tasks for trend marketers is to adopt a neutral approach to the future. They must not be biased in the interpretation of their findings. They must be able to observe and interpret trends honestly, dispassionately and without any moral, aesthetic or sector bias. They must also learn to identify and ignore any bias that might be contained in the data they receive. One of the hardest forms of bias to overturn is personal bias. It can take a number of forms: moral, generational, cultural or gender bias. For example, you might be biased towards your own gender or against certain behaviours. Whenever trend analysts describe or draw conclusions from a trend, they must check their comments for any possible bias.

It is difficult to remain neutral when dealing with either consumers or culture, both of which are key to trend marketing. Everyone will naturally have opinions on what is 'good' or 'bad' culture or on what is 'good' or 'bad' for society or for their industry. However, any such thoughts must be over-ruled. The job of trend marketers is not to search for the good in society. Their job is to search for any patterns of consumer change that are relevant to their company or clients, whether they consider those to be a positive thing or not. If they discover that a new behaviour or attitude is growing in influence, or a traditional one is diminishing, and that discovery is relevant to their company or client, then they must state it. They must also draw conclusions accordingly, no matter what their personal feelings are on the topic. If they are atheist and hear that consumers are becoming more religious, or if they are socialist and hear that more reactionary attitudes are prevailing, they must report it, and analyse it in terms of their company, not their morality. The only level at which they can judge a trend is in the implementation process, when they are determining whether a trend is good for a company's long-term future.

One way to train your mind to be more neutral is to practise seeing things from a point of view other than your own. When you read a news story in a newspaper or on a news website, try to think about it from a different point of view. If you are a Republican or Conservative, try to imagine what a story might mean if you were a Democrat or a member of the Labour Party. If you are rich, imagine what the story might mean if you were poor. If you live in the United States or the UK, imagine how someone who lives in China, India or Brazil might feel on reading the same story. Exercises such as this can help you think more openly about data.

Assumptive bias

It is essential to think differently when studying consumer change. Herman Kahn was one of the pioneers of trend prediction in the 1950s and 1960s. He followed up his ground-breaking work *On Thermonuclear War* (Princeton University Press, 1960) with a book called *Thinking about the Unthinkable* (Horizon Press, 1962). What Kahn was referring to here was thinking about something that our society or upbringing has conditioned us not to think about or does not allow us to think about. Kahn's title is a phrase that successful trend forecasters learn to live by. They must also equally 'believe the unbelievable' and 'accept the unacceptable'.

Many companies miss important and potentially beneficial trends because they make assumptions about trends based on overly traditional thinking. Companies often assume that a trend will not affect their industry or their company, or they assume that a trend will affect only a particular demographic. But successful companies or forecasters never assume: they challenge. They study, analyse and then draw conclusions.

One of the most dangerous assumptions to make is that consumers will continue to behave in the same way they always have. Trend marketers should also continually explore and challenge traditional opinion. As has been seen time and time again, consumers can change, and in quite radical ways. In fact, challenging traditional behaviours can help marketers pre-empt trends. They should try to imagine what might happen if any of the behaviours or attitudes they assume to be eternal were to change. This can help in the theoretical identification of trends (see Chapter 13).

Reported bias

Another form of bias is that manifested by observers: from experts to media sources. When obtaining data, the forecaster must consider whether sources might be biased. For instance, do they have a vested interest in reporting something? Is there a potential conflict of interest? In each case, forecasters need to study the source of the information. If it is from a primary source, then their sample size and recruitment criteria should be tested. If it is from a secondary source, how reliable is that source? Is it a reputable research company? Or is it a PR agency, brand or government department? Where possible, forecasters should go to the most neutral source possible. Where that is not feasible, they should identify and then remedy any potential bias.

KEEP AN OPEN MIND

You have to be open on all levels. We always look at different categories to see where there might be opportunities. Three years ago we introduced a toothbrush called Toothtunes. That's not a category we might have identified as in our scope of business. But it was based on understanding a trend among kids towards music. And it became one of the top-selling toothbrushes in the US last year.

Dave Capper, President Lifestyle, Music and Media, Hasbro (USA)

If something proves unfeasible, you need to be able to say 'no' and walk away.

Gavin Emsden, Food and Beverage Insights Director, Nestlé

Trend marketers need to be open to new things. To forecast consumer trends effectively, they must be open to what is happening in areas that might not normally affect or interest them. They must also be open to new ideas. Good trend marketers are generalists. This makes them good dinner party guests, as they will always have something to discuss whomever they are sitting next to! But it is also an essential attribute for a process that obtains data from such a broad range of sources and methodologies. Like anyone, I am interested in some topics more than others. I am more skilled in some areas than others. There are also certain sectors that I work more often in. But I try not to let this skew my trend analysis. I spent over 10 years in the entertainment industry, so am particularly knowledgeable about entertainment consumers. And the majority of my clients are in the media, food or financial sectors. But in the interest of trends, I spend much of my time studying the automotive, pharmaceutical and fashion industries. I am in my 40s, studied arts at college and am not much of a sportsman. Yet I am regularly to be found reading articles on youth, science and sports. To help open themselves up to new ideas, trend marketers can utilize a similar exercise to that used earlier in the chapter to eradicate personal bias. If you are a Republican, then read articles written by Democrats. If you are rich, read articles about the lifestyles of the poor. If you are US or British, read articles on China, India or Brazil.

It is not just topics that marketers should be open to. It is disciplines and methodologies too. Given the breadth of data required for prediction, trend marketers must utilize a range of different data sources and methodologies. I carry out every key research methodology in my job, from online polling to focus groups. Each of these provides different data types and can add something new to the mix. I also spend time scanning a wide range of different data sources. It is not enough to restrict yourself to a few key titles. Limiting your input will limit your output.

Trend marketers also need to be open to the opinions and advice of other people. They cannot know everything about every sector or demographic, so they will need to gain advice from experts in particular fields. These could be academics, specialists or enthusiasts. They need to be willing to listen carefully to the opinions of each group. They also need to be able to admit their mistakes. Like scientists or detectives, they will come up with theories and hunches that can help them predict more quickly, but these may not always be correct, and subsequent evidence can disprove them. If it does, they need to be able to admit that a theory was wrong and walk away from it.

BE SYSTEMATIC

Data processing

> *Having a formal, rigorous analytical process can be very useful for*
> *predictive work.*

P T Black, Partner, Jigsaw International (China)

Effective trend marketing is a systematic process. To succeed it must follow a formal path from identification via interpretation to implementation. Each stage of the process requires a logical approach. Marketers themselves must therefore be systematic in their methodology. They need to study consumers within agreed regular environmental limits. They need to analyse trends using a logical process. They need to implement strategies based on formal methodologies. Within a trend team, it is essential therefore that there are enough personnel who are methodical. Those who observe informally can afford to be less so. But those whose role is to identify data patterns, or who are charged with interpreting or implementing trends, need to be organized and efficient.

Data recording

One of the key elements of the trend marketing process is the recording of data. It is not enough just to observe trends. There needs to be evidence of them too. Management, fellow workers and clients will all require some form of evidence to convince them of the existence or potential of a new trend. The interpretation process requires a combination of data from each part of the observation process. Such data are also an essential part of the implementation process. Each part of the forecasting process will therefore require some form of data retention. Primary observation can be recorded visually via stills or video photography, or verbally using taped or written notes. To record secondary observation data, new notes can be taken or other people's can be stored. Notes must be kept of how the interpretation of a trend was arrived at, and minutes must be taken from any meetings during the strategic determination phase (see Chapter 22).

Once primary or secondary observational data have been recorded, they need to be stored in such a way that they can be easily cross-referenced or retrieved. A good trend library is an invaluable tool, and the basis of any trend forecaster's armoury. It can be used as a stimulus aid, to enable informed interpretation. It can provide evidence and evocative manifestations of a particular trend. A library today can be physical or virtual. Digitization has made it much easier to store and retrieve written and visual data. I remember being in the offices of a large fashion trend fore-caster some years ago and seeing cupboards filled with piles of photographs each held together with rubber bands. Digitization has removed the need for such a storage system. At Next Big Thing, I have a website that stores and segments our trend data. This includes statistical reports, photographs, video footage and so on. I also have a shelving system where I store any important non-digital evidence, such as paper reports, cuttings from print magazines or nightclub flyers.

The key to retrieving data efficiently from the library is the creation of a logical classification system. This is true whether you are studying trends on your own or as part of a large team. Luckily I actively enjoy cataloguing. As the son of two librarians, perhaps I have it in the genes! But all forecasters need to understand the classification process. The Next Big Thing classifi-cation system places trend data into one or more of the following four sections: sectors, demographics, locations and trends. Each of these is divided into several sub-sections. Sectors are divided into disciplines or industries such as design, food, health and home. Demographics are segmented by age (pre-teens, teens, middle youth), generation (eg millen-nials, Baby Boomers), gender, social grade (HNWIs, BC1, C2DE) and so on. Location is divided by territory, from specific nations such as the UK or Germany, to broader groups such as Scandinavia or the BRIC territories. This may seem complex, but when searching for a piece of evidence you found months ago such a stratified system can prove invaluable.

Next Big Thing consults across all sectors, demographics and territories, so our system needs to be broad in its scope. But in-house trend teams may favour a more single-sector or department-focused approach. Whatever system is used, there should be a standard structure that everyone involved in the trends process understands and can easily use. This is useful on both a practical and a theoretical level. On a practical level, any team needs to be able to locate data quickly and easily. On a theoretical level, the system-atic classification of trends helps systematize the trend analysis process. It forces marketers to determine both the source of a trend and its potential impact. It also enables them to ask the same question across different cate-gories, which aids the identification of macro trends.

INNOVATE

Innovation culture

The supreme examples of innovative brands are the ones like Apple that are happy to experiment and ready to fail. Companies that slave themselves to their consumers like Sky also make good innovators, because they're always thinking about the customer first.

Rod Henwood, ex-New Business Director, Channel 4

Innovation becomes more difficult to maintain as you get bigger. In many bigger companies no one wants to rock the boat, so it's hard to inflict real change. You have to try to keep that entrepreneurial, innovative root alive.

Tim Richards, CEO, Vue Entertainment

Trend data can prove an invaluable tool for determining and improving business strategy. However, if a company is not open to change, then any efforts made in identifying and analysing trends will be ineffective. In order to implement trend data into the business process effectively, companies need a change-friendly culture.

Each company has its own unique culture, created by a combination of traditional practices and leadership attitudes. The 'way things are done' in any company will typically determine how personnel approach any new undertaking. Some company cultures are more accommodating of new ideas and strategies than others. Large, traditionalist and state-funded companies can build up levels of bureaucracy, and policy can be hard to change. In contrast entrepreneurial companies such as Virgin in the 1970s or Apple and Innocent today are often centred around innovation. The same is true of different industries too. By their nature, sectors such as banking and the automotive industry are typically more traditional and slow-moving in their strategies than, say, the fashion or personal technology industries. And, because they have more to lose, successful market-leading companies are usually less open to change than challenger companies.

Innovation management

To create an innovation culture, you have to show it's something that's allowed, accepted and considered to make a difference. You have to reward and encourage innovation. You have to move away from 'business as usual'. You have to train people about what it means and how to do it. You have to set up forums that allow innovation to be explored. You've got to allow people the time to innovate and reward them for innovation.

Alex Owens, Director of Brand Development and Consumer Insight, Capital One

It's about having somebody with a passion that will drive trends through at all levels. And it really helps if your senior board understand what those trends are and allow you to cascade that down.

Michele Giles, Head of Insight, Premier Foods

Unless a company can accept the potential impact of a trend and be willing to change its mindset accordingly, any efforts to benefit from a trend are likely to fail. So the first step in introducing trend data into your company should be the encouragement of innovation and the reduction of internal scepticism. The natural reaction to change is fear or negativity. It is understandable therefore that personnel will initially prefer traditional behaviours and strategies to new ones. Change is disruptive. Creativity is disruptive. New ideas are disruptive. However, they are all also essential, so change needs to be seen throughout the company as a good thing. The easiest way to do this is from the top down. If senior management are convinced of the need for change and champion it from the highest level, this will aid its progress through the company. At the same time, individuals and departments need to be allowed to offer and pursue new ideas with a chance of recognition and without fear of reprisals. Regular brainstorming sessions should be run in which no idea is considered a bad one. It is also important to make the right resources available. Some companies, such as Nokia and Mindshare, have intranet sites full of trend reports, materials that make it easy for people to run brainstorms, and data on previous innovation-based successes.

7

In-house insights

TREND INTEGRATION

*It's important to have a formal structure; otherwise trends can go in one ear and
out the other!*

Liisa Puolakka, Head of Brand Identity, Nokia

After considering your attitude to trends, the next step before embarking
on trend marketing is to decide how you and your company will approach it
on a practical level. Many companies have an informal approach to trends.
They include trends on an *ad hoc* basis within the marketing process, rather
than at specific agreed stages. Sometimes they include them in communication channel decisions; at other times they include them in brand positioning strategies. But too often the decision is left to chance. No one individual
is allocated the responsibility for either identifying or integrating trends, so
it is left up to whoever hears of a trend to suggest its inclusion. But best-
practice trend marketing requires a more formal, systematic structure. To
ensure this happens, a company needs to establish an internal system that
can effectively process and integrate trends. No matter how relevant and
insightful a trend, it cannot be exploited successfully unless such a system is
in place.

TREND TEAM

*I have internally a few people that help me. There is a product manager from
R&D that collects technology trends for me. There is a person doing market
research that gathers consumer information, and a designer that I work with who*

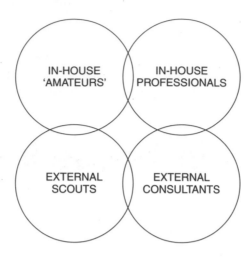

Figure 7.1 Trend personnel

collects the more aesthetic trend information. It's not part of their official job description, but their managers appreciate what they are doing, and it has become part of their daily job.

Brechje Vissers, Manager Colour Marketing and Innovation, PPG Industries (Netherlands)

You can learn a lot from the people within your company. It's almost like having your own internal scout network. We've set up a monthly forum in which we offer people from across a range of departments the opportunity to talk about the trends they've found. The sort of thing they might have just talked about casually over a coffee before, we now give them the chance to actually present.

Hanna Chalmers, Head of Research and Insight, Universal Music Group

If budgets or the skill sets of personnel do not offer the opportunity to establish a dedicated trends team, there are alternatives (Figure 7.1). Non-specialists within the organization can provide a level of trend forecasting. Trend spotting can be made part of corporate culture. This can be done by encouraging staff to look out for new trends and consumer changes and rewarding those who suggest usable trends, perhaps by instigating a monthly prize for the most interesting trend.

To bring greater formality to the process, trend marketing tasks can be added to individual staff members' job functions. Trend forecasting is an exciting activity, and can be seen as an enjoyable alternative to the daily work routine. 'Amateur' forecasters can carry out a limited amount of media monitoring. They can subscribe to and read trend websites or trend bulletins.

They can scan the internet for polling data. They can check out new retail outlets or nightclubs. They can carry out observation techniques such as vox pops and expert depth interviews. Armed with an understanding of trend development, they can interpret any trends that they do identify, to determine their relevance to the business. They can then help drive trend-based strategies through the company, armed with the evidence they have accumulated. To be even more effective, such a process can be systematized, and a set structure put in place. For instance, a specific amount of time could be set aside per day or per week for each individual to study trends.

TREND DEPARTMENT

Recruitment

> *The perfect trends team includes quantitative and qualitative researchers, data analytics people who can look at customer databases, and statistical people – having them all working in the same room on the same issue but looking at it from different points of view. The most powerful solutions I've ever found have come from mixing all those disciplines together.*

Sue Elms, EVP Global Media Practice, Millward Brown

> *In insight you have to be proactive: linking disparate pieces of information together to make something cohesive. Rather than waiting to do a specific piece of research, you should be listening to everything that's coming in and converting that into something interesting.*

Michele Giles, Head of Insight, Premier Foods

The most effective way to utilize trend data, however, is to create a specialist trends team. As change rates increase, every large company today needs a trend marketing function. The size of the team will depend on company size and budget. If you are running a small company and you already have an insights team, you can perhaps reassign roles to place a greater focus on the future, or add new trends personnel to the team. In a larger company, one or more personnel should always work full time on futures work. Global companies should certainly all have stand-alone trend teams, to sit alongside the current insight or research team.

Between them, the team needs to display the key trend marketing skill sets (see Chapter 6). They should be people and future focused. They should be generalists able to handle a range of different trends skills. They need to be able to conceive hypotheses but also know when to drop them. Different disciplines within the trend forecasting process also require specific skill sets. The identification process is the least analytical of the three disciplines. It requires instinct or 'feel' more than logic or marketing knowledge, and individuals who are good at interpersonal relations, unafraid of new social situations and with a good visual sense. The best informal trend observers are typically young, visually literate and socially mobile. Desk research, however, requires a slightly more analytical approach. The best desk researchers enjoy 'number crunching' and should have a knowledge of statistics. Interpretation requires a similarly logical mind alongside an understanding of consumer behaviour. Implementation on the other hand requires a different set of skills. To determine and implement trend-driven strategies successfully, trend marketers need to be able to convince and inspire a communal understanding and execution of trends across disciplines and personality types.

Integration

> *Insight should be at the heart of the client process. Unfortunately it is still quite siloed in many agencies. It is often seen simply as somewhere you go if you need 'research stuff'. There should be more flow through the company. Too often there's a disconnect between the people who have the information and the people who have marketing power. Insight and planning should be part of the same unit.*

Jo Rigby, Research Director EMEA, Omnicom Media Group

> *Insight is too often in the wrong part of the process to make a fundamental change to the business, so we're only able to 'tweak' an idea.*

Sue Elms, EVP Global Media Practice, Millward Brown

For trend research to have an effective impact on marketing strategies, there needs to be integration between the trend and marketing functions. The role of trends within the marketing process needs to be recognized by the rest of the company. Reporting, influencing and decision-making processes must be agreed upon. The trend marketing function must have specific, allocated budgets and budgetary controls.

To be most effective, the trend team needs to be part of the marketing department (Figure 7.2). A clear reporting structure needs to be established. Whoever oversees the trend function should report to the director of marketing or the director of insights. Part of a company's marketing budget must also be set aside for trends. Trend research can have at least as great an impact on profits as any other form of consumer research, but few companies allocate separate budgets for trends-related work. This is one reason why so many companies fail to exploit trends successfully. A

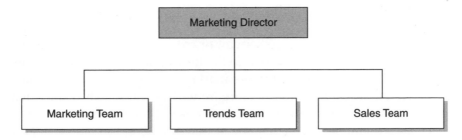

Figure 7.2 Marketing organization

formalized system needs to be put in place to sign off budget allocation and decision making. This fulfils two functions. On the one hand it ensures researchers take a responsible approach to budgeting. On the other it encourages a greater level of acceptance of that research within the company. If forecasting is done using a consultancy, then a point person needs to be allocated. It will be the point person who liaises with the external trend team, collects and distributes any materials, organizes internal attendance at meetings and so on.

Management

> *A good researcher is always identifying trends. But the thing that's much more difficult is convincing people that a trend's going to happen. And that's the key. That's what makes a researcher brilliant, that second part of the role. It's about force of personality and building relationships. It's not enough just to think of the analytical bit; you also have to be forceful and outgoing. If you can win people's trust and confidence, that's the biggest challenge.*

Hanna Chalmers, Head of Research and Insight, Universal Music Group

> *At a global level, we'll look at what the individual countries around the world are identifying as their growth opportunities or threats... One of the advantages of a decentralized company is that you get to have eyes and ears throughout the world that are motivated to keep tabs on what's keeping their local customers happy, what the competition's doing and so on. It's almost like our own little internet or scout network.*

Tom Pickles, Senior Director, Global Menu Solutions, McDonald's (USA)

Once you have set up a trend department, you need to manage it. Aside from standard personnel issues, one of the key areas for improvement is the increased utilization of insights. Insight personnel too often have to focus on specific product-led projects or day-to-day queries from other departments. The team's ability to forecast trends can be enhanced by removing such tasks from the trend-focused members of the team. This allows them time to focus on cross-sector or cross-demographic trend work, for instance transferring the responsibility for running statistical data from the insight team to others within the marketing or planning department, freeing up the insight team to run more trends-based research. Time is not the only factor in improving trend efficiency. Some corporate trends processes are simply not systematized enough. Trend marketing must follow as structured an approach as any other marketing or research function. The formal process detailed in the second section of the book offers one efficient way to deal with trend work.

Another way to enhance the effectiveness of a trends team is to improve the internal communication of trend data. Trends personnel must learn the most effective ways to drive trend data through a company (see Chapter 21). An insights team can be very good at gathering and analysing trend data. But if the team is unable to diffuse the data internally, those data will remain 'siloed' rather than successfully integrated into marketing strategies. This can happen all too often. Many companies undertake or commission costly trends research that is never used. I spoke to one head of research at an advertising agency who had delivered primary reports on Conscious Consumption, Gender Blending and the New Old that were well in advance of the trend reaching the mainstream, but that were ignored at the time by management, so missing a major commercial opportunity.

Trends develop differently in different countries (see Chapter 10). To understand national trends and international trend variations, there also needs to be communication between insight teams in different territories. Many territories will already have their own insight or trend teams, but some may not. Each territory needs to assign at least one research or marketing team member who can act as trend liaison. This person's role will be to identify relevant national trends, interpret how global trends might diffuse in that country and then feed back the information to the parent company.

8

Outsourcing insights

TREND OUTSOURCING

Of course, you always need to ground yourself in your own industry: what's worked and what hasn't, the way retailers evaluate product and their margin requirements and so on. But it's also important to have a fresh perspective from the outside, from different sectors. It's critical to have both sides. It's like having a portfolio.

Dave Capper, President Lifestyle, Music and Media, Hasbro (USA)

The best trends agencies can translate facts into opinion to create a debate, or understand the commercialization of insights and operate a consultancy-based approach. They have experience of implementation and are able to create change within an organization.

Alex Owens, Director of Brand Development and Consumer Insight, Capital One

Fresh perspective	✓
Different attitudes	✓
Unbiased opinion	✓
Additional data	✓
Specialist data	✓
Edited data	✓

Figure 8.1 Outsourcing attributes

Some companies run their trend work in-house. But others outsource some or all of it to independent consultants. Each company that uses an independent consultant has its own unique reasons for doing so (Figure 8.1). Many companies simply do not have the budgets to run their own full-service trend marketing department. For them, an in-house team is not an option, so they need to outsource some or all of their forecasting function. But it is not always a question of budget. Some of the biggest companies in the world use independent trend forecasting consultants. General Electric, Pacific Gas and Electric, and Siemens-Westinghouse have all employed the Global Business Network, a trends consultancy run by forecasting guru Peter Schwartz. Netherlands-based consultancy Trendwatching has worked with Coca-Cola, Unilever, KLM Airlines, Sony Ericsson and Bacardi. My own company has been retained by the BBC, HSBC, AOL, BSkyB, Barclays and Hachette among others. For such companies, lack of budget is not the issue. They have other reasons to outsource. Many do so because they like to gain an outside perspective. Some do so to free up their insight team for other tasks, and others because they do not have the specific personnel to analyse trends in a particular sector or demographic. Each case is different.

The most commonly outsourced segment of the process is identification. There are dozens of companies that search the globe for new trends. Some are oriented to specific segments such as design or youth. Others, like my own company, look across the board. Some use robust methodologies. Others are less formal. But all can provide a level of inspiration. There are also companies that offer independent variants on key identification disciplines. Many companies monitor print and online media. Research agency TNS, for instance, claims to scan over 10,000 media sources in the UK alone. Durrants scans 5,000 UK print publications plus thousands of news websites and newswires. Trend interpretation is also often outsourced. A consultancy might be asked to report on the implications of a particular new trend or trends. Implementation has traditionally been less commonly outsourced, and is perhaps more typically associated with management consultancies. But the situation is changing. I and other consultants have begun receiving more requests for trend implementation projects in recent years.

Trend work can be outsourced to consultants or scouts. Trend consultants are qualified professionals who can perform one or all parts of the trend process. Trend scouts are 'amateur' trend spotters who can provide examples of trends that might otherwise be out of reach.

TREND SCOUTS

The best scouts are typically intelligent, opinionated young people who work in the creative fields, who are hungry for the 'new', go out a lot and have good social networks.

Jo Peters, The Scout, Mindshare

Trends can come from a huge range of different sectors, demographics and markets. The more of these you can monitor at any one time, the more effective your trend forecasting is likely to be. But it is not possible for a single internal insights team to study every street or every club. To monitor trends globally or even nationally requires the help of others. A good way to do this is by employing 'scouts' to observe and report back on what they see. They can often identify small unusual trends very early in their development. Scouts have informed me about several cutting-edge trends I might otherwise have missed, from an interest in bicycle courier styles to Cringe Nights in nightclubs, where visitors read out the most 'cringeworthy' extracts from their teenage diaries. Although these might in themselves not be immediately useful within the business process, they can provide clues to new trends, or evocative evidence of those already spotted. Bicycle courier fashion was the first indication that cycling was becoming 'cool'. Cringe nights were an early example of Confession Culture.

A large number of scouts are typically formalized into a 'scout network'. A company can employ its own scouts, or outsource the scouting process to a dedicated independent network. Trend consultancies tend to have the biggest scout networks. According to its website, the Netherlands-based trend consultancy Trendwatching has a global network of 8,000 'business savvy people, fast-moving urbanites, slow-moving thinkers [and] frequent flyers'. Several media agencies, from Mindshare to Lowe Worldwide, now have their own global networks.

Companies can utilize their own corporate networks to locate relevant early adopters, or they can recruit them in the field during immersion or observation sessions. Once a few scouts are found in a particular city or sector, they themselves can help recruit other scouts. Scout networks require a coordinator to manage them day to day. This needs to be a person who has the ability to communicate effectively with and inspire cutting-edge individuals.

Maintaining a scout network does not need to be a costly process. Trend forecasting is considered a very 'cool' job by many early adopters. For this reason, some scouts will happily do it unsalaried, just so they can tell their peers that they are working for a trend forecaster. For others it will be enough to see their name in print as the discoverer of a trend. But some will expect more formal rewards. This can be in the form of cash or 'gifts' such as new products. Paying scouts on a regular basis can increase costs dramatically, so it is best to pay them only for one-off jobs or if they provide a useful observation. This latter method is the most cost-effective for the trend marketer. Trendwatching's scouts are rewarded with gifts from the company's 'gift gallery' whenever they identify a 'promising new business idea'.

TREND CONSULTANTS

Purpose

Outside people can have a different perspective from you. They can offer different expertise, and they might bring an extra dimension, personality- or intellect-wise.

Alex Owens, Director of Brand Development and Consumer Insight, Capital One

Outsourcing can help you to understand trends beyond your immediate category and can have more credibility.

Amanda Meers, Group Account Director, Jigsaw Strategic Research (Australia)

Trend consultancies can provide companies with useful trend data and analysis. I run a trends consultancy, so of course am not completely unbiased! But the number of blue-chip companies that utilize trend consultancies shows I am not alone in my opinion.

An independent trends marketer can offer an independent view. This can be useful for several reasons. It can provide a fresh perspective and a new set of eyes and ears. It can also remove fears of potential internal bias. Forecasters offer their insights because such insights exist, not because they have 'a political axe to grind'. Externals can also be useful in adding to your bank of identified trends. Given the rate and scope of consumer change today, the greater the input of data the better. A consultancy can be called upon to provide broad trends on a demographic a client company has yet to investigate, or to provide more detailed trends in a sector the company has only a broad overview of. Alternatively a company can sometimes be swamped with data and needs someone to edit them down to a more manageable shortlist of key trends. On several occasions I have been asked to put together a summary of key trends within a particular area or sector, with relevant analysis and recommendations. These have ranged from communal trends in Britain to luxury trends in the BRIC markets.

Choice

Trend consultancies can provide a range of identification services. Some offer primary identification services, either bespoke or off-the-peg. This can fulfil all of a company's identification needs or simply act as an adjunct to its own identification process. Such companies typically obtain their data from informal observational research. They are particularly prevalent in the fashion, design and youth sectors. They provide examples, visuals and a level of analysis from across sectors and territories. Some, such as Trendwatching, PSFK and Japanese Streets, run free websites. Others, like the Future Laboratory, Trendsight and WGSN, run subscription-based ones. Some research companies, such as Mintel, provide a web-based service that offers statistical data and complex analysis as well as visual and reported examples. Companies such as Carlin International and Fashion Trends publish regular printed reports. Media scanning too can be outsourced. Some companies specialize in print and broadcast monitoring and others in online media. The latter typically search for single words or brand names, however, so can be expensive to employ as multi-trend scanners.

The interpretation and implementation processes can also be outsourced. Interpretation is typically run as a one-off procedure. I have on several occasions been asked to provide a report or in-person presentation analysing specific trends. This will usually focus either on a single macro trend, such as Gender Blending, or on key trends in a particular sector or demographic. Although companies are more likely to employ management consultants for the implementation process, trend consultants are increasingly being asked to manage this process too. Methods such as brainstorming, workshopping and scenario planning can all be utilized successfully here (see Chapter 22).

The criteria for choosing a trends consultancy are similar to those for choosing any supplier. First check if anyone in the company has successfully employed a trend consultancy before. Has your media agency worked with one that you can utilize? Can business acquaintances or suppliers recommend one? The next step is to establish what part of the trend process you want it to provide. Each company offers a unique combination of services and skill sets. A full-service trends research company can offer any service. A specialist trends consultancy will offer certain specific services. A cool hunting consultancy, for instance, will provide you with data on new trends but is less likely to offer interpretation. You also need to choose a consultancy that matches your budget. Most consultancies will offer a day rate or a menu of deliverables. You must also establish their credibility. Some consultancies are better than others. Trend marketing is a relatively new discipline, so there are no required qualifications, league tables or annual industry polls to help a company choose. You should therefore study a company's client list and testimonials, and enquire of any colleagues as to their reputation. Once you have arrived at your shortlist, you should invite representatives of each consultancy to make a formal in-person presentation. From that you can make your choice.

Methodology

Once you have hired a consultancy, you can utilize it for a range of different functions. You can use it to write one-off trend reports, you can subscribe to its trends bulletin or website, or you can pay it an annual retainer. The decision as to which approach to take will depend on your individual needs (Figure 8.2).

Several trend consultancies offer a non-client-specific monthly, bi-monthly or quarterly trends report. It will provide this on a subscription or one-off basis. This typically includes a range of trends across different sectors and demographics. I used to publish a popular subscription-based printed bi-monthly report that combined industry-specific micro trend news with more in-depth features on cross-sector macro trends. As noted above, some trend consultancies run subscription-only websites. Such a service can be a relatively low-cost entry-level tool for companies new to trend marketing. It can also be a useful addition to the resources of an overworked insight team. You can alternatively hire a trends consultancy on a continuous basis and pay it an annual retainer to act as a virtual trends department.

Another approach is to employ consultants to write or present one-off trend reports. These can focus on single trends, sectors or markets or

MENU
One-off reports
Regular bespoke reports
Regular omnibus reports
Free website
Subscription-based website
Scout network
Interpretation
Implementation

Figure 8.2 Outsourcing options

summarize a range of key micro or macro trends. There are many occasions on which a company will need a trends report. A food manufacturer may be considering a move into a new category and need to understand new developments in it before it does. A cell phone service provider might be targeting a new consumer market such as the New Old, and want to determine the market's purchase potential or how best to reach it. A media agency might be pitching for a new client in a sector it has not worked in before.

Summary: Part 2

- Trend analysis is a new and as yet typically quite informal process.

- The many myths about trend analysis should be ignored.

- The process should be formalized into a trend marketing function.

- Trend marketing should include identification, interpretation and implementation.

- Trend marketers need to focus on people and the future.

- Trend marketers should avoid bias and be open to new ideas.

- All companies need an integrated trends function.

- Trend marketing requires a range of different skills.

- Trend teams require time, structure and strong communication paths.

- It can sometimes be useful to employ external trend consultants.

Part 3

Understanding trends

9

How trends start

TREND INITIATORS

Things like government policy and macroeconomics have a huge impact on trends. When the government announces it is building highways everywhere the impact is tremendous. Or when McDonald's or Burger King opens in a country. That sort of stuff very much affects people's lifestyles.

P T Black, Jigsaw International (China)

Once you have created an innovation culture, organized a trend marketing structure and recruited an in-house or out-of-house team, you can begin the process of identifying trends. But doing this requires a full understanding of the origins, composition and typologies of trends.

Trends thrive when the conditions are ripe and consumers are ready to adopt them. To grow, a trend requires the existence of strong behavioural and attitudinal drivers and positive social or environmental factors (see Part 5). Sociologist Henrik Vejlgaard compares trends to forest fires: they will spread only if the environment is ready.

But no matter how primed the environment is, a forest fire still needs a spark to set it off. Trends do not just appear spontaneously. They are driven by specific environmental or individual changes. What is happening around consumers affects their thoughts or actions. Trends start when an environmental shift disrupts consumers' normative attitudes and behaviours. And they typically occur as a reaction to something a consumer experiences. This can happen in one of two ways. A trend can occur when consumers react positively towards something, such as the introduction of a new product or technology. But one can also occur when consumers react *against* something. The Local Heroes trend for increased localization was a

POLITICS	ECONOMICS	SOCIETY	TECHNOLOGY
eg policy	eg Maslow	eg health	eg comms
eg legislation	eg personal	eg schools	eg transport
eg events	eg national	eg age	eg leisure

Figure 9.1 Trend initiators

reaction against the distancing nature of globalism. Those things a consumer reacts to form what I call trend initiators. They can be segmented using PEST categories into political, economic, social, and technological and environmental initiators (Figure 9.1).

INITIATOR TYPOLOGIES

Political initiators

Political initiators include government actions such as laws as well as changes in the political climate at home or abroad. The introduction of new laws or the rescinding of old ones can initiate new trends. Recent employee legislation across several markets has encouraged many consumers to improve their work–life balance and to share parenting responsibilities better across genders. The introduction of laws banning smoking in public places has prompted consumers to frequent bars less and increasingly stay in their own homes or visit friends in theirs.

Political initiators can revolve around reactions against new laws. Some consumers will react against what they see as increasing pressure to conform. Others will react because they believe their liberty is being compromised. They will subsequently behave in a way that is directly contrary to governmental or societal norms. Sometimes they do this simply to register their disapproval. At other times they do it in an attempt to change the rules. In Western countries in the 1950s and 1960s, young consumers reacted against the wealth and conformity of their society to create the hippie and anti-war movements. Today many consumers in the heartland of Middle England are reacting against what they see as the erosion of their personal freedoms: from the use of speed cameras to fuel price increases, from the reduction of pensions to the ban on fox hunting. I call these new activists Kilroys, combining a British slang term for 'every-man' with the name of television personality and ex-politician Robert Kilroy-Silk, whose views epitomized their individualistic stance.

Some political events can make people afraid for their long-term safety. This can initiate a number of different trends. Some consumers will adopt behaviours that have a direct effect on their circumstances. In 2008, fear of recession encouraged consumers to start saving again, after decades of decline. Others will change attitudes rather than behaviours. For instance they might become more conservative, seek the comfort of the home and look back with affection to what they consider a safer time. Trend forecaster Faith Popcorn spotted the trend in the 1980s and christened it Cocooning.

Economic initiators

The economic environment has a huge impact on trend creation. Consumers' relative wealth and disposable income levels affect how they think and behave. Abraham Maslow's *Motivation and Personality* (Harper & Brothers, 1954) introduced the concept of the hierarchy of needs. This is a useful guide to how economic initiators work. Consumers at different levels of economic stability have certain needs that they seek to satisfy. If an opportunity arises to satisfy those needs then they will take it. This can start a trend for anything that satisfies that need. As a consumer's economic situation improves, new needs, and therefore new trends, will develop.

A company's target market will be open to the influence of different trends dependent upon what stage they are at. Those at the lowest economic level need to focus all of their efforts on surviving. They are motivated by physiological needs such as air, food, water, shelter, sleep and sex. When an individual or a society is at this stage, new trends will arise for products or services that satisfy these needs, such as cheap food. Those who gain the economic power to satisfy their survival needs will then typically become motivated by safety needs. These are based around the desire to escape the threat of physical and emotional harm. There will therefore be a flowering of trends focused on structure and stability: the rule of law, a safe neighbourhood, job security and financial stability. The next motivator is social needs. At this stage of a society's development, trends will appear that revolve around friendship, community, social acceptance and relationships with partners and family. Those who satisfy these needs will then be motivated by esteem: the need to feel important within oneself or within a peer network. New trends for products and services that enhance recognition, social status and a sense of achievement will occur. Cognitive and aesthetic needs come next. A trend might arise for consumers to seek knowledge for its own sake: discovering and creating new things so as to understand their world better. Trends based around beauty and style too will appear. Once all these other needs are satisfied, consumers become motivated by self-actualization needs. These include moral codes, justice, freedom of self-expression and the quietness of solitude. These again will drive brand new trends.

Economic change can create trends in other ways too. Social history illustrates how consumers living through a recession will often try to avoid the reality of their lives. This can manifest itself in a trend for nostalgia or escapism. It reached its peak in the Great Depression of the 1930s, the high point for Hollywood glamour, and the oil crisis of the mid-1970s, when nostalgia was rife. A poor economic situation can create a trend for Cocooning, just as political instability can. A greater focus on the home can create further trends for products and services based around it: from increased television viewing to do-it-yourself products, and furniture sales to home entertaining. Unemployment and labour supply levels can also alter consumers' attitudes towards their working hours or their work–life balance, creating trends based around free time, stress levels and so on.

Socio-cultural initiators

Social initiators are those factors that relate to human society and its modes of organization. These include population, age, health, employment and education rates. They also include less statistically quantifiable factors such as lifestyle choices, and media and public opinion. The amount of education individuals gain will affect their attitudes, which in turn can affect their behaviours. When a cohort enjoys an increase in education, this can spark off new trends. The Baby Boomers who came of age in the 1960s typically gained a better education than previous generations. This gave them greater knowledge, confidence and expectations, sparking off behavioural trends not just in their youth but as they have aged as well. Health fears can be a strong trend initiator. When consumers become afraid of something, they will try to find ways to reduce that fear. They will typically do this by either resisting or actively ignoring that which they are afraid of. In the early 2000s, we saw consumers grow increasingly concerned over what was in their food: from genetic modification to trans-fats. As a result, purchase drivers based around health grew at the expense of price.

Trends can sometimes begin as a reaction to a contemporary social behaviour. The Extreme Pleasure trend for extreme sports, violent video games and practices such as 'happy slapping' are a reaction against the passivity prevalent in today's sedentary, distanced lifestyles. And the Wising Up trend is at least partly a reaction against the way in which society had been 'dumbed down'. Location can also affect trends. When people move into a new area, it affects their behaviours. This can happen at an individual or a group level. When consumers move from a rural area into the city, they will experience different needs. If enough consumers do so, these needs can create trends. This happened in Western nations many decades ago, and is happening now in BRIC territories such as China. The same applies in reverse: trends also occur when enough consumers move from urban to rural areas. It happened when consumers in the United States and Europe moved to the suburbs in the 1950s. It is starting to happen again, as consumers increasingly seek the calmness of a country lifestyle. This is a trend in itself, caused by dissatisfaction with urban lifestyles, but it has also helped create the Great Outdoors trend (see Chapter 10).

The media can help initiate trends, although these are typically limited to micro trends. Newspaper campaigns or coverage can shift consumer attitudes towards an event and spark off a trend connected to it. But the media are more likely to encourage a trend that has already begun. The trends for Well-being and Conscious Consumption were initiated by social and environmental drivers, but were encouraged by media editorial.

Technological initiators

I don't believe the drive for social networking and community is any different now than it probably was a hundred years ago. People always like to congregate around their interests. But it's a lot easier to do it now thanks to the internet.

Phil Guest, Managing Director Western Europe, Sulake

The introduction of a technological innovation can drive consumer usage of that innovation. For instance, the introduction of the mobile phone created a trend among consumers for mobile phone usage. The introduction of the iPod encouraged the use of MP3 players. This may seem obvious, but it is important to distinguish between product availability and consumer adoption trends, because many technologies are introduced that do not get used. The introduction of the technology itself is not what matters. What matters is the adoption of that technology by consumers. Video phones have yet to become a trend. Although the technology has been available for years, consumers have yet to want them enough to purchase them. MP3 players had been available for several years before the one-two punch of iTunes and iPods encouraged a purchase spike.

New technologies can also inspire further post-usage trends that spring from the use of those technologies. The invention of the jet engine in the 1940s had an enormous impact on society. On an immediate level, it created a trend for HNWIs to travel abroad more often, but it had other consequences. As the rich vacationed more, travel was increasingly featured in films, books and news reports. This led to a broader consumer interest in other countries, manifested in the purchase of more exotic, travel-related products and services. Purchase of foreign food grew. So too did 'jetsetter' lifestyle products: from exotic rugs to fondue sets. As the cost of flights fell in the 1970s, air travel became possible for more mainstream consumers. As they began to travel more, there was growth across a range of products, from cameras to travel books. In recent years, constant usage of the mobile phone created a demand for mobility in other areas. On a practical level, it has encouraged the uptake of MP3 players, portable DVD players and smartphones. On a broader level, it is encouraging consumers to seek more mobile lifestyles. Today consumers are increasingly interested in 'travelling light'. They are demanding shorter contract terms, putting more possessions in storage and increasingly renting products: DVDs, cars and even handbags.

10

Trend typologies

TYPOLOGY TRAITS

We just launched a new product called Miller Midnight in Russia recently, which is a black easy-drinking lager. It is a brand new piece of product development that has been developed to meet a Russian consumer need. Russian consumers are extremely innovation hungry right now. They have a passion for innovation and new and fresh ideas… and that's an attitude trend. But we also respond to trends in other areas: trends in flavour, trends around fragrances, and so on.

Andy Routley, International Brand Marketing Director, Miller, SAB Miller

Once initiated, trends can manifest themselves in different ways. Some trends are based around consumers' behaviour. Others are based around

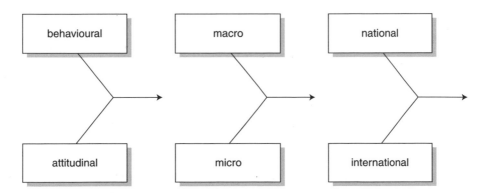

Figure 10.1 Trend typologies

their attitudes. Some trends have a greater impact than others. Some affect more markets than others. In order to exploit trends for strategic purposes, it is necessary to understand the different types of trends that occur. Each time a trend is identified it must be further defined, in order to enable correct analysis and commercial utilization. Is it a micro or macro trend, a behavioural or attitudinal trend, a national or international trend? (see Figure 10.1.)

Understanding the typology of a trend will provide vital clues as to its relevance, potential growth and usefulness. For instance, it is important to understand how big the future impact of a trend is going to be, in order to estimate the importance of it to your market or customer base. Some trends just affect a single sector. If a trend is confined to the food sector, say, then those within the food sector will need to react to the trend but those in other sectors will not. The same is true of trends that affect a single demographic, such as teenagers, or a single territory, such as the UK. For companies that target those markets, such a trend is important. For others it may not be. But if a trend has the potential to spread to other markets, then companies outside those sectors will need to be aware of it too. A trend that starts in the food sector can spread rapidly to others, as happened with trends such as Hectic Eclectic.

BEHAVIOURAL VERSUS ATTITUDINAL

Behavioural trends

> *We're trying to find better and better ways to communicate with people and the most effective places to communicate to them, so we focus on media and channel behaviour trends. But we also need to know attitudinal trends. How are people feeling about marketing when they're out? Are they paying attention? Are they giving their permission? They've all got a mobile phone, but how do they feel about getting ads on it?*

Sheila Byfield, Leader, Business Planning, Mindshare

Consumers can change in two ways. They can change their attitudes towards something or they can change their physical behaviour. Typically the former drives the latter.

Behavioural trends are changes in the ways that consumers behave. Consumers can change their behaviour in a number of ways. They can change what they do, how much they do something, when they do it and where they do it. The Are You Experienced trend is seeing consumers beginning to choose experiences over possessions. Americans now spend almost as much on eating out as they do on food for home consumption, and the US eating-out market has risen above a half-trillion dollars in total sales for the first time.[1] In the UK out-of-home food purchase has actually overtaken that in-home. It rose by over 100 per cent from 1992 to 2004, almost double the increase in spending on fresh and processed food and drink products,[2] and is now worth £17.7 billion.[3] In China, it has yet to reach such levels, but it is growing massively. The country's catering industry saw revenues rise by 22 per cent in 2004: well over twice the expansion speed of China's gross domestic product.[4] Meanwhile there has been a massive sales growth in experiential games such as karaoke-based 'Singstar' and the dance game 'Dance Dance Revolution'. Independent reports suggest Nintendo's new 'physical' console Wii has sold over five times more than the PS3. Sales of the console are higher than even Nintendo itself forecast. Experiential activities right across the leisure sector are proving increasingly popular, from spas to holidays. Experience gifting too is a growing market in Europe and the United States. It is now worth over $60 million worldwide and is growing 20 per cent annually.[5]

Behavioural trends are the 'holy grail' for trend marketers. Predicting them correctly and early enough provides the knowledge and time a company needs to adapt its strategy accordingly. They can have a direct impact on sales. If consumers decide they will stop buying one type of product and buy another, then sales of the former will fall. As noted above, the trend for healthy eating directly affected soft drinks sales. The trend for fast fashion also reduced sales of designer clothing. If the trend for consumers in the United States and the UK to take fewer car journeys continues, it will reduce the revenues of garages, oil companies and ultimately automotive manufacturers. Behavioural trends can also do more than this. They can necessitate change to marketing and sales strategies. As consumers have increased their online spending, not only has it directly affected physical retail sales; it has also forced companies to alter the entire way in which they market products.

Attitudinal trends

The way people understand society, where they fit into it and what they've got to contribute to it, informs trends relevant to the specifics of business. Such attitudinal trends translate into behaviours by defining what is and what isn't seen as acceptable.

Andy Shaw, Product Development Director, BT Agile Media,
British Telecom

Attitudinal trends do not have as immediate an impact on sales as behavioural trends. Consumers may change their attitude towards something without changing their behaviour. However, attitudinal trends are vital trend analysis tools. Spotting and correctly interpreting attitudinal trends are a hugely important part of trend marketing. They can help in brand positioning, product response and behavioural prediction.

The best way for brands to identify what will or won't work in tomorrow's marketplace is to get under the skin of their customers. This means understanding the 'why' as well as the 'how' of change. Identifying attitudinal trends can provide information on future purchase drivers and aid brand positioning. Attitudinal trends indicate which marketing methodologies, creative content and tone of voice customers will respond best to in future. If customers are starting to care more about the environment, for instance, they are more likely to respond well to marketing that stresses a company's green credentials. Such trends can also indicate potential consumer response to a new product range.

Importantly, attitudinal trends also offer clues that help in the prediction of future demands and behaviours. Attitudinal trends typically prefigure behavioural trends. Consumers usually change their attitude towards something before they change their behaviour around it. Consumers did not begin eating more healthily without reason. They did so because there was a growing attitude among them that it was important to eat healthily.

It was in fact attitudes that drove the Are You Experienced behavioural trend. After the materialism of the 1990s, consumers have been showing a growing interest in 'being' rather than just 'having'. In the major economies of Europe, as few as 10 per cent of consumers now consider that they are 'a person who wants to have a lot of money/expensive things'. Two-thirds of Russians disagree with the statement that they would be happier if they had more money. Half of all global consumers agree that 'the time it takes to become financially successful is not worth the time it takes away from other, more important things', the highest levels of agreement being in India (65 per cent) and Italy (64 per cent).[6]

The automotive industry is regularly affected by attitudinal trends. Much of the success of Volkswagen in the United States in the 1960s was due to a shift away from traditional 'big is better' attitudes. More recently, female consumers' greater sense of independence and entitlement has encouraged greater automotive purchase among this cohort. Consumers' growing concerns over the environment have also led to a demand for more energy-efficient cars, and a growing interest among young people in customization led to the introduction of a greater variety of models.

MICRO VERSUS MACRO

Micro trends

Trends that affect a relatively small number of consumers are known as 'micro trends'. The difference between micro and macro trends is similar to the difference between microeconomics and macroeconomics: '[Microeconomics is a] study of economics in terms of individual areas of activity (as a firm, household, or prices). [Macroeconomics is a] study of economics in terms of whole systems especially with reference to general levels of output and income and to the interrelations among sectors of the economy.'[7]

Micro trends are larger than fads but smaller than macro trends. Political consultant Mark Penn describes them as: 'small under-the-radar forces that can involve as little as one per cent of the population, but which are powerfully shaping our society... the hundreds of tiny shifts in attitude and behaviour that combine to create consumer change'.[8] They are typically regional or national, and are usually based around a single sector or behaviour. And they can be numerous. Penn's book *Microtrends* lists 75 of them. And the Trendhunter website, for instance, recently offered 'the 507 micro trends this week'!

Micro trends can be useful in themselves, especially for targeted or short-term marketing tactics. New micro trends such as fixed-wheel bikes or the 1980s revival could provide inspiration for an advertising creative, or promotional or sponsorship activity. But they also have another highly useful attribute. As with attitudinal trends, they can be an effective predictor of future activity. They offer clues to macro, global and cross-sector behaviours. Few micro trends operate in isolation. Many of them are the small, early manifestations of a large trend. Trends analysts identifying several micro trends based around a similar theme will realize that they might have stumbled across the beginnings of a new macro trend. A few years ago I found several separate trends such as revivals of knitting, folk music and poker that I thought were micro trends, but soon realized were part of a macro trend for 'old-fashioned' pastimes and behaviours that I christened Traditionalizing.

Micro trends can also be driven by macro trends. The Hectic Eclectic macro trend is seeing consumers trialling a wider range of behaviours. This means consumers want to do more in the same amount of time, creating a demand for products that help them stay more alert. Consequently energy drinks from Relentless to Red Bull are seeing massive sales. So too are 'energy gums' like Jolt. The popularity of hot caffeine drinks is growing in Brazil and China, and Coca-Cola has created Blak, a 'cola coffee'. As people spend more time experiencing more, there will also be a micro trend for products that aim to hide the signs of tiredness, such as L'Oréal Europe's Infallible range.

Macro trends

It helps to be able to consciously understand the broad [macro] trends in society, the trends around the way people are thinking and perceiving, and the way that informs reality. These are real trends that have practical consequences.

Andy Shaw, Product Development Director, BT Agile Media, British Telecom

Macro trends are the most powerful trends. They are all-encompassing shifts that typically influence a wide range of sectors, markets and demographics. They can rarely be confined to specific sectors or demographics. They are based around key consumer needs and attitudes. Macro trends are typically the summation of a number of micro trends. In this they are like a paradigm: 'a philosophical and theoretical framework; an outstandingly clear or typical example or archetype'.[9] They represent a broad, simple theme that can be summed up succinctly. Examples include: 'greed is good', 'small is beautiful', 'the young generation' and so on. This ties in with the more recent meaning of the word 'macro': 'a single computer instruction that stands for a sequence of operations'.[10]

One example of a new macro trend is the Great Outdoors trend: a renewed interest in outdoor pastimes and the countryside. This is affecting a range of different sectors. The rural population in Britain is now growing eight times faster than that of inner cities.[11] Over a third of first-time house buyers want to live in a village or market town, compared to just 12 per cent who want to live in a city centre and 14 per cent who want to live in the commuter belt.[12] The trend is composed of several micro trends. One of these is the trend for Natural Fitness. Cycling, running and walking are all on the increase. Britons bought 13 million bicycles in 2005, and spent £3.78 billion on bicycles and a further £657 million on accessories such as helmets, lights, pumps and locks. Britons spent £120 million on dedicated cycling holidays in 2006: up 30 per cent year on year.[13] Seventeen per cent of Britons now prefer using bicycles to cars or public transport.[14] The trend is also affecting choice of leisure pursuits. The Camping and Caravanning Club saw membership rise 10 per cent from 2002 to 2005. Retail too is being affected. There was just one farmers' market in the UK in 1997; now there are more than 500.[15] A quarter of Britons now use local markets,[16] and almost a third buy from farmers' markets and 90 per cent would like to. Supermarkets are being redesigned to look more like markets. Heinz has even produced a range of soups under the 'Farmers' Market' name. There is also a growing demand for the rural in design. References to plants, flowers and animals are proving popular in fabrics and interiors. Ruralism is a strong trend across a range of other sectors too: from Cath Kidston country-style cookware to the rise of garden fête chic among today's urban early adopter 20-somethings.

INTERNATIONAL VERSUS NATIONAL

International trends

> *It can be really useful to obtain data from different countries. It offers a different perspective on a topic.*
>
> Stephen Dalton, *The Times*

Trends can transcend national borders. International trends thrive in nations that share similar socio-economic traits or have reached similar stages of societal development. Some trends cross over into so many territories that they can be referred to as global trends. Like macro trends, they are typically based on strong behavioural drivers such as safety or status enhancement.

Some develop simultaneously in several territories at approximately the same time. The trend for bicycles described above is spreading across the UK, the United States and much of Europe simultaneously. But most begin in one or two countries and in time spread to others. For instance, a growth in the number of weddings was first manifested in the UK and has now spread to Russia. It looks set to grow elsewhere as the Traditionalizing and New Puritan trends encourage more consumers to seek comfort in traditional attitudes and activities.

There are now over 3 billion mobile users in the world.[17] That represents over half of the entire world population. Between them they send 2 trillion text messages a year.[18] But the trend began with a handful of consumers in just a few cities. It took time for it to spread elsewhere. But once it did, it was quickly adopted, eventually spreading to cover the globe. By 2006, the average mobile ownership rate per country had reached 80 per cent.[19] But over 50 nations now have cell phone subscription penetration rates higher than their population.[20] The rate is a massive 163 per cent in Hong Kong today,[21] and the average rate in Western Europe is 110 per cent.[22] The trend is not restricted to the developed nations. More people in China own a mobile than in any other country in the world. There are now over 500 million active mobile phone accounts there.[23] Russians own 115 million phones, the third biggest mobile ownership rate in the world. India is the largest growth market, with over 5 million new phones bought each month. The country is expected to reach 500 million subscribers by the end of 2010.[24] Even in some of the very poorest countries, consumers are leapfrogging traditional fixed technologies in favour of mobile technologies. In countries such as the Sudan, the vast distances between communities and the absence of technological infrastructure mean that the satellite-enabled capabilities of mobile phones and laptops are often the only way for consumers to enter the digital world. Mobile phone usage is clearly now a truly global trend.

By studying trends that are currently taking place in one or two territories but are starting to spread elsewhere, marketers can make judgements about trends in their own countries. They can determine if a trend might reach them and what impact it might have. They can determine how consumers in different territories might or might not adopt new trends, and what the implications might be. They can learn from the way brands in other countries have successfully adapted their strategies to retain consumer demand. This is as important for national as for global companies. A national telecommunications company, for instance, needs to understand how new technologies are being accepted by consumers in 'early adopter' nations to understand how consumers might do so in its own country. It needs advance warning of how consumers in other countries are reacting to change, and it can pick up early on design and product trends by studying consumer responses to design in different territories.

National trends

There are nuances that make things more relevant to some markets than others. Trying to reach younger consumers in the UK is very different from reaching the same consumers in South Africa, for instance. Broadband penetration is extraordinarily high in the UK. A viral, digital approach works with them. But it is much lower in South Africa where more traditional advertising forms such as television are still extremely effective.

Andy Routley, International Brand Marketing Director, Miller, SAB Miller

Two different trends in two separate markets can sometimes look similar, and it is only with rigorous analysis that you can understand how different they are. There is interest in organic food across the world, but it is for different reasons. In the West it is popular mostly because of concerns over nutrition and anti-corporatism. In China it is much more about personal safety. There is an enormous fear of local companies not observing regulations and using dangerously toxic levels of pesticides on their foods. So in the West, products from small,

independent local manufacturers seem healthier. But in China the opposite is
true. A mother will say 'I need to see the Coca-Cola seal on that package'!

P T Black, Partner, Jigsaw International (China)

Some trends can thrive in some territories but may not spread into others. Businesses have become more adept at understanding different cultures in a business context. But as the world moves ever faster into tomorrow, it is no longer enough to understand how territories traditionally react to particular marketing approaches. Marketers now need to understand how they will react in the future. To know how to implement trends overseas it is important to understand how different cultures influence, and are influenced by, trends.

Every country has its own individual traits that impact on consumer attitudes and behaviours. Territorial traits develop over many years. They are typically based on a range of factors: environment, climate, moral codes, laws, infrastructure, foreign policy and so on. Trends need certain environmental or social conditions in order to thrive (see Part 5). If those conditions are found in a particular territory, the trend is likely to grow there. If they are not, then it is not. A trend like the New Old trend, for instance, which is seeing a greater hedonism among Grey Consumers, will be of great interest to Western companies but will have little impact in China. The trend is based on the ageing of the youthful, rebellious Baby Boomer generation. But this segment does not exist in China: those who grew up in China in the 1960s and 1970s led a very different life. Conversely there are segment-based trends in China that will not appear in the West, such as the Haigui, those who went overseas to study or work and having returned now straddle both worlds, or the Baofahu, those who have become suddenly very wealthy thanks to foreign investment.

Even trends that do spread globally can often also manifest themselves differently in different countries. Attitudes towards green issues, for instance, differ greatly from country to country. Seventy-six per cent of Chinese consumers have bought a green product but just 32 per cent of Americans have. Just 18 per cent of Russians claim to recycle but over 50 per cent of Chinese do. In fact the territories most concerned over climate change are South Africa and Brazil.[25] The reasons for international trend differences are often connected to environment or history. Polls might suggest that Scandinavians are not as overtly concerned over climate change as some nations, but that is perhaps because it has become such an ingrained part of their lives. The same can hold true of the role of women in society. Scandinavians and many Eastern European nations have employed women as regularly as men for so many years that women's rights are of less immediate concern. Trends concerning changing gender roles will therefore have less impact there.

Although each territory is different, there are some generalizations that can help. Trends spread more slowly in larger countries such as Russia or the United States than smaller ones like Britain. They also spread more slowly in countries with limited physical, media or communications infrastructures such as Africa and China. Consumers from countries with greater disposable income levels will be able to trial and adopt new innovations more. Those at later stages of socio-political development will typically be more interested in the idea of the new, and thus in new trends.

National trends share some characteristics with micro trends. They can be useful in themselves in those territories where they do exist. A Japanese trend will be useful in Japan, a Scandinavian trend in Scandinavia. But, like attitudinal and micro trends, they can also be predictive. They offer clues about potential future global trends. A trend that begins in the Netherlands might be confined to that territory if it is based on specifically Dutch characteristics and conditions, but if it is based on consumer traits that can also be found in other similarly industrialized nations then it might easily spread to other parts of Northern Europe and the United States. And if it is based on traits common to consumers in more territories, it could become a global trend. The Living Apart Together trend, for older partners to maintain their own homes even when they are in a partnership, began in the Netherlands but has since spread across Europe.

CONFLICTING TRENDS

Opposing trends do not need to cancel each other out. When it comes to cooking, the zeitgeist has changed. It's no longer seen as 'woman's work' and looked down upon. It's seen as a good thing, part of being a good parent. But at the same time people are getting busier, or at least having more demands on their time, so they don't have the time to cook, and they seek convenience.

Michele Giles, Head of Insight, Premier Foods

Two opposing trends can exist at the same time. Typically each will exist among different types of consumers. For instance, some consumer typologies may follow a traditionalist trend while others are following a more future-facing one. In such cases, trend marketers need to determine which trend their particular customer base is likely to follow (see Chapter 23).

But a single consumer can also adopt or be influenced by two opposing trends simultaneously. Consumers who feel a greater urge to spend time preparing a meal may also be under time pressure that pushes them towards convenience food. The trend marketer's job here is to determine how these two opposing trends will resolve themselves. For instance, will consumers enjoy the idea of cooking and purchase more cookery books but actually end up eating convenience food? Or will they look for products and services that enable them to cook from scratch more quickly?

NOTES

1. National Restaurant Association, 2006
2. Office for National Statistics, 2005
3. Mintel, 2007
4. Chinese Ministry of Commerce, 2004
5. Unity Marketing, 2007
6. Synovate, 2008
7. *Merriam Webster*, 2008
8. Mark Penn, *Microtrends*, Allen Lane, 2007
9. *Merriam Webster*, 2008
10. *Merriam Webster*, 2008
11. Office of National Statistics, 2006
12. Standard Life/Next Big Thing, 2006
13. Mintel, 2007
14. Churchill Insurance, June 2006
15. National Farmers' Retail and Markets Association, 2005
16. Food Standards Authority, 2006
17. International Telecommunication Union, 2008
18. Research and Markets, 2008
19. Netsize, 2006
20. Informa, 2007
21. Office of the Telecommunications Authority in Hong Kong, 2008
22. Informa, 2007
23. ITFacts, 2007
24. Telecom Regulatory Authority of India, 2007
25. Synovate, 2008

11

Where trends occur

SECTORS

The nature of trends means that they can pop up anywhere. The spark can come from anywhere and catch on in unexpected ways. People don't live in just one sector. Trends that are found in one industry can impact another. Companies make mistakes when they only trust their industry. You need to look at trends across all sectors and put those in the context of individual sectors.

Craig Thayer, Managing Editor, Mintel Inspire,
Mintel International Group (USA)

There are typically a number of trends taking place within a particular sector at any one time. Studying the impact of trends on a single sector such as food illustrates the high number of trends that can affect an industry, and the different ways in which they can manifest themselves. Consumers today typically take a greater general interest in what they eat than they used to. Trends such as Wellness and Hectic Eclectic have created both threats and opportunities for a huge range of brands across the food industry. The last 10 years have seen consumers changing traditional behaviours: avoiding 'unhealthy' brands and trialling new foods across a range of categories.

The Wellness trend that began in the late 1990s saw a major shift in consumption patterns. Cholesterol, fats, and sugar and preserves consumption declined.[1] A greater number of consumers claimed to be eating more vegetables, salads and fruits than in previous years.[2] As fruit and vegetable sales rose, confectionery and carbonated drink sales fell.[3] As noted previously, health concerns drove high juice sales. Even snack consumption became healthier, with sales of nuts rising and those of crisps and other savoury snacks declining.[4] Sales of brands that were perceived as healthy thrived. Those that were not declined. By 2005 the fastest-growing grocery brands in the UK were those that claimed health benefits.[5] For some this was terminal, but others were able to slow and even halt that decline, through a combination of product innovation and trend-based marketing initiatives. Companies from McCain to McDonald's used the trend as an opportunity, finding success with campaigns based around health.

Meanwhile, as consumers became more aware of what was in their food, they began to trial more. The Hectic Eclectic trend saw consumers enjoying a wider range of products and experiences. It drove growth in more experimental food consumption. Consumers across regions began consuming a wider variety of types and regions of food. By the mid-2000s, 45–50 per cent of French, German and Spanish consumers and two-thirds of Britons claimed to be positively interested in trying new food products and brands.[6] Fifty-nine per cent of French, 64 per cent of Germans and 68 per cent of Britons claimed they 'like foreign food'.[7] Eighty-three per cent of Britons now consider it important 'to be open-minded' about trying new products and experiences.[8] Two-thirds are 'positively interested' in trying new food products and brands, half like to try out new food products, and a third 'often buy' a new brand 'to see what it is like'.[9] This provided huge opportunities for brands to expand their product offerings. Ethnic food, for instance, has benefited. In the Netherlands, the number of foreign cuisine restaurants in the country grew by 19 per cent from 1995 to 2002, whilst the number of traditional Dutch restaurants increased by just 2 per cent.[10] Demand for exotic foods too has risen. In Britain the market for exotic juice and juice drinks, for example, grew by 16.5 per cent from 2004 to 2005.[11] Now a new Micro Sourcing trend is deepening the trend, encouraging consumers to demand products sourced from very specific places. There is now a market for gourmet sea salt sourced in particular areas, with Hawaiian Red, Black Lava and Tahitian Vanilla varieties all proving popular. There is also a new market for different types of honey such as Tasmanian Leatherwood and Spanish Rosemary.[12] Dairy products from a single herd or flock are proving popular too. One company has found success selling cheese from sheep living in the tiny Partick Fell region of Yorkshire in Northern England. Premium juice manufacturer James White even has a range of apple juices each based on a single traditional British apple variety, such as Cox, Russet and Bramley.

These are just a few of the many trends that have affected the food sector recently. Elsewhere the Trading Up trend has seen mainstream consumers regularly purchasing luxury foods. Are You Experienced has driven a growth in out-of-home consumption. Traditionalizing is encouraging consumers to seek out 'old-fashioned' foods and food brands. Some of these trends began in the food sector, but others began elsewhere and spread to food.

Food is not an isolated example. A range of industries has been affected by similar trends in recent years. For instance, the Micro Sourcing trend is not limited to food. Givenchy was inspired by the vintage wine market to introduce limited-edition specifically sourced scents for their Harvest series, made from flowers harvested in a single region in a single season. Traditionalizing has encouraged a wealth of different pursuits in the leisure industry, from bowling to burlesque performance. And the Hectic Eclectic trend is affecting consumers across most major industries.

Many marketing executives consider trends are only important in certain sectors or with particular demographics. For instance, some believe that trends can only affect fashion-based industries. Others consider them useful only for youth markets. But consumer trends can affect any industry or market. Sectors as diverse as leisure, interiors and health have all proven vulnerable to trend influence. Leisure has seen a huge range of micro and macro trends. Micro trends include the rising popularity of genealogy, traditional dancing classes, poker, outdoor fitness, food and health-focused holidays. Macro trends like Come Together, a trend for greater communality, have manifested themselves in everything from online gaming to amateur soccer leagues.

Fluctuations in house prices are an economic trend, but the way they affect consumption is a consumer trend. As prices rose, houses were seen as investments to be improved before sale, and home improvement product sales thrived. The amount of money spent on DIY in the UK rose by 75 per cent in the 10 years to 2006.[13] But, as prices plateaued and the uncertainty over future values increased, house sales stalled. Because of this, consumers are increasingly viewing their home as a place to live rather than just as an investment. When decorating their homes today, consumers are less concerned with attracting potential buyers and more concerned with creating an environment they like. They are therefore becoming more adventurous with paint colours, furniture and so on.

Meanwhile consumers in the health sector are becoming increasingly self-sufficient. The Help Yourself trend is seeing them supplementing visits to their doctor. More of them are looking to pharmacists or online sources. Over 60 per cent of British internet users have gone online in search of health information, and over 21 million people have been influenced by health information gleaned online.[14] Sales of self-diagnostic products have increased by almost 30 per cent in the last five years alone, to reach annual sales of £99 million. A massive 60 per cent increase is expected in the market to 2012, with sales expected to reach £158 million.[15] The late 2000s even saw the launch of an over-the-counter fertility test that costs £80 and provides results in an hour. Under Pressure is proving another influential health trend, as anxiety levels rise across the world. Men in particular are increasingly anxious. Three-quarters of today's British males will experience some form of stress, depression or anxiety at some point in lives. Over half feel it at least once a month, and almost half once a week.[16] Hypertension is also having an impact in BRIC territories such as China and India.

Even those industries that might seem on the surface to be immune from consumer trends rarely are. The construction industry, for instance, can be just as affected by trends as any other. The trend towards single-person homes has driven construction industry strategy for decades. But the Sandwich Families trend is creating a new market for larger houses. More and more middle-aged consumers are finding themselves with dual care responsibilities, for teenage children and elderly parents. Young people in Northern Europe are increasingly adopting Southern European behaviours: staying at home longer, attending university near the family home and so on. Approximately 60 per cent of British 20- to 24-year-old males now live with their parents, and 40 per cent of 20- to 24-year-old women do.[17] Many undergraduates are choosing to live at home. Even those who do leave home to go to university often return after they have graduated rather than buying or renting new homes. On top of this, many households are taking on a physically or financially ailing grandparent. Approximately 15 per cent of Britons with unretired parents expect to have to support their parents financially in their retirement.[18] Meanwhile another trend, Going Father, is creating a demand for a new type of home I have christened the Dad Pad. These are apartments for singles with an extra room or facilities for a child. They are designed for those separated parents, typically fathers, whose children do not live with them but who visit them regularly. The flat is not the child's permanent home, but must be comfortable enough for weekend visits. The demand for such homes will grow as today's fathers take a greater interest in their children. Working practices too can be affected by trends. The Work–Life Balance trend has encouraged greater flexible working patterns. Today in the UK alone, 2 million people work all day from home, and another 8 million spend at least part of their week doing so.[19] Even the financial services sector has been affected by trends. Card-based payments have grown at the expense of cheques and cash. More and more consumers do the majority of their banking online. The Spend Spend Spend trend has seen a long-term shift away from saving, although there have been signs recently that this may be diminishing. No sector is immune.

SEGMENTS

Differences

When it comes to trends, market segmentation is hugely important. It's really useful in a cross-functional organization for everybody to be aware of what the priority customer segments are out there and what the trends are within them.

Tom Pickles, Senior Director, Global Menu Solutions, McDonald's (USA)

Fifty-five-year-old women don't want to go to the cinema and see a bunch of 18-year-olds any more. Knowing that, it's not hard to understand why Mamma Mia *was one of the highest-grossing movies in UK history!*

Tim Richards, CEO, Vue Entertainment

Many trends have an impact across consumer segments. But others are limited to a single demographic cohort. As with national and sector trends, this is because each demographic has different needs, occupies different social environments and has developed in different ways. Those in a younger age cohort or earlier life stage will have different priorities to their older counterparts. Women will typically have different attitudes and needs from men.

Gender

Macro trends will typically affect both genders, but they will often affect each differently. I have already noted the different manifestations of the Gender Blending trend across the two genders. But the trend has had further consequences for men. As women become more independent, many young males in emerged nations have become confused about their own role. They are in a state of flux, caught between the vanity of Metrosexuality and the machismo of Retrosexuality. The New Gent macro trend is seeing a shift towards sophistication and knowledge as a way to bridge the gap. In an increasing number of male social situations knowledge, from pop quiz trivia to traditional skills, provides strength without the need for violence. Wine and speciality beer sales are increasing as traditional beer sales fall. A shift away from the New Lad is driving down sales of men's magazines across the United States and Europe. Grooming, tailoring and even social etiquette are becoming more important, although the renewed popularity of beards and moustaches shows this is not just a continuation of the Metrosexual trend. For many, the new role models are the 'playboys' of the 1950s and 1960s, from James Bond to the Rat Pack. They are considered to have been strong but intelligent. They knew how to handle themselves in a fight, but also what temperature champagne should be served at!

There are also many gender-specific micro trends. Roller derby is just one example. It is a dangerous contact sport played on roller skates on a roller skating rink. It has recently experienced a revival in the United States and Europe specifically among 'alternative' 20-something women. It is traditionally a unisex game, but all-female teams have revamped the game as a punkish spectator sport. Players adopt names like Dinah Mite or Rayna Terra, and wear ironic or provocative outfits along with regulation padding, and play to a soundtrack of loud punk rock.

Age

There are many trends that are age-specific. Age can have a huge effect on the different ways many trends manifest themselves. The Silver Surfers is a trend occurring among Grey Consumers for greater use of the internet and other personal technology. It is part of a broader cross-demographic trend for increased technology usage. But it has very specific characteristics relevant only to this particular demographic.

As typically happens with technology usage, internet use was initially limited to teenagers and 20-somethings, but later 'aged up' to the Grey market. Today more than a quarter of all European over-55s regularly use the internet.[20] Approximately 35 per cent of all European 55–64s and 15 per cent of the 65-plus group access the internet at least once a week.[21] The fastest growth in e-commerce today is among the over-55s. Nearly a quarter of European over-55s will be shopping online by 2010.[22] In the UK, the over-55s are the fastest-growing shopper group. The over-55s now spend more online than even the 35–44s, with an average of over £500 per head per annum.[23]

Older consumers are even starting to take to social networking. Over-35s accounted for more than half of all visitors to MySpace in the United States in 2005. There are already a growing number of websites and portals with information and services for seniors on health, travel, insurance, financial investments and other topics of interest. Other 'youth' internet activities are proving popular with them. Fifty-six per cent of Irish 45–65s use YouTube, and 36 per cent use Skype.[24]

Social grade

Some trends are confined to particular income groups. The 2000s saw the rise of the Trading Up trend, where low net worth individuals (LNWIs) began purchasing across more premium product ranges than in the past.

The rise in champagne sales provides a strong indicator of the trend. In Spain, champagne consumption has increased by 50 per cent since 1998. The French now drink 125 million litres of it every year. Global demand for champagne has risen so much that the French government has had to increase the borders of the official champagne region in order to cope. In Britain, champagne sales grew so much that the hypothetical 'standard basket of goods' used by the Office of National Statistics to determine the cost of living was changed to include champagne, as well as other such premium products as flat-screen TVs, digital camcorders and wine boxes.

There are many other diverse examples. In the Middle East, consumers have switched from baking bread to buying it. There has been a sharp rise in the consumption of *premium* ready meals in France. The size of television screens grew each year across Europe in the mid-2000s; television manufacturer Sharp believes the average main TV in Europe will be 152 centimetres by 2015. Sales of the Netherlands' *Miljonair Magazine* and tickets to its annual Miljonair Fair have risen as LNWIs copy the lifestyles of today's HNWIs.

The Trading Up trend has affected sales in emerging markets too. Premium cosmetics brands such as Clinique and Estée Lauder are enjoying exceptional value growth in China, growing 91 per cent and 60 per cent respectively in 2005 alone.[25] The Indian wine market has risen 126 per cent by volume since 2001, and is set to expand 97 per cent in the next five years.[26] Seagram recently launched its first Indian wine brand.

Relationships

Trends can also occur in specific family or relationship segments. There have been several interesting parental trends in recent years. One of the most important is the growing role of fatherhood seen in the Going Father trend. There has been a growth in 'fully involved dads'.[27] British fathers today spend an average of two hours per day interacting with their child or children compared to an average of just 15 minutes in the 1970s.[28] Ninety-three per cent of fathers now take time off around the birth, and over a third take more than two weeks' paternity leave, up from just 22 per cent in 2002. Books on fatherhood are proving popular, such as *From Lad to Dad: How to survive as a pregnant father* by Stephen Giles. And there is now even a high-profile pressure group, Fathers 4 Justice, that champions fathers' rights.

Another parental trend is Reverse Pester Power. This is the purchase of products for children that represent the parents' own tastes. These include baby clothes with rock band logos on them, DVDs of the films that the parents used to watch when they were young, and video games both parent and child can enjoy. Many parents are now taking their children with them to concerts by their favourite bands. Others are taking their children to mother-and-daughter film screenings or yoga classes.

As for relationship trends, Living Apart Together, which began in the Netherlands, sees older couples not moving in together but keeping their own separate apartments. Meanwhile singles are increasingly looking for partners on the internet. One out of every eight marriages in the United States in 2007 took place between couples who had met online.

Culture

Culturally and ethnically segmented trends are becoming increasingly important again in Western nations. The growing number of Hispanic consumers migrating to the United States, coupled with a decreasing birth rate among non-migrant Americans, has increased the percentage of Hispanic consumers in the United States. They now make up 20 per cent of New Yorkers and 40 per cent of Angelenos.[29] By 2015 the Hispanic population in the United States will have spending power equivalent to 60 per cent of all Chinese consumers.[30] Because of this trend, the market for products targeting the US Latin market has soared across a range of industries: from TV and film to music and fashion. More and more diverse sectors are exploiting the trend. McDonald's now pipes closed-circuit sports programming into Hispanic bars. Weight Watchers in Chicago holds Spanish-language sessions. Marvel launched a comic featuring Latin superheroes the Santerians. There is even a US consultancy, Iconoculture, that specializes in Hispanic trends. Other US migrant markets too are growing. With Indians now the largest Asian ethnic group in Washington, Bollywood concerts there are attracting audiences of up to 10,000 people. Ethnic cultures are also proving popular with indigenous populations, especially with those leading-edge culture fans keen to avoid the mainstream. For instance, in the Balkan Beats micro trend, Middle and East European gypsy music is proving popular with early adopters in New York, London and Berlin.

Some trends that begin among ethnic communities will spread into other segments. As with national and sector trends, although some demographic trends remain limited to a single demographic, many begin in one and then spread to others. The trend for Speed Dating began in New York's Jewish community but soon spread to non-Jewish New Yorkers and then to consumers across the globe. It also inspired a range of other 'speed' trends, such as Speed Flatmating, in which consumers try to find the perfect flatmate.

NOTES

1. DEFRA, 2005
2. Food Standards Authority, 2006
3. DEFRA, 2005
4. *Independent*, 2006
5. ACNielsen, 2006
6. Mintel, 2006
7. Mintel, 2004
8. Datamonitor, 2005
9. TGI Europa, 2005
10. Royal Dutch HORECA Association, 2003
11. IRI Soft Drinks Flavours, 2005
12. ACNielsen, 2005
13. Halifax Building Society, 2006
14. Economic and Social Research Council, 2007
15. Mintel, 2007
16. Men's Health Forum, 2006
17. Office of National Statistics, 2002
18. YouGov, 2005
19. Office of National Statistics, 2005
20. Forrester Research, 2006
21. nVision, 2007
22. Future Foundation, 2007
23. Verdict, 2005
24. Amarach Research, 2008
25. Euromonitor, 2007
26. Euromonitor, 2006
27. Equal Opportunities Commission, 2002
28. *Independent*, 2005
29. US Census Bureau, 2003
30. McKinsey, 2007

12

Trends versus fads

AVOIDANCE

Before you make any strategic change in your business model based on a theorized trend, you need to confirm whether it's going to last or it's just a fad. Fads by definition are more short-term – typically more fashion driven. Real trends are more related to long-term behaviours, to how people actually live… Sometimes it can be worth appealing to fads as a promotional tactic. It's a great way to make you fashionably relevant. But you shouldn't change your basic business model to do so. It's more like icing on the cake.

Tom Pickles, Senior Director, Global Menu Solutions, McDonald's (USA)

Fads are short-term, like what colours are in at the moment. A trend is something significant. It has proof behind it and has at least a two- to five-year lifespan. And it actively impacts on or changes people's lives.

Liisa Puolakka, Head of Brand Identity, Nokia

Some people confuse trends with fads. In fact even some trend forecasters have been known to. But this is dangerous. There is a big difference between a trend and a fad. It is vital that marketers distinguish between them. Trends and fads are very different not just in their manifestations but in their consequences and the opportunities they afford.

Data on consumer change can offer important practical insights into the development and future behaviour of a market, but in order for such data to be valuable for marketers the change must affect a large number of customers for a sustained period of time. It must be a trend and not a fad. Far-reaching strategic shifts depend on far-reaching consumer change. Fads offer insights only into what a few consumers will be doing for a short time.

This might be useful for occasional short-term, focused marketing tactics, but fads must never be used on their own for long-term strategy or planning.

The factors that distinguish genuine consumer trends from fads are cause, impact and durability. A trend grows organically owing to specific social, environmental or psychological drivers. It typically affects more than one industry or demographic cohort. It lasts for a minimum of two years, barring unexpected socio-economic events. It is driven by consumer needs, and it has an impact on future change, as consumer behaviours build constantly on each new trend. A fad is typically driven by the media or by a brand. It lasts for a season or at the most a year. It rarely has roots in a strong consumer need. It typically affects just one demographic or industry sector, and its impact rarely moves outside the sector. It does not have an impact on future behaviours. It is a forgettable 'blip' rather than a stage of development to be built on later.

CREATION

Hype

The most common type of fad is the marketing-led or 'playground' fad. This is a behaviour or product that is popular for a brief time before being passed over for another behaviour or product. Growth is typically based on peer pressure and status. The most famous example is probably the hula hoop. Based on a traditional dancing implement, this plastic toy was heavily marketed in the United States in 1958. Because of some strong initial success it was heavily featured in the media, and it became suddenly hugely popular. In fact an alleged 25 million were sold in just four months over the summer of 1958. But, as its popularity was based upon marketing and not consumer needs, sales quickly fell away. By the end of 1959, the product had all but disappeared. Another fad popular around this time was the dance the Twist. It became popular thanks to marketing campaigns by first the dance-based music television show *American Bandstand* and then New York nightclub the Peppermint Lounge. The dance did have a slight consumer-led element. It appealed to the growing demand among some consumers for a means to express their new-found hedonism. Because of this it lasted longer than the hula hoop, but it too soon became unfashionable. Since then short-term, marketing-led fads have appeared regularly: from Slinkys and Rubik's Cubes to the charity wristbands of recent years.

Fads can also be created by a strong PR-led campaign. I began my career in the PR department of Sony Music, working with artists from Michael

Jackson to Alice Cooper, so am very aware of the ways in which products or individuals can be hyped. Much of what appears in the media is there to entertain. And today, with the growing proliferation of outlets, there is more media space to fill than ever. Subsequently some of the 'trends' reported in a newspaper can be based more on the comments of a PR person perhaps or the research findings of a particular brand than on robust behavioural data. Public relations companies can sometimes exaggerate or even occasionally fabricate a trend that places their brand in a favourable light. For instance, a company that manufactures salt might play down any trends that suggest consumers are avoiding high-salt food and might try to find, or even 'create', evidence of a 'pro-salt backlash'. Upon finding what appears to be a new behaviour in a media source, it is therefore essential that trends analysts ask themselves whether this might be a 'manufactured' trend. Trend marketers should never dismiss any story out of hand, but should be cautious and test its reliability thoroughly. Marketers should be particularly wary of 'trends' that focus on a single brand. The increased purchase of a particular product is rarely if ever a trend. The popularity of, say, Cabbage Patch Dolls in the 1980s was generated by good above- and below-the-line marketing. The publicity and profile around the dolls created a short-term sales fad, but it was not a trend.

Marketers should also be wary of media-created fads. Announcing a new trend can help sell more copies of a publication. Front-page stories presenting statistical 'evidence' of dangerous new behaviours excite interest or fear and can increase circulation. But a good trend marketer will always study the reports such evidence is based on. Figures that offer genuine insights into consumer change can sometimes be left out of a newspaper report because they do not support a particular editorial stance or are not considered newsworthy. Trends are often written about in features sections and seen as entertainment rather than news, so the levels of validity normally applied to news stories are not necessarily required of them. The media can also sometimes talk of the 'death' of a trend they spoke of a year ago, even if in fact the trend has not yet reached the mainstream. Marketers must be careful to draw their own conclusions.

Fashion

> *Newness in fashion is there to ensure people continue to make purchases. Fashion people are constantly looking for information that can give them newness in store. That's why fashion trends change more quickly and more often than consumer trends.*

> Alison Hughes, UK Agent, Carlin International

Knowing what young, 'trendy' consumers in early adopter locations across the globe are wearing, listening to, looking at or playing has always been of vital importance in the fashion industry. But only part of this information will ever be of use for marketing non-fashion products. Whether, say, stripes or short skirts will be fashionable next year might be useful information for a fashion forecaster or fashion buyer, but it typically offers few insights for other sectors. That is because it is a fad and not a trend.

Fashion 'trends' are typically based at least loosely on changing consumer attitudes. But they do not represent genuine consumer change. Fashion styles are typically only variations on long-term consumer trends, not trends in their own right. The regular turnover of new fashion styles is actually a marketing tool. It is a way to drive consumers to recurrent purchase. Its purpose is to sell more clothes, not to guide long-term strategy. The fashion industry learned in the late 19th century that consumers would be more likely to buy a new garment if they thought their current garments were no longer fashionable. Fashion 'trends' were initially created once per year. This became once every six months, to take account of the difference between summer and winter attire. Seasonal trends became the norm from the mid-20th century onwards. But recently, with the growth in consumer change rates and product turnover, new styles are being introduced every few weeks. Clearly consumers do not change this frequently.

IDENTIFICATION

It is essential that marketers are able to distinguish between trends and fads, but the difference is not as distinct as might be expected. It is wrong to assume, for instance, that if something is 'trivial' it is a fad, or to assume that if something is 'important' it is a trend. Both trends and fads can be found across a range of different sectors and behaviours. 'Ephemeral' behaviours such as tattoos and piercings or the sending of text messages are now too established to be considered fads. On the other hand fads can regularly be found in such 'serious' areas as health and business. 'Fad' diets are common, and many consumers might trial them for short periods. The business community has often been influenced by management 'fads'.

At the development stage, fads and trends follow similar development processes. The initial manifestations of trends and fads can appear very similar. The early adopters of the cell phone were mainly senior executives, for whom it was an important means of keeping in contact with both office and clients. Phones then were cumbersome, impractical and expensive. Who can forget the image of pinstriped executives holding these 'bricks' up to their ear? Early cell phone usage could easily have been dismissed as a fad – phones looked 'gimmicky' and were expensive and cumbersome – and many commentators at the time did dismiss them. But after a few years prices fell. Models became lighter and more user-friendly, and sales soared, not just in the West but in every nation across the world, and over half of the population of the world own a cell phone.[1]

To establish whether an instance of consumer change is a fad or a trend, marketers need to monitor it over time and across sectors. If a development can be observed in several industries at the same time, then it is more likely to be the beginnings of a trend than a fad. If it continues to grow, even slowly, then it may eventually reach the mainstream. It is also important to determine if a trend has the *potential* to grow: to establish if it satisfies basic consumer needs, or if current environments might encourage growth (see Chapter 20).

UTILIZATION

Fads should never be used for long-term strategy. Confusing a fad with a trend can have disastrous consequences. A company that bases long-term strategy on consumer behaviour that quickly fades will waste a great deal of time and money. But there are two ways in which fads can be useful. They can be used for tactical marketing and short-term NPD. They can also indicate the potential existence of a genuine trend. In fast-turnover industries, products or services based on fads can sell. A company could have made money from selling hula hoops or Slinkys if they had picked up on the trend early enough. A brand that picks up early on the popularity of a faddish television show such as *America's Next Top Model* will gain sales advantage by sponsoring or advertising in the show, or using imagery pertaining to the show in short-term marketing campaigns.

Fads can also offer clues to the existence of a trend. I call such fads Forward Fads. The success of *America's Next Top Model*, for instance, though a fad in itself, was evidence of a growing fascination with short-term fame. The Twist was an early indicator that Americans were ready to shed the conservatism of the 1950s and enjoy the hedonism of what was to become the Swinging Sixties. The Retro Chic fashion trend offered early signs that consumers were starting to look back to the past; and the demand for a more authentic style suggested that the importance of price as a purchase driver might be waning. The popularity of rubber wristbands among schoolchildren in the mid-2000s may have been a fad, but it gave an indication of a growing sense of responsibility among them.

NOTE

1. International Telecommunication Union, 2008

Summary: Part 3

- Trends are created by shifts in consumer environments.
- Trends have political, socio-cultural, economic or technological causes.
- Trends can be segmented into several categories.
- Trends can be behavioural or attitudinal, micro or macro, international or national.
- Two opposing trends can influence consumers concurrently.
- Trends can occur across all sectors.
- Trends can occur in every demographic.
- Trends and fads are different.
- Companies should not base long-term strategy on fads.
- Fads can provide clues to future trends.

TREND MARKETING

Part 4

Identification

13

What to look for

WHAT TO STUDY

This section of the book details the three stages of the trend marketing process: identification, interpretation and implementation. To determine how to identify trends necessitates a return to the definition of a trend: 'a long-term change in consumer attitudes and behaviours that offers marketing opportunities'. The first key word here is 'change'. Trends are the manifestation of change. In order to identify a new trend, marketers need to look for any signs of change among consumers. These can be changes in behaviour or changes in attitude. They can manifest themselves in consumer activity, display or conversation. Evidence for them can be found in statistical reports or magazine polls or on the street. To discern instances of change, trend marketers need to study consumers across a range of demographics and environments. They also need to employ a range of methods. In her book *The Popcorn Report* (Doubleday, 1991) trend forecasting pioneer Faith Popcorn calls the process 'brailling the culture'. She describes how researchers should 'scan today's culture for signs of the future... "brailling" the culture, reaching out to touch as many parts of it as possible – to make sense of the whole... compensating for tunnel vision by developing a different sensitivity, a "feel" for what's going on'. The second key word is 'consumer'. To identify instances of consumer change, marketers need to observe consumers.

WHO TO STUDY

Consumers

A trend without any sort of understanding of who the customer is is just a line on a chart.

Mark Broughton, Research Insights and Knowledge Manager, Global
Product Development, Alliance Boots

Consumers lie at the heart of any marketing trends research. What consumers are going to think or do tomorrow is the key issue that such research needs to answer. It follows logically that the way to observe trends is to look at consumers themselves. It can also help to study those individuals who influence them and those who study them. All consumer groups can provide evidence of change, but it is more useful to study some groups than others. Trend marketers should study four key typologies. These are the innovators who create trends, the influential individuals who spread them, the consumers who are the first to adopt them and the experts who can spot them (Figure 13.1). If you observe one of these typologies adopting or describing a new behaviour, it can give a strong indication that that behaviour may become a trend.

Innovators

We look at architects, furniture and product designers, people like that, people who have their eyes and ears open all the time looking for anything that's new and innovative, people who pick up on things before Joe Bloggs does. They could be in books, film, art, music – anything creative. They live, eat and breathe innovation. It's part of their everyday lives, so it's quite natural for them to be able to sense certain things early.

Alison Hughes, UK Agent, Carlin International

CONSUMERS	OBSERVERS
innovators	journalists
influentials	academics
early adopters	researchers
	entrepreneurs

Figure 13.1 Who to study

Innovators are those creative individuals who first express a new artistic idea or mood. Professional innovators include artists, writers, filmmakers, musicians, and product and graphic designers. But there are many amateur innovators who can help initiate trends. These are those typically youthful and subcultural consumers who create for their own pleasure outside their working lives. Both groups have a history of adopting trend behaviours and attitudes early. Studying the changing attitudes and behaviours of creative people is a good way to discover future trends a long time in advance. What creative people are doing today gives an indication of what less creative people may be doing tomorrow.

Influentials

When you're targeting a group, consider who it is they look up to, whose values they admire, or who they would have wanted to be when they were young. And then actually study those people, because what they're doing now your target market may well be doing in future. If you are targeting housewives who wish they had more time and money so they could spend more time preparing food, then you should look at the people who do have the time and money to prepare food. Look at what they're doing now, because that's what the housewives could be doing in future, and that might be buying organic, cooking from scratch or growing their own vegetables.

P T Black, Partner, Jigsaw International (China)

There are two problems with observing innovators. They are a large, diverse and individualistic group, so it is only possible in practice to study the behaviours of the most high-profile of them: the 'coolest' subcultural cohorts in a city, perhaps, or the most respected creative professionals. Also not all of the new behaviours they adopt actually grow into trends. Luckily it is not always necessary to observe the very first instance of a new behaviour in order to pick up on a trend early. Innovators may be the first to adopt a particular behaviour, but they are not necessarily the ones who create a *trend* for it. A trend occurs only when a new behaviour is adopted by a significant number of people. It is therefore important to study those who influence adoption too: the influentials.

Innovators come up with an idea or adopt a new behaviour. Influentials are the ones who spread that idea to others. What an innovator does may not become a trend, but, as long as it has the right adopter attributes, what an influential does typically will. A trend creator may come up with just one idea and stick with that for years, but a typical influential regularly spreads a range of trends. Influentials are therefore at least as important an obser-vational subject for marketers as innovators. It does not matter exactly who the innovator was who encouraged influential celebrities like Gwyneth Paltrow, Jennifer Lopez, Madonna and Christy Turlington to take up alternative exercise regimes such as yoga in the late 1990s. What did matter was the fact that these influentials had shown an interest. It was their interest that would encourage more mainstream consumers to take up such practices. Once trend forecasters had identified that such influentials were starting to adopt yoga, they would have been able to predict that the practice would become popular with the mainstream. Of course, if they had been able to identify before the influentials took it up, that would have been even better.

Influentials do not need to be world famous. They just need to be a source of aspiration. There are many high-profile influentials such as television personalities, film stars, sportspeople, models and journalists. But the influential typology also includes those individuals within a particular consumer cohort whom others look to for their behavioural or attitudinal cues (see Chapter 17). Influentials are not limited to individuals either. They can also include media outlets. For instance, three-quarters of British women believe that the media are the most prominent factor in making them more environmentally friendly.[1]

Early adopters

Early adopters are the first consumers to adopt a new trend. They are typically the people whom more mainstream consumers turn to for advice on new products or services. The image that many people have of an early adopter is a young, style-focused consumer who is the first to trial any new, 'cool' product. We see such types staring out at us from the pages of style supplements. But this describes only a certain percentage of them. Early adopters are not necessarily the 'coolest' consumers. The characteristics of an early adopter will actually differ from industry to industry, and from trend to trend. Many are far from style focused, may only buy new products in a single sector, and do not care how 'cool' a product is. For instance, the early adopters for many food trends are 30-something housewives (see Chapter 17).

Observers

One thing there should be more of is bringing outside creativity into your business, to do it in a way that mutually benefits you and them. That could be involving customers, or it could be involving small start-up companies.

Andy Shaw, Product Development Director, BT Agile Media,
British Telecom

We have some great tie-ins to academics. Our business development managers are constantly talking to them about the latest technologies, the latest sociological and cultural elements.

Mark Broughton, Research Insights and Knowledge Manager, Global Product Development, Alliance Boots

Observing individual consumers is a good way to pick up on trends, but it can be time-consuming. Studying or interrogating those who themselves observe trends can reduce the amount of time spent on physical observation. These include academics, journalists, entrepreneurs and market researchers. Observing them can be done in two ways. Virtual interrogation involves simply reading articles such individuals write or watching presentations they give, but to gain the greatest information you should practise real-time interrogation, which involves speaking directly to them.

Trend forecasters and journalists have much in common. Both typically spend their lives searching for interesting new information about consumers. Both need to find statistical and example-based evidence for their stories. A trend forecaster and a journalist investigating the same new trend will typically search the same data sources, sift through the same cuttings and interview the same individuals. The reports or stories they write may share similarities too. Because of this, they can make good allies. Trend forecasters can tip journalists off about a new trend, providing them with a ready-made article topic. They can also offer quotes to give that article added robustness. Journalists can provide forecasters with relevant and robust data in return. There are two sorts of journalists who are particularly useful. The first sort is those who specialize in a single sector. The second is those who cover broad consumer or trend-related topics. I regularly speak to journalists, either by telephone or in person, and have learned a great deal from them.

Trend forecasting can benefit from combining the practical with the theoretical. There are hundreds of academics across the globe currently working on research projects related in some way to consumer trends. Some might be working on marketing projects, others on social projects. The information they obtain during this process can be invaluable to a trend marketer. A physical or online search can provide information on current academic projects, reports, articles and papers. Sometimes reading such articles will provide you with all the information you need, but if you locate a report that particularly interests you it can be advantageous to contact the author and ask if he or she is willing to discuss the project with you. Authors will not always be willing to do so: some do not like to mix academic work with commerce. But others will, especially if you can share some of your own information on the topic with them. I have obtained some fascinating information this way. Academics can also prove useful contacts later in the process. They may obtain further data in future that can be of help. They might even act as advocates in future communications campaigns.

As I will show later, the virtual interrogation of research company reports can provide a good source of trend data (see Chapter 14). But real-time interrogation of researchers can also be useful. Companies across a range of different sectors can each benefit from a single macro trend. Companies currently researching a trend may be interested in working alongside researchers in non-competitor sectors to analyse such trends.

When a new trend appears, there will often be one or more entrepreneurs trying to take advantage of it. They will typically pick up on the trend early because they are specialists within the relevant sector or they have an affinity with the culture or cohort involved. They too can provide useful information. Their company can provide a case study to be utilized in a trend presentation or strategy determination session, but it can also sometimes be worth making direct contact with them. There may be competition issues between your own company and themselves and, if so, you may not want to discuss the topic together, but a trend can often start in a sector other than your own, so you will not always be in competition.

WHEN TO STUDY

There was a formalized trend part of the brand planning process that was done on a regular basis, but there could also be an ad hoc element as well. Something could come up where someone thinks 'Trends will be a key part of this project that I'm working on.'

Camilla Vickerage, Founder, Sweet Shop Research (ex-Research Manager, ICI Paints)

You can look for trends on a one-off or an ongoing basis. I call these different processes single sweeping and constant sweeping. Single sweeping involves a one-off exploration of the trendscape. It can focus on a single trend, sector or cohort, or it can cut across topics to identify a range of key trends. It can be done regularly, occasionally or when a trend input is required. One problem is that each time you sweep you have to catch up on any trends that have occurred since the last sweep. It also means you might miss a vital trend that occurs between sweeps. One way around this is to employ a trends consultant to run such sweeps for you, particularly if the sweep is focused on a non-core activity. Constant sweeping can prove a more valuable and cost-effective method in the long term than running single sweeps. It can be done in different ways. A company can divert particular personnel to the task on a full-time or part-time basis, or in a roster system, or they can subscribe to a trends website or regular trends bulletin. Companies should where possible maintain at least some level of constant sweeping to inform more focused single sweeps.

HOW TO STUDY

Practical identification

I look at magazines and internet sites. I speak to a variety of people. I go to seminars. I read specific trend magazines and a variety of different design and interiors magazines.

Brechje Vissers, Manager Colour Marketing and Innovation, PPG Industries (ex-Senior Trend Consultant, Philips) (Netherlands)

Trends can be identified via observation or deduction (see Figure 13.2). Practical identification is the study of consumer activity, statistical data and media sources to obtain physical evidence of change. Active evidence might include the types of websites or retail outlets consumers are visiting, the food and drink they are consuming or the leisure activities they are pursuing. Statistical evidence could be government figures on the rising number of teenagers doing part-time jobs, or a research company study on the growth of e-tailing. Media evidence could be an article in the specialist press on the micro-sourcing of dairy foods, or the rising number of national newspaper articles on the dangers of trans-fats.

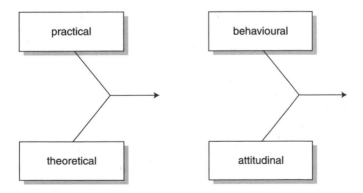

Figure 13.2 Identification methodologies

Theoretical identification

Trend marketers can limit themselves to practical identification, but this can be very time-consuming. A proactive theorem-based approach can speed up the process considerably. By studying recent consumer patterns, marketers can come up with theories on what is likely to happen next and then search for evidence for it. I call this theoretical identification. It is vital to run at least some practical identification alongside the theoretical, to ensure you do not miss any unexpected events. No matter how good trend forecasters are, they cannot anticipate absolutely every trend before it begins, but utilizing some theoretical identification can certainly save time. It falls into three categories: analogous, logical and hypothetical.

Analogous identification follows directly from observational identification. Observing one trend or event can sometimes suggest further trends. To determine what these are requires an understanding of how such trends have behaved in the past. If you know that the movements of behaviour X and behaviour Y correlate in some way and you observe that X is changing, then there is a strong chance that Y might also be about to change. The divorce rate in the UK rose relatively constantly throughout the last decades of the 20th century, but quantitative secondary observation at the start of the 2000s showed a slight fall. This was interesting in itself, but it also provided us with a springboard for several other potential observations. If the divorce rate was now falling, could the marriage rate be growing? If so, was it growing more among the young or the old? If it was among the latter, might that indicate a reversal of the long-term trend for having children later? Might other more traditionalist lifestyle behaviours be on the rise? Testing these theories using observation techniques, it became clear that the trend away from divorce was part of a larger trend. It proved to be the first evidence of consumers returning to more traditional social attitudes.

Logical identification is a form of detective work. It involves a search for clues based around known consumer behaviours. Consumers typically follow traditional patterns that have been observed over time (see Chapter 18). By understanding these behaviour patterns, a trend marketer can propose logical identification theories that can be tested by practical research. Forecasters should look, for instance, for evidence of needs-based change drivers. During a recession, for example, several trends typically occur. Consumers typically start reducing their spending in some areas but not in others. They will usually be wary of spending money on 'big ticket' items such as cars, sofas or houses, but they will increase their purchase of low-cost products that boost their self-image, such as lipstick or a night at the cinema: so-called 'small indulgences'. They will also look to things that enhance their sense of safety. These can be products and services for the home, or those that evoke a 'safer', more traditional time: from comfort food 'like grandmother made' to old-fashioned games and traditional TV formats. Equally, when a major health scare occurs, consumers typically grow increasingly afraid. They take more interest in safety and health issues. They reduce their international travel. They focus more on family and friends.

Maslow's theory of a hierarchy of needs can be useful here (see Chapter 9). If a society or consumer cohort is at what Maslow calls the social needs stage, for instance, then consumers are likely to follow trends that revolve around friendship, community, social acceptance and relationships with partner and family. Trend marketers should therefore look out for trends based in these areas. But if consumers are at the safety stage then trend marketers should search for safety-based trends. Many attitudinal changes and some behavioural ones are cyclical. For instance, style-focused consumers may favour maximalist interiors now, but at some point in the future they will react against this and seek minimalism again. By determining how far through the cycle a trend is, marketers can estimate when they should begin to look for signs of change in that trend (see Chapter 19).

Hypothetical identification utilizes what Einstein called 'thought experiments'. Such experiments determine what might happen under a particular set of circumstances: testing a theory in the imagination rather than in a laboratory. For instance, what would happen if A grew larger than B, or X moved closer to Y? Typically this will be inspired by or based upon trends observed previously or that have manifested themselves in areas outside the current focus. I used hypothetical identification to identify the Conserva-Teens trend, which sees many of today's young Westerners becoming more conservative in their outlook. I was running a study on how Generation X were adapting to adult life stages. While exploring Gen X attitudes to parenting, it occurred to me that these might have an effect on the long-term attitudes and behaviours of their offspring. A reaction against one's parents is a natural stage of child development. A reaction against predominantly conservative parents, for instance, was one of the drivers for the hedonism and iconoclasm of Baby Boomer teenagers. But what if one's parents were not conservative? What if they had enjoyed, or were even still enjoying, hedonistic lifestyles? What if their cultural tastes were not *passé* but actually 'cool'? How would a child react against them? The only way to react would be actually to become more conservative. What better way to truly upset cool, liberal, hedonistic parents than to become, say, an opera-loving religious accountant! I determined to test this theory, and found that there were indeed some early signs that teenagers were becoming more conservative. Levels of youth drinking and drug taking were starting to fall slightly, while anxiety levels were on the rise. There was even some evidence of increased church going among the young both in Europe and in the United States. I have closely monitored the trend since and have seen it grow from strength to strength. It is now set to be a key trend for the 2010s.

Theories alone, of course, are not enough to base company strategy on. Once you have identified a trend theoretically, you must go into the field or search through polling data to try to find physical evidence to prove it. I call the process of seeking physical evidence for theoretical trends 'reverse identification', to differentiate it from the more regular process of 'practical identification'. Once I noticed the growth of strong retro and vintage trends in the fashion industry, for instance, I ran reverse identification to look for evidence of similar trends in other sectors. Unsurprisingly I started finding it in such areas as interiors and early adopter food and drinks packaging. But I also began to find it in more surprising sectors such as technology, where some early adopters were purchasing retro phones and wooden computers: early evidence for the Soft Technology trend.

Behavioural identification

Behavioural change is easiest to observe. Behaviours can often simply be noted and then extrapolated. They do not necessarily need more analysis than that. For instance, if you know how many more consumers bought products online this year than last, and how many more bought products that year than the year before, then you can simply extrapolate the data ahead to predict how many more will buy online *next* year.

Attitudinal identification

Identifying attitudinal change is more complex. It is typically less concerned with numbers, so change levels are not so well delineated. But the process is just as systematic and can offer even more effective data on the future. The way consumers behave and the products they buy and consume provide a wide range of non-verbally communicated meanings about themselves. Interpreting such meanings falls into the social interpretation or semiotics field. Semiotics or semiology was first used within the field of linguistics. It was defined by its creator, Ferdinand de Saussure, as 'a science that studies the role of signs as part of social life'. Semiotics enables researchers to interpret behaviours attitudinally, which in turn provides clues as to future behaviours. For instance, consumers will buy a product because it fulfils one or more of their needs: practical or emotional, intrinsic or learned, conscious or subconscious. The consumption of a product therefore tells you something about the needs of the person buying it. Purchasing products from high-profile premium brands that display prominent logos suggests that the purchaser is concerned with materialist values such as social status. The level of popularity of a product can therefore indicate changing consumer attitudes. If sales of such designer brands decline, this can indicate some respective decline in such materialist values. To gain an understanding of attitudinal change, trend marketers should analyse any products that are proving either much more or much less popular. What does their rising or falling popularity say about new consumer attitudes?

NOTE

1. IPC, 2009

14

Statistical data

FINDING DATA

It's important to combine different methodologies – expert opinion, 'street' obser-
vation, media observation and so on. You need all of those to get a balanced
view. Supporting data from a range of different sources will help you understand
the trend better.

Liisa Puolakka, Head of Brand Identity, Nokia

Trend analysis is an interdisciplinary activity where you're looking at a symphony
of information. A lot of different pieces of data come through and you try to sift
through that to find the story. We do depth interviews, home visits, accompanied
shopping and online surveys, plus we look at government statistics, census data,
industry reports and of course the media. It's less about the individual methodol-
ogy and more about just getting good answers.

P T Black, Partner, Jigsaw International (China)

Whether the purpose is observational or theoretical, behavioural or attitudinal, trend marketers can use a range of different methodologies to identify trends. They can run informal observational research and study
consumers in the field; they can run formal observational research such as
focus groups or street polls; they can run secondary research, by scanning
available polling data; or they can monitor the media (Figure 14.1). Each
methodology is valid. But some may be more relevant or practical than
others, depending on budget, sector and business question. Those with
lower budgets may have to focus more on statistical secondary research
rather than formal observational research. Those in a style- or leisure-

STATISTICAL	OBSERVATIONAL	MEDIA
Paid for eg research reports Free eg government reports eg annual reports eg press releases	Formal eg focus groups eg ethnography Informal eg clubs, arcades	News media eg mainstream consumer eg alternative consumer eg business Non-news media eg films eg TV drama eg books

Figure 14.1 What to study

related industry might benefit more from informal observational research than will financial services or automotive companies. But an automotive company will still need some element of observational research to inform any design or NPD questions. For business questions based around consumer motivation, an input of formal qualitative research will be required.

A multi-methodological approach typically works best. It is difficult to find evidence of a trend. The more methodologies you employ and the more sources you scan, the more chance you have of identifying a trend. Identification methodologies fall into two broad categories: statistical and observational. The former is quantitative and offers the robustness of large numbers. The latter is qualitative and offers the depth of motivational understanding.

Quantitative research is the process of asking a large group of consumers the same defined set of questions. It can provide evidence of change across a large group such as a product market, demographic or national population. It can be done face to face, by telephone or online. By its nature it can be quantified and compared. It provides traditionally robust data, and particularly appeals to those who are used to gaining information numerically.

FUTURE DATA

Consumers won't always know what they want. Steve Jobs always quotes Henry Ford's saying 'If I'd asked my customers what they wanted, they'd have said "A faster horse".'

Dave Capper, President Lifestyle, Music and Media, Hasbro (USA)

The iPod's a good example. No one actually said 'Oh, I want a little music thing that I can carry around in my pocket.' You don't always know what you want until someone presents it to you.

Camilla Vickerage, Founder, Sweet Shop Research (ex-Research Manager, ICI Paints)

The traditional quantitative research process needs to be adapted or 'future-proofed' for use in trends research. Like all traditional forms of consumer research, quantitative research was designed to provide data on present or past behaviours. That is because consumers can provide robust data only about those two areas. Respondents in quantitative or qualitative research can explain with great accuracy what they were doing or thinking yesterday and what they are doing or thinking today. They cannot be relied upon to say with any accuracy what they will do or think tomorrow. The most that can be expected is for them to state what they *expect* to do tomorrow, but this is rarely accurate. They may expect to act in one way, but circumstances or subconscious influencers may intervene to make them behave in another way entirely. Even a professional forecaster or marketer can find it hard to accurately predict the future. It will be many times harder for non-professionals such as research respondents to do so.

One way to future-proof quantitative research is to utilize and then extrapolate from time series data. A time series is a collection of specific data items obtained via repeated measurement over a particular period. Comparing results over time can determine if there is evidence of a trend – if a behaviour has increased or decreased, if X or Y is more prevalent today, and so on. Primary time series data can be obtained by rerunning a previous research campaign. For instance, if you asked beer drinkers about their key purchase drivers this year and then ran the same questionnaire on a similar sample next year, you would be able to compare this year's results to next year's to obtain the data you need. It is also possible to extrapolate likely future data from that. Secondary time series data can be obtained from research companies that run regular polls using the same sample criteria and the same questions each time. It is also sometimes possible to compare two similar polls, even if they were conducted by different companies. This can become necessary when there are no time series polls available. But such polls need to be close enough to bear rigorous comparison, and any differences in sampling criteria or question route must be noted when the evidence is presented.

Another way to future-proof primary research is to create a questionnaire that enables a future-facing interpretation of the data. This can be done in several ways. If you want to understand how consumers might utilize a product they have not yet used, and the product is similar to one that they might already have used, then you could ask them how they have used the previous product. Their responses will enable you to draw intelligent conclusions about how they might use the new product. For instance, I was asked by book publishing trade publication *The Bookseller* to gauge how consumers might respond to an e-book reader. To do this I asked respondents questions about their usage of other mobile devices such as cell phones and iPods, and interpreted the results accordingly. Alternatively, if you are interested in how respondents will utilize product X or service Y in the future, you can ask them questions about how they used X or Y in the past and then ask them how their usage has changed since then. By comparing the two responses, you can extrapolate how respondents might behave in the future.

PRIMARY DATA

The most effective way I've found for identifying trends early is through commissioning fresh research. That's when it's most convincing – when you can present it as research that's just been done and you can really see something happening. Every time you commission strategic research you develop a richer understanding of your consumers, and you can sometimes even identify trends that aren't related to the research you're doing.

Hanna Chalmers, Head of Research and Insight, Universal Music Group

It's vital to get constant feedback from our customers. When we're not getting unsolicited feedback, we'll run focus groups of our own.

Phil Guest, Managing Director Western Europe, Sulake

Primary research is the process of obtaining original data about a topic. It is also referred to as field work or field research. This is because it is typically conducted 'in the field': in actual situations, not as an experiment or theorem in the laboratory or office.

The easiest, most relevant and cheapest place to begin any primary research is among your own consumers. This can be done in several ways. Those with access to customer data can interrogate it to establish relevant behavioural patterns. Those without it can use other evidence of their customers' behaviour. Studying product sales data, for instance, can offer clues as to possible trends. If certain products are selling well, what is it about them that might be particularly popular in the current climate? For instance, are the cheapest products selling best, or is it the most hard-wearing? If so, what does this say about potential trends? If, say, your lightest and smallest products are selling, could this be because consumers are focusing on portability? If products in single colours are selling well, could that indicate a return to a more minimalist aesthetic? Such information on its own cannot offer robust evidence of a trend, but it can serve as a clue and prompt a targeted reverse identification campaign.

Companies are now beginning to use their consumers for more interactive research. In June 2006 *Wired* magazine coined the term 'crowdsourcing' to describe a form of communal creation in which customers contribute to new product development. Technology companies, from computer manufacturers to games developers, have been at the forefront of the trend, creating consumer-accessible beta sites and encouraging customers to send in their own designs. Website Mosh.Nokia.com allows customers to test new products. The beta site for Joost, the IPTV service created by the founder of Skype, had a million unique visitors ahead of official launch. The trend is now spreading outside the technology industry. Japanese furniture and clothing manufacturer Muji ask customers to pre-evaluate their designs before production. In the Netherlands, dairy products producer Mona uses recipes sent in by its consumers as the inspiration for new desserts. In Finland, Country King's new tractor tyres are developed in close cooperation with farmers. By opening the NPD process up to consumers, companies are allowing a greater level of consumer trend input.

Companies are not limited to researching their own customers of course. Quantitative data can be found by polling any number of different respondent groups. The type and number of consumers researched are dependent only on budgets and availability. Non-customer quantitative research can be run in person, by telephone or online. It can help determine how current products, services and trends are faring among consumers. How do consumers feel about X or Y today compared to yesterday, or compared to Z? It is typically a costly process, however, so many companies rely on secondary research for much of their trend data.

SECONDARY DATA

Paid-for data

Secondary research is the process of collating and synthesizing already existing research. A company may not have the resources to run its own primary research, but there is no excuse for not utilizing research that others have already obtained. Secondary research may not be as immediate or evocative as primary research, but it is typically cheaper and less time-consuming. It enables even small companies to utilize data obtained from large samples, and it is more likely to offer time series data than new primary research.

Secondary research information can be obtained in two ways: paid for or collected free. The former is typically the easier to obtain. But the amount of fee-based information obtainable will be limited by available budgets. Research reports are available on a massive number of topics. Whatever one's interest, there is likely to be a report available somewhere on the topic. Some offer broad overviews, such as 'Green living'[1] or 'Global healthcare'.[2] Others offer more specific product or market analysis, such as 'Trends in kids' nutrition'[3] or 'Dishwashing products in India'.[4] Some are one-offs; others are annual or biannual updates. Paid-for data are available from professional research agencies. They can also be purchased from trend consultancies. Every country has a range of different agencies. Most countries will have a market research organization that can provide a directory of research agencies. There are also online report brokers that provide a huge range of reports from many different sources.

Good research reports are rarely cheap, so must be purchased carefully. Given the costs of reports, it is advisable to utilize them only for topics that are of immediate concern. That can be a specific trend such as green consumerism or a market such as cosmetics. When purchasing, it is typically advisable to go to the most established companies, although it can sometimes be worth taking a chance on reports by new low-cost companies. It is important to establish exactly what information the report will contain. Most professional reports will have a detailed contents list. It is also important to ensure the report includes time series data or at least information that is comparable to otherwise available data.

Research companies themselves can offer help in sourcing the right data. A few years ago I was asked to put together a report on the Hectic Eclectic trend for broadcaster UKTV. Britain, often considered overly traditional and even xenophobic in its eating habits, was becoming much more open to new foods. Determining if this was happening faster in the UK than elsewhere required statistical data on consumption habits across a range of different territories. However, information on the eclecticism of eating habits was a specialist field, and I found few reports that focused specifically on it. In the end, I was helped by an executive at research agency Datamonitor, who spent time searching its database to determine the most cost-effective data sources.

Free data

The internet is the journalist's best friend. In the past, research was much harder and more time-consuming. I used to have to pull cuttings from a company's library, which was a hit-or-miss affair, or I'd have to read whole books to find one good quote. Today I can find a range of things so easily.

Stephen Dalton, *The Times*

Not all statistical data need to cost money. A careful search can provide a great deal of free information. Good trend marketers have a lot in common with good investigative reporters (see Chapter 13). A lot can be learned from their techniques. Like a journalist, a trend marketer needs to keep a bank of key sources. Some of these will provide universal information. Others will be sector- or market-specific. Data can also be found by searching online or in a library. This will be easier for some topics than others. The earlier you pick up on a trend, or the more obscure the topic, the less information there will be available. The advent of search engines such as Google has proved hugely beneficial to those looking for free data.

Government polls can be a useful source of data. Commissioned by individual government departments, they are typically available free. Adding your name to departmental mailing lists will provide regular press releases that detail any research that has been conducted and the most relevant statistics from it. Commercial companies often run polls, the top-line results of which they are willing to share. Magazines also often conduct polls of their readers, and these can sometimes offer useful insights, especially among younger audiences. For instance, youth magazine reader surveys in the early 2000s provided me with early clues as to the changing social attitudes of teenagers.

Data about the sales of individual products and services can be obtained from a company's annual report, and data on new products can be obtained from company press releases. You can obtain these by searching for them online, by signing up to company or PR mailing lists or by looking at the press, media or investor relations section of a company's website. Most research companies offer some of their research free. If you search their websites, you will often find a separate section that provides gratis data. This will typically be older data, and may be located in an archive section. If there is no such section, you can obtain some data by reading the press releases that can be found in the press section.

TESTING DATA

When studying quantitative data, trend marketers must always try to avoid potential bias. Most poll data obtained directly from long-established global research agencies can be trusted to be accurately and fairly obtained, but it is always worth checking the methodology section of any report. The data to be most wary of are those produced by or on behalf of a particular manufacturer or brand. That is because such polls can sometimes be carried out just to find a specific result favourable to the brand.

There are several ways to test the veracity of a poll. You should always verify the size of the sample a poll is based upon. The larger the sample questioned, the more credibility can be placed on the findings. I spoke to someone recently, from a health-related shoe company, who admitted that the efficacy of their product is based on a sample of just 10 people. Clearly data based on a sample this small will be of little use and should be discarded. Marketers must also be careful of claims based on small *percentages*. A 100 per cent increase in the number of people doing something sounds impressive, but that might simply mean that, instead of 2 per cent of a group behaving in one way, now 4 per cent are doing so. The same holds true for smaller samples within a large sample. Imagine a group of consumers that use products W, X, Y and Z. The figures may show that more people like W than X. But if 90 per cent of people use only Y or Z, then the sample of those who actually use W or X is in itself too small to take meaningful data from. Where possible, recruitment criteria should be checked too. The sample should be representative of the market being tested and not biased towards a particular typology or attribute. The wording of questions or multiple-choice answers in a poll should also be studied. Sometimes researchers can 'load' a question so as to obtain a more favourable result.

The way that researchers word their results when writing a report can also be manipulated. Words like 'only' or 'as many as' can be inserted into reports to make the reader think that the figure is either surprisingly low or surprisingly high. Forecasters should always mentally remove such phrases and then rephrase the figures quoted. If a report states that 'As many as 25 per cent of people do X', that might seem impressive, until one removes the first three words and reverses the figure. At that point you realize that three-quarters of those polled do *not* do X. Be careful too of comparisons between two data in a times series. Always try to obtain all of the available data. Comparing figures from, say, 2007 and 2003 might suggest a major shift in a particular behaviour, but the researchers may have chosen those two particular years to compare simply because they were the most extreme, or most favourable to their brand.

NOTES

1. Mintel, 2008
2. Synovate, 2008
3. Datamonitor, 2008
4. Euromonitor, 2007

15

Observational data

THE BOARDROOM

Marketing people always want to see the numbers, but if you want to innovate that's not always possible, so I try to convince them in other ways.

Brechje Vissers, Manager Colour Marketing and Innovation, PPG Industries (ex-Senior Trend Consultant, Philips) (Netherlands)

At Kraft the culture has traditionally been numbers driven. You need to build a case, to define the size of the opportunity. But the more we work with trends, the more people are understanding that you may not have a number yet. They will now be more accepting of something that has been proven in previous examples, or that's happened in another territory.

Bruno Montejorge, Senior Brand Manager, Kraft (Brazil)

Marketing and strategic decisions are typically based on statistical data. This can be sales figures, market share, economic growth rates and so on. Decisions based on trends, however, may by necessity involve much softer data than marketers are used to. Hard data such as statistics might perhaps offer the most robust verification of any trend, but it is not always possible to find such verification. In order to spot a trend early enough to exploit it successfully, it is sometimes necessary to find other types of evidence.

Not having numbers can worry some people, but a lack of statistical evidence does not mean a trend does not exist. In fact, if there is a wealth of statistical evidence for a trend, you may be identifying it too late. If there is a large amount of polling data currently available on something, it is typically because researchers have already identified that trend.

The identification of a trend requires some evidence, of course. No marketers should base a major strategic decision on 'gut instinct' alone, no matter how experienced in trend marketing they are. Convincing others to accept a trends-based decision will require some form of evidence too. With no statistical evidence for a trend, the best way to prove it is with observational data.

THE LIVING ROOM

Focus groups

We regularly hold focus groups on various topics. This helps us monitor the attitudinal pulse of our customers. Occasionally, we'll notice that ideas which first appeared to have only limited relevance begin popping up in the discussions more and more often. This might flag an emerging trend or shift in attitudes that really warrants a response.

Tom Pickles, Senior Director, Global Menu Solutions, McDonald's (USA)

At Levi's we did 'youth panels'. These were panels of young people that we spoke to twice a year. We ran them in the key cities in Europe, and it helped us to get an idea of how our strategy should change or develop.

Helene Venge, Global Director, Business Development,
Lego Group, Denmark and ex-Head of Digital Marketing, Levis Europe

Though quantitative data deliver robustness, there is nothing as evocative as observational or qualitative data. Qualitative research should always be used if the purpose is to explore consumer attitudes or motivations. This is especially true in relation to new products or services. Formal observational research is done via in-depth, typically face-to-face, interviews. These can be conducted with individuals in single depth interviews, or with groups in focus groups or listening posts. Focus groups are useful to trend marketers for gauging current attitudes to find clues as to potential future behavioural trends. A good moderator uses the group environment to develop a discussion that provides greater insight into motivations than single depth interviews would. The questions used in qualitative research need to be future-proofed in the same way as for quantitative research (see Chapter 14).

Most qualitative research is conducted with consumers, but trend marketers can also utilize non-consumer respondents. Expert depth interviews, for instance, can be used to gain data on a trend. One useful multiple depth technique is Delphi research, developed by RAND scientists in the

1960s to aid futures studies. A moderator interrogates a group of experts about possible futures in a series of rounds, alternating between individual and group input, to obtain both unique and consensual responses.

Ethnography

I think the best way to convince people of a trend is to get them to experience it – to go and be with consumers, to go to events and experience what researchers are talking about first-hand. When I worked at Unilever we had regular consumer immersion programmes. I worked on a low-income consumer project there, and the first two weeks I spent entirely in people's homes in Eastern Europe, with an interpreter, watching how they lived their life. I think buying reports only offers you so much. It's much more about what you experience yourself.

Andy Routley, International Brand Marketing Director, Miller, SAB Miller

Even just sitting down in the Arndale Shopping Centre and watching how people are dressed or how they're walking can provide insights.

Wayne Garvie, Director of Production and Content, BBC

Other formal observation techniques centre around ethnography. This is the exploration of a particular demographic or community through long-term field work. Traditional scientific ethnographic research typically involves spending a year or more living with the community, but in modern consumer research such field work typically involves days or hours rather than years.

Ethnographic research can take several forms. The most popular for trends research are immersion and accompanied behaviour. They are similar practices in which researchers spend time experiencing or observing a particular behaviour first-hand. The former involves researchers spending time in an environment where a new trend is being practised. This could be a nightclub or a sports venue. In the latter, researchers will accompany respondents as they take part in a particular behaviour. The most common example is accompanied shopping, in which researchers observe and converse with respondents as they shop.

Ethnographic research can be undertaken by a researcher and the results presented to key company stakeholders, but it can also be undertaken by the stakeholders themselves. Watching or even taking part in a new sport or club night can be an excellent way for people to understand a new trend. For instance, when I worked on a music trends project for Siemens a few years ago, its product development team wanted to understand what tomorrow's consumers might be looking for from a music phone. I spent the day with a marketing partner talking them through new music trends, and in the evening took them to some cutting-edge clubs and up-and-coming-artist concerts, where they were able to see those trends for themselves.

THE STREET

I'll just have my eyes open whenever I'm going out, and I'll listen to other people's conversations as well. It's all about testing the temperature of consumer attitudes.

Camilla Vickerage, Founder, Sweet Shop Research (ex-Research Manager, ICI Paints)

I'm always interfering with people when they're shopping. It's really easy. You just say something like 'I've never tried that brand; what's it like?' or 'Have you ever tried this brand, and how does it compare?'

Sheila Byfield, Leader, Business Planning, Mindshare

Observational research can also be carried out in a less formal manner. Informal research cannot offer the robust evidence of formal research, but it can offer insights or 'snapshots' that work alongside formal research. As it is based upon strong visuals and real-life anecdotes it can often be more evocative and inspiring than formal statistical data. It is particularly useful for identifying innovator or early adopter trends. It can also offer clues as to future behaviours. It is in the informal observational research stage that cool hunting and scout networks are best employed.

Many new trends can be observed informally. In fact, that is how consumers themselves typically pick up on trends. Half of all consumers claim to get their knowledge of new styles from observing what others are wearing.[1] I have run focus groups for several magazine publishers in which mainstream consumers have readily admitted to obtaining much of their information on new trends, ideas and behaviours from informally observing others. In fact, much of the process of trend diffusion is based upon consumers observing each other informally (see Chapter 17).

Data on behavioural change gained via a conversation in a bar or the observation of a new fashion style cannot provide robust evidence of a trend, but it might offer a stimulus to more formal research. Observing a consumer doing something new can stimulate marketers to look for further evidence of such behaviour, to determine whether it might be a trend. It can also be used as stimulus material in presentations or strategic determination workshops (see Part 6). Tim Richards, the managing director of Vue Cinemas, told me how observing an older couple deciding not to go into a cinema because it was too bright and loud was the inspiration for his making his own cinema chain environments more accommodating for a broader audience group. Dave Capper of Hasbro told me that the initial inspiration for the company's hugely successful U-Dance toy came from observing how children enjoyed playing with a musical instrument called a theramin in a museum.

Informal observation should, where possible, be accompanied by some formal research such as depth interviews. This will provide context. If you spot someone in a club wearing something unusual, it is better to ask the person his or her motivation in doing so rather than make what might be an incorrect assumption. For instance, if someone is wearing an army uniform, is it as a mark of aggression, as an ironic protest against growing militarism, or just because the person thinks it makes him or her look attractive?

The most important tools for informal observation are a stills camera, a video camera, a tape recorder and a notebook. There is no way of knowing when you are going to come across evidence of a new trend, so it is vital to keep a notebook and camera on you at all times. You can stumble across a new trend indicator at any time: while out shopping, walking along your local high street or attending a concert. There is nothing more frustrating than spotting evidence of a new trend when you have no means of making a note of it. I remember observing two early adopter consumers actually playing badminton in the middle of a Soho side street one evening. This was an excellent illustration of a trend called Urban Playtime I was working on for brewer SAB Miller. But unfortunately I had neither my stills nor my video camera with me, so the opportunity was lost. It was not something that people were likely to believe unless I had photographic evidence!

To observe consumer behaviours effectively, trend marketers typically need to locate themselves in an environment where early adopters gather. The informal observation process will typically combine visual reportage and depth interviews. Out-of-home behaviours are obviously easiest to observe. In-home behaviours too can be observed but, given the nature of the environment, that is best done using formal ethnographic techniques.

The choice of locations will depend on the topic being researched. Suitable settings can include shopping centres, nightclubs, sports venues and public parks. Underground events and club nights can prove a valuable trend environment. The manner in which such events are presented and the themes behind them are typically a manifestation of the changing interests and attitudes of the innovators and early adopters who have organized them. Such events can thus provide early evidence of new trends, but it is also important to study less cutting-edge environments such as shopping centres and public bars, to identify new mainstream-led trends and to establish how far early adopter trends are spreading into the majority.

It can also be useful to attend trend-related seminars and conferences. These can provide genuine insights. You must of course choose seminars carefully, as they can be expensive, but they can be a good place to hear and interrogate trend observers across a range of sectors. Trade fairs provide good opportunities to observe new or potential product-related trends. Most industries hold annual trade and consumer fairs. These can be a great way to see what the industry in question believes will be of interest in the coming year.

My favourites are the trade fairs for the food, book, toy, interiors and car industries. When I go to these I always return with some new insights. A few years ago I was compiling evidence of a peculiar new trend. Younger people were exploring traditional pastimes in the Traditionalizing trend, yet personal technology was selling better than ever. How were these two diverse behaviours going to resolve themselves? It was while visiting a trade show that I began to understand. The Ideal Home Exhibition is Britain's biggest consumer show for the home and interiors industry. Walking around, I noticed several examples of products designed to traditionalize or even hide technology products. These included wooden computers and sideboards with flat-screen TVs that sank down inside at the push of a button. It was clear that the functionality of the technology was still important, but that the products themselves were perhaps becoming less attractive. Here was the first evidence of an important trend I later christened Soft Technology.

THE INTERNET

Virtual observation is the study of consumer attitudes by monitoring virtual conversations on forums, blogs and social networks. As with any informal research, it can offer only pointers or one-off examples of trends, as evidence is based on a small sample of consumers, but it can provide highly valuable stimulus material. It can be particularly useful in providing initial insights on a new consumer cohort. As with any qualitative technique, data need to be interpreted carefully. Forums are typically inhabited by like-minded individuals. Trust levels therefore tend to be high. An individual may be more honest on a forum than they would in a more formal interview or focus group, but some of their comments may simply be an attempt to impress others in the group. Virtual observation is currently being developed into a more robust process. Global brands are tracking potential market threats using keyword searches, and US intelligence services are increasingly utilizing an analysis of online and media trend data to make predictions of potential terrorist activity.

Virtual observation helped me gain an initial understanding of the Mod Squad trend for product customization. At a car show I noticed groups of youths inspecting each other's cars. I talked to some of them and was introduced to the practice of modifying or 'modding', in which young car enthusiasts personalize their cars. Intrigued, I obtained the addresses of some of their websites and scanned them. Reading alone provided a huge amount of information, but I decided to create a more formal qualitative element. I added my own comment to several of the blogs, explaining who I was and why I was interested in the topic. I made it clear that my interest was not prurient and that I was genuinely keen to learn more about them. I then asked if they would be interested in answering a few questions. I received several replies. This information served as the basis of a questionnaire, which I used in more formal quantitative research at further motor shows. I have kept in touch with some of the modder groups, and they provide me with updates not just on modification but on broader trends in the automotive and youth sectors.

NOTE

1. Yankelovich & Partners, 2003

16

Media monitoring

HOW TO MONITOR

Media monitoring

One of the first things I do every morning is spend half an hour going through blogs and news articles. It's a habit that I've got into just to see what the latest thinking is, what the analysis on different markets is, what people think are the emerging trends, what the shifts and the predictions are.

Mark Broughton, Research Insights and Knowledge Manager, Global Product Development, Alliance Boots

I subscribe to a lot of different websites, from cool hunting websites through to some of the trend websites, and I always read the newspapers and watch the news, and I search around people's blogs. If I come across an emerging trend then I'll read whatever's been written on that.

Camilla Vickerage, Founder, Sweet Shop Research (ex-Research Manager, ICI Paints)

The media are an important source of consumer data. Scanning the right media sources can help marketers to identify or verify the existence of a trend. It can also provide data that aid in establishing the future development of a trend. Like trend forecasting itself, media monitoring was used first by the military and then by intelligence agencies, before filtering down into the commercial world. The scanning process was used by Allied military intelligence officers during the Second World War, to try to learn more about events in occupied territories. They called the process 'scan, clip and review'. After the war it was used by US intelligence agencies, to gain a better understanding of attitudes within the Soviet bloc, but soon it began to be used by commercial concerns, to gain a greater understanding of market change. It is now an important part of many companies' media communications policy.

Behavioural monitoring

The media can be monitored in two ways: behaviourally or attitudinally. Behavioural monitoring falls into three categories: open, evidentiary and coverage monitoring. Open monitoring is the process of scanning the media landscape with an open mind. Researchers study media sources to discover any stories that might indicate the existence of brand new consumer change patterns. They are not looking for specific trends, and do not limit their search to any individual trend, sector or demographic.

In contrast, evidentiary monitoring focuses on specific topics. Its purpose is to identify further evidence of pre-identified trends. Identification is not just about finding one example of a trend. It is an iterative process. The more evidence you have for a trend, the more confidence you can have in its existence and the easier it will be to implement trend-based strategies internally (see Chapter 21). Here researchers will have a list of trends they are searching for evidence of. These will typically be what the brand or consultancy considers the most important or relevant trends. Whenever they find a story that relates to one of them they will file or note it before continuing with their search.

Coverage monitoring involves identifying the amount of space or airtime that is given to a new trend. The process is popular with PR agencies that need to know how much coverage a particular press release or client is receiving. It can be useful for identifying new consumer attitudes. Media stand or fall by the number of viewers, listeners, visitors or readers they attract. The more editorial they provide on the topics that most interest their target consumer, the more consumers they are likely to attract. This means that the best media will cover only topics they strongly believe their consumers are interested in. If they cover a new topic, this suggests they have reason to believe their consumers are showing a new or renewed interest in it. This is not robust evidence in itself, but it can provide a good indicator. Coverage monitoring can be used to quantify media coverage empirically over time. I spoke with one major FMCG brand that employed a PR agency to monitor eating trends in the media. It was able to use this information to obtain empirical evidence on the growth of concerns over obesity (Figure 16.1).

Alternatively multi-use monitoring combines all three processes at once. A trend marketer monitors media sources for new trends and for

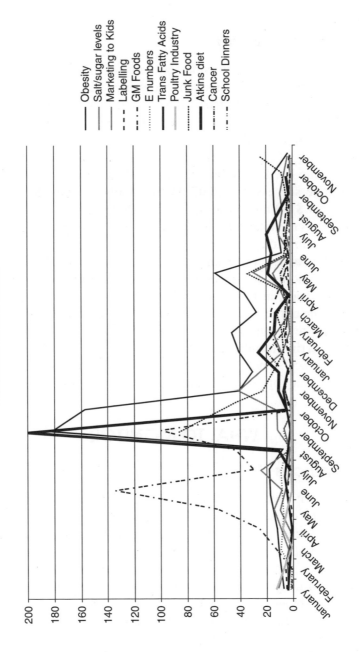

Figure 16.1 Coverage monitoring

evidence of already-identified trends, and also to see how much coverage a trend is getting. This can be useful for small companies with restricted time or budget.

Attitudinal monitoring

Media monitoring not only provides evidence of behavioural trends, but it can also offer clues to attitudinal change using sociological interpretation. Non-news-based media are particularly open to semiotic interpretation. Consumers are more likely to make subconscious, attitudinal choices when consuming non-news media.

The popularity of a particular film, for instance, can provide evidence of new trends. The low-key, intimate, independent film drama *Juno* was one of the surprise successes of 2007. With a budget of just $7.5 million, it grossed almost $150 million in the United States alone, and even won an Oscar for best screenplay. On one level it provided an early indication that early mainstream audiences across the globe might be tiring of the bombast of blockbusters and were looking for content that offered advice on relationships. On another it provided further evidence of consumers' growing demand for advice, in this case on relationships and parenting. The fact that the heroine of the film is an 'alternative' youth who decides to keep her child despite the suggestions of her parents offers more evidence of the Boundary Blurring trend. Juno's parents are Baby Boomers who take a liberal, pro-choice stance, but Juno's actions offer an example of the new conservative values of the millennial generation: the Conserva-Teen.

WHAT TO MONITOR

Media sources

'Media' is a word with a variety of meanings today, dependent on the speaker and the context. Trend marketers need to consider the term in its broadest context: as any content created to inform or entertain consumers. There are typically thousands of media sources in each developed nation, amounting to millions across the globe. These range from national TV broadcasts and daily newspapers with viewer numbers and circulations in the millions, to blogs with a few thousand regular readers. One of the first things a trend marketer must do is establish a library of favoured media titles. This should include the most authoritative titles across all key influencer fields. These should be a mix of news and non-news, consumer and industry media. It is also important to study media from across as wide a range of channels as possible. Given the proliferation of consumer internet use, online media today can provide as much data as print or other offline media.

Media sources can be segmented into news media and non-news media. The two typologies serve different purposes and need the utilization of different observational and interpretational methodologies. News media include newspapers, magazines and factual broadcast media. Non-news media are those editorial products that are not news or fact based. They include films, books, video games and non-factual broadcast media such as dramas or game shows.

A distinction should also be drawn between consumer and business media. The former provide news and entertainment content for consumers and can be used for all kinds of behavioural and attitudinal monitoring. The latter offer news stories about and for a particular industry and should be used for open or evidentiary monitoring only. Another subdivision is that between mainstream and alternative media. The former are the equivalent of the authorized biography, the latter the unauthorized one. Both are valid, but provide different types of data and require a different interpretation process.

Consumer news media

Consumer news media sources can be broken down into mainstream consumer, specialist consumer and alternative consumer media. Mainstream consumer news media sources typically feature a wide range of topics and are more concerned with the breadth than the depth of their information. National and regional newspapers, listings titles, news websites and regular television news broadcasts typically fall into this category. They provide a good edited source of consumer behaviour data.

To obtain more detailed, sector-based information, the forecaster needs to monitor specialist consumer media. These include magazines, websites and TV shows dealing with interest-led topics such as fishing or football, or targeted at demographics such as young children or older women. They can range from magazines on yachting to websites on skateboarding or TV shows on cooking. They can be the first place to hear about a trend in a particular sector. Extrapolating such trends into your own sector can offer clues as to potentially relevant trends.

Alternative consumer news media can provide early warning of new trends. New ideas typically originate at the margins. Alternative media can be the first place to hear about a new trend. The alternative media sector has grown considerably recently, thanks to the reduction in start-up costs offered by the internet. There has been a proliferation of alternative publications not seen since the flowering of such titles in the 1960s after the introduction of cheap mimeographing machines. Alternative websites range from consumer-created mainstream ones such as Wikipedia to one-person 'think piece' blogs. Fringe publications can provide early evidence of new trends. I was inspired to investigate what became the Arty Crafts and Conserva-Teen trends by two great US fringe publications, *Bust* and *Vice* respectively. Another reason to study fringe publications is their readership. They can be the 'bush telegraph' of the trendsetter community: the forum for early adopters to air their concerns. Behaviours and attitudes that are first voiced here can grow into trends. Trends that are picked up and spread by early adopter media will grow faster than those that are not. The most cost-effective way to identify key alternative media is to ask experts within each sector for their favourite media sources. Blog search engines such as Technorati and Google Blog Search can also provide a shortlist of sites that can be investigated further.

Business news media

Business news media are produced for industry professionals and can be segmented into industry media, which focus on specific sectors, and methodological media, which explore different disciplines across a range of sectors. Most marketing executives will be reading some of the industry publications targeted at their own industry, but scanning should not be limited to one's own sector. Trends can begin in any sector, so it is important that marketers scan business news media from across a range of different sectors. Reading outside one's own sector is also a useful discipline for avoiding bias. Methodological media offer advice and information on a single methodology or discipline as it manifests itself across different sectors, from marketing to research. They often run features on changing consumer attitudes or behaviours. They can also offer information on the ways in which marketers are targeting new markets or reacting to behavioural changes. This can be useful during the implementation process when attempting to determine new trends-based marketing strategies (see Chapter 24).

This segment also includes specialist trends media. These range from opinion blogs to larger websites and print publications. They can provide useful data to input into the trend forecasting process, acting as a virtual scout network. A few are the work of enthusiastic amateurs, but most are run by trends consultancies. Some can be accessed free, providing trend data as a means of stimulating future paid consultancy work. Others require an annual subscription (see Chapter 8). Global trend bulletins, for instance, provided evidence of the Extreme Pleasure trend in which consumers, distanced from physicality by technology and numbed to novelty by constant access, were seeking more and more extreme experiences. Such bulletins described 'anger bars' in China, where customers were allowed to beat up the bar staff to release their frustrations of the day. Given enough notice, the specially trained staff were able to dress up as any character that the clients wished to attack. They also described how wealthy Russians were setting up complex, expensive and sometimes dangerous hoaxes for each other as surprise treats. For instance, when one wealthy businessman turned 30 recently, his friends organized for him to be kidnapped by armed police. Such information might have been hard to obtain otherwise.

Non-news media

Non-news media include non-factual print and broadcast content as well as films, video games and books. They offer insights into the mind of contemporary creative artists as well as providing clues to future consumer behaviours. Creative individuals form a large part of the innovator segment. They are often the first people to pick up on a trend. What is of interest to them now may become of interest to more mainstream individuals in the future (see Chapter 13). Observing the books, artwork, plays, television shows and films they create can give an indication of topics that interest them now and might interest other adopter categories in the future. It also offers an indication of changing consumer tastes. If what is popular today differs from what was popular in the recent past then conclusions can be drawn about how attitudes have changed. This can be done using the attitudinal identification process (see Chapter 13).

Non-news media monitoring is best practised as a three-stage process. An initial scan of relevant industry media will offer upfront information on forthcoming products, for instance what new television shows, films or books will be launched in the coming months. Next, the most important of these should be read or watched, to gain a better understanding of what trends they might be encouraging or reacting to. If this is not feasible, then scouts should view them and report back, or reviews should be studied. Finally, the popularity of all such products should be monitored, using industry media or research services, for the purposes of attitudinal identification (see Chapter 13). For instance, if reality or game shows are becoming less popular and documentaries more so, what might this suggest about changing consumer attitudes?

It is also possible to use non-news media to uncover evidence of new early adopter trends. Sites like YouTube were the source for examples of 'gonzo' or non-organized sports that provided the first evidence of the

Extreme Pleasure trend. In tube surfing, individuals were filming themselves on skateboards or other objects 'surfing' down escalators in subways. In ghost riding, the driver or passengers of a vehicle would exit it while it was still moving and dance on top of or beside it. Video sites also offered evidence of less positive manifestations. Happy slapping, in which youths filmed themselves or their friends inflicting injury on random strangers and then uploaded them, started in the UK and quickly spread into European territories such as France and the Netherlands.

Books can also provide inspiration. Steven Johnson's *Everything Bad Is Good for You: How today's popular culture is actually making us smarter* (Riverhead, 2005) described how, despite headlines about 'dumbing down', most successful entertainment products among youth today actually necessitate greater intellectual interaction than previously. To understand television shows like *CSI*, *24* and *Lost* or play video games like *Final Fantasy* and even *Grand Theft Auto*, young people need to retain and analyse large amounts of data and solve complex puzzles. This inspired me to investigate what became the Wising Up trend, in which consumers demand more depth from media and marketing alike.

Summary: Part 4

- Trends can be identified using a variety of different methodologies.

- Trends can be identified across a wide range of consumers, industries and countries.

- Trends can be identified using observational or theoretical methods.

- Trend research needs to be future-proofed.

- Trends can be identified using primary and secondary research.

- Trends can be identified using statistical and non-statistical research.

- Statistical and non-statistical data are both useful.

- Statistical data can be free or paid for.

- Non-statistical research can be formal or informal.

- Trend data can be effectively obtained across a range of media.

Part 5

Interpretation

17

How trends spread

WHERE TRENDS SPREAD

Identifying a trend is the first step in the trend forecasting process but, to make use of a trend, trend marketers need to interpret it. This will enable them to determine how it might develop and what impact it might have on their company. To do this requires the implementation of formal criteria based on an understanding of the way in which trends are adopted.

Trends typically follow a systematic adoption process. Theories differ as to the exact ways in which trends spread from one consumer group to another. However, most experts agree about the basic principles of trend development. Consumer A behaves in a new way. Consumers B and C observe this and copy consumer A. Then consumers W, X, Y and Z copy consumers B and C. This process is known as trend diffusion. In scientific usage, diffusion is the process whereby liquids or gases intermingle and move from an area of high concentration to an area of lower concentration. As for liquids or gases, when people who have adopted trends mingle with those who have not, the trends move from a small concentrated group to a broader mainstream one. The typologies of those who adopt a trend at a specific point in the diffusion process also follow a standard pattern.

WHO TRENDS SPREAD TO

Adopters

The key opinion leaders for most brands are probably only 20–30 people. Then there's another layer of maybe a few hundred 'lesser' opinion leaders. Then you've got your early adopters who are your next wave, which depending on the size of brand and market could be several thousand consumers. And then you've got your followers. And the approach you take to successfully connecting with them must differ for each.

Andy Routley, International Brand Marketing Director, Miller, SAB Miller

There is a difference between early adopters for technology and ones for, say, food or cleaning products. The tech geeks admit that when it comes to laundry questions they go to their mothers. Their mothers may generally be seen as very conservative, but it is they who are actually the early adopters for laundry products, and they who are looking for innovations in this area. It is true in other sectors too. The guy who always buys the latest phone might not be the first to buy a new car.

Bruno Montejorge, Senior Brand Manager, Kraft (Brazil)

Trends diffuse from one adopter typology to another in a prescribed pattern. A creative individual adopts a new behaviour or attitude. This is observed and then copied by a number of forward-thinking, novelty-loving consumers. The trend will then be taken up by more traditional and risk-averse consumers. Those who create the trend are known as the innovators. Those who copy them are known as early adopters. The next group to adopt a trend is the early mainstream. If it continues to grow it will be adopted by the late mainstream and then finally by the laggards.

Innovators

Innovators are the very first people to adopt a new behaviour or attitude. It is to them that the early adopters look for their trends. Professional innovators range from filmmakers to product designers. Amateur innovators are those individuals who enjoy creating for its own sake outside of their working lives. Innovators are generally individualistic, are unafraid of the negative opinions of others, enjoy novelty and are less afraid of uncertainty than any other cohort. Their drivers for adoption are typically attitudinal rather than behavioural. They may be naturally curious, so try something new just to see what it is like. They may get bored easily, so seek a rapid turnover of new experiences or products; they may simply have a natural aversion to the status quo; or they might like the status that comes with trend creation.

Early adopters

Early adopters do not come up with trends, but they actively seek them out and take risks with adoption. It is they whom early mainstream consumers turn to for advice on new products or services. They typically share many traits with innovators. They too are generally individualistic, favour novelty and are unafraid of uncertainty or the negative opinion of others. They adopt early for the same attitudinal reasons that innovators do: out of curiosity, boredom or the desire for status. This latter is particularly important for them. They also adopt trends for specific behavioural reasons: because they have either the means or the need to do so. Early adopters are therefore not always driven by curiosity or novelty. They might have the money to try new things or the contacts to obtain them gratis. For instance, the rich or those within the technology industries will be the first to obtain technology products. They might have the free time to trial something that requires many hours to practise or understand. This is one reason why computer services have been picked up by the very young and the very old: two cohorts that have a lot of time on their hands. Importantly, they may simply have a greater need for a new product or service than anyone else. For instance, those who are busy are likely to trial a time-saving product before those who are not.

Early mainstream

Early mainstream adopters are not the first in a cohort to pick up on a trend, but they pick up on it before the majority of consumers do. They are the individuals whom the late mainstream turn to for advice on new products or services. In any market, only a few friendship groups will include an early adopter, but the vast majority of them will include at least one member of the early mainstream. This group is interested in new products and services, but they are much less adventurous in adopting them than early adopters. They take a practical approach to innovations and will typically deliberate for a long time before deciding whether to adopt a trend. They are an important link in the adoption system. Once a trend reaches them, it can offer genuine strategic opportunities. But the transition from early adopters to early mainstream can be a difficult one. In his book *Crossing the Chasm* (HarperCollins, 1991), Geoffrey A Moore describes how he believes the 'chasm' that exists between these two adopter cohorts stops many innovations from gaining success.

Late mainstream

Late mainstream consumers make up the majority of customers in any market. They are more risk-averse and sceptical than the early mainstream. They prefer to feel completely comfortable with and certain about an innovation before adopting it. The group is heavily influenced by media, societal and peer pressure. The gap between adoption by the early and late main-stream can be lengthy. Once a trend has reached the late mainstream, every company in the sector that trend is relevant to should be exploiting it.

Laggards

Laggards are those traditionalist consumers who are the least interested in change and the most risk-averse. They are very slow to pick up trends. Many trends actually never reach them. For instance, although most people in the West take internet usage for granted, there are still many in even the most developed territories who do not have access to the internet. Further, over 50,000 Britons still watch black-and-white television.[1] Laggards are typically older than other consumer types, so find new products and serv-ices of less interest or harder to accept than young ones. They can often come from lower social grades, so simply cannot afford to trial new trends.

Although each adopter type follows general principles, it is dangerous to generalize too greatly about their demographic constitution. The young and those with the highest disposable income typically constitute a high proportion of the earlier adopter groups, but this is less true in sectors where trends move more slowly or where style or novelty is less important. Young people are typically more interested in new products generally, but they often do not have the money to adopt them, and it is left to older, wealthier cohorts to do so. This has been the case with products such as the iPhone or 3G networks. There are also many new trends that will not inter-est young people. For instance, the young will usually be less interested in trends in the household, home or financial sectors. Lower grades may typi-cally be unable to afford new products, but new products are not always expensive, especially within the digital sector. This is true of ringtones or pay-as-you-go phones. Some theorists have argued in the past that lower social grades do not have media access to new trends, but today that is rarely true. From *Hola* to *Hello*, publications targeted at LNWIs regularly feature new trends. Such publications helped spread trends such as Well-being and Trading Up to the late mainstream.

HOW TRENDS SPREAD

Trend diffusion

The question of what drives trends from one adopter cohort to the next needs to be broken down into two separate questions. The first is 'How do trends spread?' The second is 'Why do trends spread?' The reason *why* a trend spreads lies in the inherent qualities of that trend. I deal with this in Chapters 18 and 19. *How* it spreads is due to the influence of individual consumers, and I will deal with that here.

Most experts agree trends spread via some form of diffusion. They also typically agree that trends move from early adopters to mainstream consumers and then to laggards, and they agree that there are certain qualities or circumstances that will encourage the take-up of a trend. What they find harder to agree on is which individuals or groups encourage trend adoption.

Trend diffusion theory is a relatively new concept. Its roots stretch back to the early 20th century, but its key texts did not appear until the 1950s. Perhaps because of this, again there is no single agreed theory. The good news for trend marketers is that the different theories are not mutually exclusive from the point of view of forecasting. Each theorist agrees that trends are more likely to grow if they are sanctioned by admired individuals. What differs is that some believe they are individuals known personally by the adopting consumer, whereas others believe they are individuals typically 'known' only through the media. There is also disagreement as to whether those influencing individuals play an active or passive role. But trend marketers do not need to take sides in this matter. It is enough simply to know the key points of each theory in order to determine how a trend develops (see Chapter 20). It is only when trying to *influence* the adoption of a product or service that a marketer needs to take sides – and that is not part of the job of a trend marketer (see Chapter 5).

Trickle-down

The first attempt to understand how trends spread was trickle-down theory. It was introduced by French sociologist Gabriel Tarde in the early 1900s. Tarde was the first person to show how trends moved down through society from one level to another. He claimed that it was the richest consumers who established trends. It was they who were able to purchase the latest products and services and, owing to the rigid societal hierarchies in place at the time, poorer consumers looked to the rich for their opinions and followed their tastes. Social history suggests this theory was accurate at the time. Up until the 19th century, trends were typically spread by high-profile individuals who frequented one or more of the important royal courts in Europe. This was true of fashion styles from the court of Queen Elizabeth I of England to the era of Count d'Orsay and Beau Brummell. The father of the modern fashion industry, Charles Frederick Worth, became influential only when he was made dressmaker to the court of Napoleon III. From here his influence 'trickled down' from the aristocracy to early mainstream consumers. It held true too in other design-led manufacturing sectors. In 1765, Wedgwood created a new earthenware form, which he initially called 'creamware'. The British queen, Charlotte, ordered a set and, sensing a publicity opportunity, Wedgwood renamed it 'Queen's Ware', in her honour. Sales soared all across Europe, encouraging a trend for household pottery that reached into the mainstream.

Trickle-down theory in its most literal sense is less relevant today. It still has validity in those emerging markets where similar societal values still hold, but it has generally become a less influential part of trend diffusion as societies have developed. In most developed markets, societal hierarchies have changed a great deal in the last two centuries. Purchase and lifestyle movements in Western societies today are typically more meritocratic than aristocratic. Consumers do not necessarily look to the richest segments for their opinions. They will look to the opinion of whomever they consider the most valid, regardless of social standing. Trends now go up and down throughout society, 'bubbling up' almost as often as they trickle down. People from all social grades can influence the trend process. Trends can come from underground and low-income cultures too. Society is also more complex today. There is no single barometer of taste. What is considered fashionable or aspirational can differ from one consumer cohort to the next, and the richest consumers do not always buy into the latest trends or even buy the latest products. The principle behind trickle-down, however, formed the basis for one of today's most strongly held trend theories.

Innovation diffusion

Everett M Rogers used trickle-down theory as the starting point for a new theory of diffusion in the early 1960s. In his hugely influential book *Diffusion of Innovations* (Free Press, 1962) he developed a theory that showed how trends trickled 'through' a society or community rather than 'down' it. Rogers established many of the central premises of standard diffusion theory. He explained how diffusion worked, identified the adopter typologies, from early adopters to laggards, and established the association between the attributes of innovations and their rate of adoption. Any study of trends is by necessity informed strongly by Rogers's work. The present volume is no exception.

Rogers's ideas were developed further by others. Biologist Richard Dawkins's *The Selfish Gene* (Oxford University Press, 1978) introduced the concept of meme theory, in which ideas, habits and fashions pass from one person to another by learning or imitation in a manner similar to that of a virus. Malcolm Gladwell developed Rogers's and Dawkins's theories in his own highly successful book *The Tipping Point* (Little, Brown, 2000). He further explored the attributes of opinion formers, popularized the concept of trend diffusion as a viral process, and took the concept of trend diffusion into the mainstream.

Networks and trendsetters

Rogers and his followers believe that consumers are most influenced to adopt trends by opinion-forming early adopters within their own social networks, but some trend theorists have challenged this. US sociologist Duncan J Watts has questioned whether opinion formers have as great an influence as Rogers believed. In works such as *Six Degrees* (Norton, 2003) he puts forward an alternative theory based around networks. He agrees that trends spread through personal influence, but he does not believe they travel only from opinion formers to non-opinion formers. He believes they spread through the interaction of *all* the members of a network.

Recently Danish sociologist Henrik Vejlgaard has questioned whether active personal influence is actually the most influential factor in the diffusion of many trends. He believes many trends today are spread more through consumers' observation of innovators or early adopters, whom he calls 'trendsetters', than by the active persuasion of opinion leaders. In effect, Vejlgaard's theory was a development of Tarde's theory. In it, consumers imitate those they look up to. But today that is not the aristocracy: it is the 'new aristocracy' of celebrities, creatives, media sources and high-profile early adopter consumers. They are analogous to the influentials described in Chapter 13. Vejlgaard uses the dance the Moonwalk to illustrate how important celebrity is in the spreading of trends today. Entertainers such as Sammy Davis Jr and Cab Calloway performed the dance in the 1940s, but observation was limited to their theatre audiences. It was not until Michael Jackson performed the dance on a television show in the media-saturated 1980s that it became the 'overnight sensation' that millions across the globe believe Jackson himself created.

Celebrity trendsetters range from musical artists such as Madonna to fine artists such as Damien Hirst, from sportspeople such as David Beckham to celebrities who are 'famous for being famous' such as Paris Hilton. Their personal behaviours and attitudes have inspired trends from fashion, hair and beauty to cars, gender roles and travel. The growing success of celebrity product ranges offers evidence of the growing power of celebrity, but the 'new aristocracy' is not limited to celebrities. All that is required is an influential audience. This could be the readers of a newspaper column or the viewers of a television show. On a more minor level, it could simply be fellow club goers, or even just one's school friends.

Multi-driver diffusion

All the theories above have validity, but some have more validity for particular trend typologies or consumer cohorts than others. Tarde's trickle-down theory is still applicable in several developing nations. Many of Rogers's findings about the nature of diffusion can be usefully applied to any trend, but others are today only applicable to innovation-based trends. When it comes to cultural trends, Vejlgaard's adoption theories can often be more appropriate. A good approach for a trend marketer to take is to consider what I call 'multi-driver diffusion'. This is an inclusive, holistic approach that takes the best from each theory. The rest of Part 5 describes that method.

NOTE

1. *The Times*, December 2005

18

Active trend drivers

ASSISTANCE ATTRIBUTES

When establishing our business model, we had a big discussion over how people would react to new technological developments. We wanted to ascertain whether people would shift their behaviours to new technologies or simply adapt their use of old ones, and we determined that it would be the latter. So we decided we should put our initial investment there: into what people are comfortable with, what is ubiquitous, what is easy to access, what the people know and are familiar with. It was absolutely the right thing to do… and it really paid off for us.

Andy Shaw, Product Development Director, BT Agile Media,
British Telecom

Having considered how trends move from one adopter cohort to another, the next step is to understand *why* they do so. There are active and passive reasons. The active reasons are connected with the specific qualities of the

ASSISTANCE ATTRIBUTES	NEED ATTRIBUTES
simple	status
cheap	health
visible	money-saving
communicable	time-saving
continuous	safety
trusted	excitement
practical	peace of mind

Figure 18.1 Active attributes

trend. The passive reasons are connected to the environment the trend is being launched into. This chapter will focus on active trend drivers, and the next on passive ones.

The active reason a trend grows is because it has qualities that appeal to consumers. It might have attributes that make it easy for consumers to adopt it, such as simplicity, visibility or practicality, or it might have qualities that appeal to basic consumer needs, such as value for money, safety or status (Figure 18.1).

Some trends are more visible or communicable than others. The more visible a trend is, the more likely it is that consumers will copy it. Some trends are connected with products or behaviours that are displayed, whereas others are less visible. Clothes, cosmetics, hairstyles and music are more observable than home furnishings, sports equipment, banking or food. This is one reason why fashion and personal technology trends typically spread faster than interiors or finance trends. You can see what people are wearing or using when you pass them in the street, but you can only see what furniture they have if you enter their houses, and you know what financial services they use only if you discuss the subject with them. Trends connected with appearance, such as changes in colours and materials, are also typically easier to see. If a trend is media-friendly it will be seen by a greater number of people than one that is not. The latest personal technology product is more likely to gain publicity than the latest mortgage. The same applies to products that have a celebrity endorsement.

Some trends are more expensive than others to adopt. This is either because the product or pastime itself is expensive, or because it requires the purchase of other products in order to utilize it. The more expensive a trend is, the fewer consumers will trial or adopt it. One reason text messages and ringtones took off among the young was their low unit price. The easier or cheaper it is to trial a product prior to purchase, the more people will use it and the faster it is likely to be adopted.

Some trends can be too complex for mainstream adoption. The more knowledge a trend requires prior to use, the slower the adoption rates will be. Such complexity can be product or concept based. Genuine complexity refers to how difficult it is actually to operate the product. Conceptual complexity is more concerned with the ideas behind a product or service. For instance, what can the product do better than its predecessors? Conceptual complexity is one of the key reasons that sales of personal video recorders were initially slow. The services the product offers, such as the ability to pause live television, are not easy for consumers to understand. The iPod is evidence that this holds true in reverse. The simpler a product, the more people will try it. A broad product trend sometimes does not gain mass appeal until a simplified version of it becomes available.

There had been a number of unsuccessful MP3 players launched into the market before the iPod took off.

Trust is another key issue. Consumers need to be able to trust that a trend will not harm them either financially or physically. It needs to appear safe and reliable. Where the innovation has been created and who has created it can affect adoption rates. It helps if the innovation shares attributes with previously trusted ones. An innovation needs to be of practical use too. Topless swimsuits were heavily publicized in mass media sources in the 1960s, and commentators suggested they were going to be very popular. But they could not be worn in public, so unsurprisingly failed to sell. An innovation should also offer a perceived advantage over its predecessors. If it is a manufactured product, then the competitive intensity of the manufacturer will also have an effect.

The dislocation level of a trend, how different it is to previous trends, can affect its speed of adoption too. There are three types of innovation: continuous, part-continuous and discontinuous. A continuous innovation is simply the modification of an existing product or service. It does not require users to change their behaviour before adoption, so it is likely to be adopted quickly. A part-continuous innovation may be a brand new trend, but it does not force adopters to alter their established patterns of purchase or use. A discontinuous innovation, however, is not only new; it also requires adopters to alter their behaviour patterns. This is likely to slow adoption rates, especially if there is a high level of complexity involved in adopting the trend. This is true of practicalities such as behaviour but also of attitudes. For a trend to be broadly adopted, it should be compatible with consumers' current practices, cultural beliefs and value systems.

If a trend has strong trend drivers but does not have the necessary assistance attributes to diffuse to the mainstream, what typically develop are variants of the trend that *do* have positive attributes. The drivers for the Extreme Pleasure trend for extreme pastimes were strong. Increased rates of technology usage were making many consumers' lives more uniform and predictable, distancing them from physicality and 'reality'. Meanwhile, constant access was numbing them to traditional novelty. A 'been there, done that' attitude was driving many consumers towards more and more extreme versions of favourite pastimes.

There was also a growing need to relieve the tensions of modern living. Road rage and other examples of what psychiatrists call intermittent explosive disorder were on the increase. So too was hypertension, not just in the West but in China and India too. Yet, by their very nature, extreme behaviours rarely diffuse far. Such extreme trends were only likely to be taken up by early adopters, who enjoy the thrill of new, 'edgy' behaviours. Mainstream consumers are typically put off by such trends' negative need attributes. Such activities do not increase feelings of safety: in fact, quite the reverse. They are also often morally at odds with current behaviours. So instead some mainstream consumers adopt 'softer' versions of the specific elements of the trend. The violence of white-collar boxing, one example of Extreme Pleasure, was popular with early adopters, but too dangerous to be adopted widely. The result was a re-popularizing of the safer traditional form of the sport. More men and women are boxing competitively now. Eighty thousand engage in the sport recreationally in Britain, and over 100 new clubs have started up in the last two years.[1] Meanwhile a more 'acceptable' version of the entire Extreme Pleasure trend evolved: Cruelty Culture. In this, consumers enjoyed other people's extreme behaviour *voyeuristically*. This ranged from reading the 'misery memoirs' of writers such as Dave Pelzer to watching the 'torture porn' of movies such as *Hostel* and *Saw*.

NEED ATTRIBUTES

Consumer drivers

We have to consider how our strategy ties in with what the core consumer insight is, what the need we're addressing is, and how that need will develop over a three- to five-year term.

Mark Broughton, Research Insights and Knowledge Manager, Global Product Development, Alliance Boots

When developing a new product or service you need to have a real sense of how it might tap into a trend or a new behavioural trait or economic need.

Andy Shaw, Product Development Director, BT Agile Media, British Telecom

Need attributes are the qualities of a trend that appeal to eternal or contemporary consumer needs. The more such qualities a trend has, the more likely it is to spread to the mainstream. Need attributes can be based on a product or service's utilitarian or functional product attributes and benefits. These will be particularly important if the trend is such that consumers are making a rational decision about it. But many innovation consumption decisions will be based on more than just functionality. Hedonic and emotion-driven drivers can be at least as powerful. Some adoption drivers are universal – they hold true for all consumers – but some adoption drivers exist only among certain cohorts, as different markets, demographics and segments have differing needs, demands and drivers.

Universal drivers

My belief is that absolutely everything must be embedded in social dynamics. The question I ask every time I hear about a potential trend is 'Why would someone want to do that?' For something to succeed it needs to make life easier, more convenient, more enjoyable or offer greater status. And if it doesn't, then the chances are it won't take off.

Sheila Byfield, Leader, Business Planning, Mindshare

Trend drivers are typically based around the lower level of the needs pyramid. Generally a trend is likely to last if it makes life easier or more satisfying, if it enables more informed decisions in filling an established need, or if it allows people to set their standards a little bit higher within their financial capabilities.

Tom Pickles, Senior Director, Global Menu Solutions, McDonald's (USA)

Universal adoption drivers are typically based around a perceived benefit. Do consumers believe that adopting a particular trend will provide them with something favourable that they do not currently possess? This can be a physical benefit, such as an improvement in health, functionality or circumstances, or the saving of time or money. It can also be an emotional benefit, such as increased status, confidence or self-image, a sense of excitement, or peace of mind. Conscious Consumption, for instance, the trend for more ethical purchasing, provides health benefits and appeals to consumers' self-image and peace of mind. The Convenience Story trend, in which consumers are looking for services that simplify and ease their lives, improves functionality and saves time. The Natural Fitness trend improves health, saves money and builds self-image and peace of mind.

The relative importance of particular adoption drivers will of course differ dependent upon the circumstances of the potential adopters. It can be affected by the level of time, the amount of money and the ability to receive information consumers have. It will also be affected by consumers' attitudes, motivation, values and lifestyle. It can be affected too by their environment, from their social class to their family situation, or the degree of their personal involvement in the innovation.

Specific drivers

Personal motivations, drivers and the tools you use depend on what age and life stage you're at. With social networking, when you're 12–16, it's all about how many people you know. Then when you get a bit older, you become a lot more selective, so your network of friends narrows.

Phil Guest, Managing Director Western Europe, Sulake

Consumers' ages affect what they are interested in, what they consider 'appropriate' and what they are physically capable of doing. Those going through adolescence will have different needs and aspirations to toddlers or retired people, so they will be more or less likely to adopt particular trends. Consumers are also affected by outside events. There are the life-stage events that consumers experience at certain points in their life: becoming or losing a parent, perhaps, or moving in with a partner. There are also specific events that affect every generation at once, such as wars or economic downturns. As with age, the life stage or generation a consumer belongs to will affect the relative importance of drivers such as interest, appropriateness and capability.

This can help the prediction process in two distinct ways. If you are targeting a particular demographic and know what age, life stage or genera-tion they are, you can include the related trend driver dependent on whether they fall into that segmentation or not. Alternatively you can work out which ages, life stages or generations are most likely to be open to a particular trend, and then choose to target only the consumers within those. You can also use life-stage and generational drivers in cross-demo-graphic trend prediction. Knowing how many consumers in any given market are of a particular age and knowing approximately when a life stage takes place mean that you can gauge how many people are likely to be passing through a life stage at any one time. You can then build this into your calculations. The same is true of generations.

A similar approach can be taken with gender, culture, income or atti-tude. Men may be driven less by family safety than women. South Americans may be affected more by status attributes than Australians. Low-income households may be driven more by value than those with high incomes.

Evolving drivers

> When you're in hard times economically, the functionality of a product is
> increasingly important.

> Sheila Byfield, Leader, Business Planning, Mindshare

Even universal drivers are not immune to change. They will evolve slightly owing to environmental factors. Universal drivers such as money and status can become relatively more or less important depending on factors such as economic outlook. Their composition can also change. What constitutes status, for instance, can evolve over time.

There are other drivers that grow or diminish much more strongly owing to external factors. Their number is growing because of accelerated rates of change. As explored earlier, traditional gender and age boundaries are blurring (see Chapter 2). Life stages too are changing. We are reaching some of them later, such as childbirth and house purchasing. We are reaching others earlier, such as our first job. We are also passing through some of them more often than we used to. In previous centuries, we might have got married only once, but now many are doing so twice or even three times. This of course means we are also getting divorced more often, and returning to the single life stage more regularly. Such changes affect the way in which our needs, and therefore those factors that drive us, develop.

The way that changing consumer drivers affect trends can be illustrated by studying historical attitudes towards an activity such as tanning. Rich consumers in the 17th and 18th centuries tried to make themselves look pale, but those in the 19th and 20th centuries tried to make themselves look more tanned. In both cases the driver was the same. Consumers were behaving in a certain way because they wanted to enhance their social status, but the nature of the behaviour changed because the environment changed. More recently, social status has become a weaker driver as attitudes towards health and wealth have grown in importance.

Up until the 19th century, pale skin typically identified a person in Western countries as belonging to a wealthy minority. The poor typically worked outside, so their skin would become naturally tanned. A tan made you look like a farm labourer. Because of this, many rich people actively kept out of the sun, and many others emphasized their pallor by putting powder on their skin. Here social status was actually a barrier to tanning. There was no reason that consumers rich or poor might have wanted a tan. Companies launching tanning-related products would have failed. Trend analysts could have confidently predicted that tanning trends would not grow.

But the environment changed in the late 19th century. With the Industrial Revolution, many low-income consumers began working indoors. Farming became less common. This caused a complete reversal in attitudes to tanning. Now the rich were no longer the only ones who spent their days indoors. They became the only ones who could afford to spend their days *outdoors*. The way to show their higher social status was to cultivate their tans. This trend was encouraged in the 20th century by the introduction of the passenger liner and the invention of the jet engine. This enabled the rich to travel regularly to hot destinations, where they were able to increase their tans. The media coverage that ensued in the 1960s encouraged poorer consumers to emulate the tanned look of the rich. They began to buy fake tan and sought holiday destinations with tanning opportunities. Consumer demand for tans created a whole micro-industry based on tanning beds and tanning salons, as well as a demand for tanning-related cosmetics products. This influence spread into other sectors such as the holiday and fashion industries. Tanning opportunities helped drive the demand for hot holiday locations. Clothes that showed off a person's tan became more popular. The importance of social status meant that tanning-related trends were predictably popular for several decades, and tanning trends grew.

But three recent environmental changes have since drastically affected consumer attitudes to tanning. Firstly, it has become easier to obtain a tan, which has devalued its status, so now it is increasingly important what the quality of the tan is. It takes more time or money to develop a 'good' tan. The trend for products that provide such a tan has grown at the expense of standard tanning products. Secondly, scientists learned that prolonged exposure to the sun could be dangerous. This tied in with greater general consumer concern over personal health issues. The combination created a new micro-industry based around sunscreens, fake tans and spray tans. It also encouraged a trend away from beach holidays towards more cultural ones. Cultural destinations saw a 50 per cent increase in value sales from 2000 to 2005.[2] Consumers are now more wary of exposing themselves to the sun. Social status has waned compared to the drive for safe health. Consumers still want good tans, and if they can obtain them safely they will do so. Tan-based trends that depend upon exposure to the sun will typically fail, but those that can be obtained safely are likely to succeed. Finally, there has been a growth in the 'nouveau riche' and 'nouveau celeb': people who have risen quickly from poor backgrounds to either wealth or celebrity. This has devalued the idea of wealth and celebrity among some consumers. The fact that many of these people sport good tans has in turn devalued the very status of tanning. This means that, for the first time in decades, even safe tanning-related trends may be on the wane.

NOTES

1. *Guardian*, 2007
2. Euromonitor, 2006

19

Passive trend drivers

PASSIVE DRIVERS

The success or failure of a trend is based not just upon the active qualities of the trend and the passive qualities of the market environment. Trends can succeed or fail dependent on whether or not they have qualities that actively appeal to consumers (see Chapter 18). But their success is also dependent on whether the market environment is appropriate for them. There are a number of factors outside the trend itself that act as drivers or barriers to its growth. These are the environmental or social factors that will act upon a trend as it develops.

These passive drivers can accelerate a trend by encouraging uptake. They can also slow it down or even stop it altogether. A trend might occur at a time when conditions are not ready, or it might run contrary to traditionally held beliefs. If so, it is likely to stall. Alternatively it might be perfectly suited to the current social or technological environment, in which case it is likely to grow.

Passive drivers can be grouped into four categories. I call them the 4 Cs (Figure 19.1). They are constants, cycles, calculables and chaotics. Constants are those environmental factors that do not change. Cycles are behaviours or attitudes that run in established patterns. Calculables are those things the outcome of which is unknown, but that an estimated calculation can be made about. Chaotics are unexpected events that can have an enormous impact on trends but cannot be planned for. Anything that is a constant or part of a cycle can typically be predicted accurately. Calculables can be predicted, but with less accuracy. The arrival of chaotics cannot be predicted, but their outcomes can.

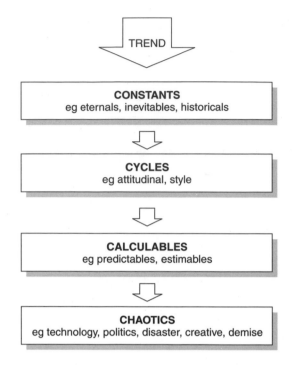

Figure 19.1 Passive attributes (the 4 Cs)

CONSTANTS

Eternals

> *The problem is, many people don't consider the things that people have always done. You need to look at what's the same as much as what's different.*

Annie Freel, Head of Knowledge, McCain Foods

Trends are based on change but, when determining the potential of a trend, it is essential to be aware too of those factors that do not change. Constants provide the foundations for trend predictions. They are the things we know do not change. They can be natural constants. We 'know' the sun is always hot and illuminating. When the sun shines on us, we become warmer and we can see more clearly. When the sun stops shining, we are less warm, and we need artificial light to see. There can also be consumer constants. Consumers have certain basic needs and will look for products that fulfil them. A constant, by its nature, will always remain the same. As long as you can establish something as a constant, you do not need to *predict* how it might develop in the future. You already 'know' that it will be the same as it is now and can plan accordingly, including it in any calculation as a 'given'.

Eternals are those constant factors that always hold true. They include natural and technological laws. A country's environmental infrastructure is an eternal. So too are some elements of its social and utility infrastructure. Eternals will retain their qualities over time, except in exceptional circumstances. Typically it takes a chaotic to change them. Global warming is currently changing 'eternal' temperatures, and the propeller and the jet engine voided the 'eternal' law that humans could not fly. Eternals can be predicted with extreme accuracy, at least in the short and mid-term, but they are so hard-wired into our brains that we typically take them for granted and do not even see them as predictions. They must of course be factored in, but a marketer is likely to do that naturally.

Inevitables

Inevitables are constant not because they are eternal or 'natural', but because something has happened in the past that renders them unavoidable. There is continuity between the past and the future. Once an event has happened, it cannot 'un-happen'. And some of the occurrences subsequent to that event can be predicted with certainty.

Baby Boomers are a good example of an inevitable. During the 1930s food and utilities were expensive so parents were wary of having too many children. During the Second World War, many husbands were away for long periods fighting in other countries, so they and their wives had fewer opportunities to conceive. At the end of the war, the economic situations in most countries improved, and newly reunited couples 'made up for lost time'. As a result, many countries, especially in the West, experienced a sudden growth in the number of births: a baby boom. This lasted for over a dozen years, creating the Baby Boomer generation. Such an environment had implications for the future that are not only clear in hindsight; many of them could have been predicted in 1945. They were inevitables.

Boomers typically grew up with a sense of privilege and a lack of want. Their parents' newly improved economic situation enabled them to give the children most of what they asked for. Those who grow up in a time of wealth tend to feel financially secure and adopt a 'live for today' attitude, so are more likely to spend than save. Better education gave them greater knowledge, confidence and expectations. Their parents were predominantly conservative, and the Boomers' continued hedonism and iconoclasm are to some extent a reaction against this. As they gained or were allowed more freedom, they became used to it and demanded it from brands. The era they grew up in exalted youth, from President Kennedy to the Beatles and beyond, and saw remarkable social, technological and political changes. Boomers are therefore particularly open to products that offer to extend their youth. Used to change, they have found it easier to adapt to new concepts, products, technologies and trends than their parents have. When it comes to purchase and consumption behaviours, their upbringing means they typically admire novelty, believe they deserve 'the best', and have a strong sense of financial justice. The remarkable popular culture explosion encouraged an enjoyment of popular culture that has remained with them.

Historicals

Insight is typically the key source for trend prediction. But trend analysts can also make use of hindsight. As futurist Edward Cornish states: 'Futuring can be thought of as the art of converting knowledge of the past into knowledge of the future.'[1] Similar events can reoccur through history. If these reoccurrences are regular, we call it a cycle and we can use it in our predictive calculations, but if they happen irregularly they can still help in the prediction process. If we know the way something happened previously, we can anticipate how it is likely to happen a second time. Historicals fall into two categories: case studies and social history.

For those considering innovation, it can prove highly effective to study the history of companies that have succeeded or failed with innovations in a similar area in order to understand why they did so. If they succeeded, was it just luck or was it due to certain factors that can be replicated? If they failed, did they innovate too late, or did they fall into traps that needed to be avoided? The first point of reference will be case studies in competitor and same-sector brands, but marketers should also study other-sector brands that share similar markets or attributes, or that are sold in similar ways or within the same environments.

Trend marketers should also study social history. Most eras echo the past in some ways. Forecasters should search previous eras for similar circumstances, environments or trends, and then explore what happened in those eras. A good knowledge of history is helpful, but an intelligent online search will typically reveal some useful data. The economic problems of the late 2000s echo two previous eras: the 1930s and the mid-1970s, both times of economic decline. In both instances, consumers sought to 'escape' their economic struggles through entertainment and leisure pursuits. In the 1930s they 'escaped' poverty by experiencing virtual wealth in glamorous Hollywood films. Stars like Clark Gable and Bette Davis made consumers forget their poverty by giving them a glimpse into a more sensational, upmarket world. The mid-1970s was an era of prime-time nostalgia.

Consumers 'escaped' the problems of the present day by a virtual retreat into the past. Television shows and films that harked back to the economic boom years of the 1950s were hugely popular: from *Happy Days* to *American Graffiti*. From such temporal analogies, marketers can predict that trends offering glamour or nostalgia might be more likely to succeed in the current economic climate than those focused on the future or the hardship of, say, the 'misery memoirs' genre.

It can also help to study recent international social history if a particular trend has already developed somewhere else. For instance, if a trend began in Western countries but is beginning to spread to BRIC or emerging nations, a study of how the trend developed in the West can provide strong clues as to how it might develop elsewhere.

CYCLES

Everything has its time line. If you're still doing the 'same old same old', then eventually sales will start dropping off. The burlesque thing, for example, this sort of overtly sexy sassiness, has been around for ages, but it can't go on indefinitely. It will reach a point where it's got to change, and these things typically go to the complete flipside. So we'll see people start talking about more discreet sexiness, perhaps the return of the boyish look, or of masculine coats.

Alison Hughes, UK Agent, Carlin International

Another reason for studying the past is to try to identify potential new cycles. Cycles are those behaviours or attitudes that run in established patterns. The way that the sun rises in the east every morning, moves across the sky and sets in the west that evening is a natural cycle. Another is the cycle of plant growth: from seed to flower. Nature is full of similar cycles. Consumers can behave in a cyclical manner too. Consumer cycles can exist at a macro and a micro level. Styles can move from minimalism to maximalism and back, or from monochrome to colour. Consumers can also move from a demand for big products or concepts to small ones, or from materialism to spirituality and back again.

Cycles are useful for marketers because, like constants, they are predictable. They move in prearranged patterns. You can predict how something will behave in future if you can establish two things: if it is part of an established cycle and, if so, then where in that cycle it currently sits. Once you have answered these two questions, you can predict with some accuracy how that behaviour or attitude is likely to develop.

Consumer cycles can be behavioural in their manifestation but are typically attitudinal in their motivation. Many are based on the concept of reaction. Sir Isaac Newton's third law of motion states that for every action there will be an equal and opposite reaction. This is also typically true of consumers. For many people, there is something boring or improper about doing 'what everyone else is doing'. For them, excitement or moral superiority is to be gained from doing something different. Many trend innovators fall into this category (see Chapter 13). One of the key trends cited by Malcolm Gladwell in *The Tipping Point*, for instance, is reactive. At the height of the trend for the Urban Cool style, a few style-conscious urban youths reacted against the mainstreaming of 'cool' training shoes. They did so by wearing Hush Puppies, a shoe previously associated more with laggards than early adopters.

Generational cycles are another good example of a reactive cycle. Children born to conservative parents are likely to react by behaving in a more hedonistic and iconoclastic manner. Many of them continue at least an element of that behaviour past adolescence and even into parenthood. The only way for their *own* children to react against that will be to display behaviours and attitudes similar to their grandparents'. This is the stage in the cycle we are in today in many Western nations. Many young people today are reacting against the hedonistic iconoclasm of their Baby Boomer and Generation X parents by pursuing more conservative or traditionalist pursuits. This is driving the Conserva-Teen trend.

The way in which products are adopted too typically follows a cyclical pattern. A product enters the market, the market grows, the market matures and then sales decline. Trends also follow a cyclical pattern. They are picked up and then dropped first by early adopters and then by the early mainstream. Once they have reached the mainstream, many early adopters will have dropped them for being unfashionable or overly popular. But once they reach the laggards, they have become so far 'beyond fashion' that some early adopters will consider them of interest again.

Styles also typically run in cycles. Reactive fashion styles are part of the fashion marketer's armoury. The more different a style is from another, the more new items must be bought. Styles such as short or long skirts will become fashionable, then unfashionable and then fashionable again. Style cycles have narrowed with the advent of fast fashion. One traditional fashion cycle that still appears to hold true, however, is the 20-year rule. Several fashion theorists have noted that clothing and entertainment styles reoccur or are revived approximately every 20 years. The culture of the 1950s was revived in the 1970s, from quiffs and roller blades to bands such as Sha Na Na and Showaddywaddy. Psychedelic 1960s fashions were revived in the 1980s. The trend for 1970s themed club nights began in the 1990s. This is partially age based. Fashion early adopters are typically aged from 16 to 24. They are therefore not old enough to have lived through 20-

year-old culture and fashions and can be excited to 'discover' them. If a trend is less than 20 years old, those early adopters will have already lived through the trend, so will be less interested in reviving it.

CALCULABLES

Predictables

Calculables are trend drivers that, although not inevitable, can be predicted to at least a certain level of accuracy. There are typically more calculables than any other factors. Calculables are usually based on constants or current statistics. The more closely you monitor current PEST trends, the more accurately you will be able to predict them. We know how many people were born last year, both in our own country and in others. We also know how many people turned 50, how many died, how many contracted cancer, how many moved house and so on. These are recorded facts. They do not provide us with information on what will happen in the future, but they do provide calculable data that can be used to help predict it. They can be determined by multiplying a known statistic by one or more variables. The fewer variables, the easier it is to predict an outcome accurately.

Calculables can be divided into 'predictables' and 'estimables'. Predictables are events that have not yet occurred but that can be relatively accurately predicted. They involve fewer variables than estimables do. Predictables can range from trends based on life expectancy to those based on recent events. For instance, if we know how many children were born in the UK this year, we make a calculated prediction as to approximately how many children are likely to be starting primary school in five years. Predictables also include trend diffusion situations. If a trend proves popular with a particular celebrity or trendsetter, we can predict that it will be adopted, or at least trialled, by those who have previously been influenced by this individual.

Estimables

Estimables are among the least predictable factors. The number of variables attached to an estimable is usually very high. They are typically new situations for which there is no historical precedent. The greater the number of variables, the less accurate any prediction is likely to be, so factors such as time frame and level of detail required can affect the accuracy of such a prediction. The further into the future you look, the less accurate a prediction is likely to be. It is harder to predict what will happen in a year than what will happen tomorrow. It is harder still to predict what will happen in two, five or even 10 years. That is because there are so many more variables. I know how many people are alive now and have a good idea how many will be alive tomorrow, but it is hard to predict accurately how many will be alive in 50 years. It is harder still if I need to know more details about them, such as how many of them will be suffering from a debilitating disease or still in work.

In the example above, the number of children starting primary school is a predictable. That is because it is relatively rare for children to die in the UK between birth and the age of five, and the minimal death rate within these years can be utilized in the calculation. But, as children age, more variables come into play. It is harder therefore to predict the number who will go to university. This therefore becomes an estimable. Children have to begin school at five years old but they can leave it at any time between the ages of 16 and 18. This can depend on a number of social, economic, personal and parental variables. The behaviour of children aged between five and 18 also makes their death rate harder to predict. A great deal could happen in the next five years that might affect schooling, but a lot more could happen in 16 years. If more detail is required, such as the number starting school in Manchester or Michigan, the number of boys starting school, the number of children born to single mothers starting school and so on, an accurate prediction will be even harder to achieve.

CHAOTICS

Chaotics are those chance events that cannot be predicted, but can have a huge impact on consumers when they do occur. They are low-probability but high-impact events. Some trend forecasters refer to them as 'wild cards'. Their manifestation itself is unpredictable but, once they have occurred, their future impact can to some extent be predicted. They can occur in several fields. They can be political events, disasters, innovations, creative products or unexpected deaths.

Politically driven chaotics include acts of terrorism. The impact on the families of those who die is of course immense, but they also typically have a massive impact across consumers. It can temporarily diminish the economic and political influence of a country. Financial markets can be affected. The tourism industry can suffer. They can affect foreign policy decisions that can have their own further trend consequences.

Recent examples of disaster-based chaotics include the tsunami, avian flu, the credit crunch and global warming. Such events can affect behavioural and attitudinal trends. In the unstable period after a major natural or political disaster, trends that promote security will be boosted but ones that require a long-term investment will typically be less popular. Disaster chaotics are typically negative, at least in the short term. But they can occasionally have a positive impact on trends. The tsunami did have a positive long-term effect on trends for charitable giving, and was one of the factors behind the rise of Conscious Consumption.

Chaotics based around innovation can have a huge impact on consumer behaviours. They are different from incremental innovations. They are not simply variations on a current product, as camera phones or music phones are on standard cell phones. They are brand new products that appear to come out of the blue. Chaotic innovations with far-reaching effects include the internal combustion engine, the jet engine, the PC, the CD and the cell phone. Creativity can produce unpredictable but influential products too. These range from television programmes such as *Big Brother* or *The Jerry Springer Show*, which encouraged a greater voyeurism among consumers, to exhibitions such as 'This Is Tomorrow' in London in 1956, which launched the Pop Art movement. Creative events rarely have enough impact to *create* a trend, but they can certainly accelerate the growth or diffusion of one.

Sometimes the death of a high-profile individual can have an unexpected impact on consumers. This is particularly true if the death is unforeseen. The death of President Kennedy encouraged the United States to reassess itself in the months following the event, encouraging the growth of the civil rights movement. A collective national sadness then drove US consumer demand for more positive products, which helped the success of the Beatles, the miniskirt and other products of Swinging London. In the UK, the death of Princess Diana in 1997 prompted an outpouring of grief that ultimately encouraged a national trend for greater emotional openness: particularly surprising in a country not known for its sentimentality. The death of General Franco in Spain helped open up the country's citizens to the influence of capitalism. The death of John Lennon in 1980 prompted a reassessment of the Beatles, encouraging a renewed interest in Baby Boomer nostalgia products and ultimately helping drive the sales of the new CD format a few years later.

NOTE

1.   Edward Cornish, *Futuring*, World Future Society, 2004

20

Predicting trends

TREND PREDICTION

Necessary prediction

If you're in marketing, you can't afford to wait until consumers ask the question. You should be looking at the topic already. We were doing qualitative groups on health even before the public debate on healthy food began. We had been monitoring media and consumer attitudes to health and had already seen the concerns mounting.

Annie Freel, Head of Knowledge, McCain Foods

There's a value to having breathing space in a particular market. With Channel 4, we were able to learn lessons by being ahead of the game. We got an awful lot out of being alone in the market amongst our peer groups for six months or so.

Rod Henwood, ex-New Business Director, Channel 4

So far I have focused on the present. The initial identification of trends is typically based upon observing what is happening today, especially as compared to what happened yesterday. We might observe consumers playing or purchasing in a particular new way, or we might note a statistic that shows consumers are using one medium or marketing channel more than they did last year. This is very useful. It shows that an old behaviour or attitude has stopped and a new one begun. It can act as a warning to companies to cease or adapt strategies that are based on behaviours or attitudes that are now out of date. But the key to trend marketing is to predict how today's trends will develop *tomorrow*. This is important for two reasons. It helps determine the relevance and potential impact of a trend, and it provides enough time to prepare for it.

Only by correctly analysing the way in which a trend will develop can a company determine the effect it might have on its business. The more that is known about a trend, the better it can be predicted. If I plant a healthy seed I can predict that it will grow. But the more I know about the seed and the conditions it is growing in, the better I can predict its growth patterns. It helps hugely if I can determine what type of plant it is or the way in which similar plants have grown in the past. It also helps if I know about its environment: its soil type and how often it is watered. If I can answer such questions, I can comfortably predict the plant's growth patterns: how big it is likely to grow or how long it will take to flower. So it is with trend prediction. The more information you have, the more effectively you can predict an outcome.

The earlier you pick up on trends, the more time you have to adapt them before they reach the mainstream, and the greater the chance you can adapt them before your competitors. Information about trends needs to be obtained a long time in advance of any new strategic change. The earlier you can spot a trend the better. It takes time to adapt. Product launches and marketing campaigns are not instantaneous. Some products and services can be updated faster than others, but they all take time to develop and need to be planned and agreed months or years up front of launch. By the time the majority of consumers have moved in a particular direction, it may be too late to respond effectively. The speed with which you identify and analyse a trend is thus very important.

Systematic prediction

Trend prediction is deterministic. Its outcome can be predicted because its causes either are known or repeat previous patterns. So the best way to predict the future is by looking at the past and extrapolating forward. The American Marketing Association defines trend extrapolation as the 'projection of patterns identified in data about the past into the future'.

In statistical terms, extrapolation refers to the extension or projection of a numerical data line. If a series of numbers runs in a standard pattern, future numbers can be predicted. If an experiment has shown consecutive increases of 10 per cent each time a particular ingredient is added, then the next time that ingredient is added another 10 per cent increase can be expected. But extrapolation need not be limited to numerical data alone. It can be applied to behavioural or attitudinal data too. For instance, historically the level of consumer spending has grown in inverse proportion to the cost of living. From this it can be extrapolated that, when the cost of living rises, spending levels are likely to fall.

Today numerical extrapolation is regularly done through computer modelling. The modelling process first came to prominence in the 1970s when MIT professor Jay Forrester developed a computer model that dealt with global variables like population and pollution. Since then, as computer technology has advanced, it has become an increasingly efficient process. Intelligence services in the United States have allegedly created computer models to predict potential terrorist threats utilizing global media inputs, but to my knowledge there has yet to be a model that can accurately predict trends. That is partly because modelling is still based on the input of numerical time series data, not cross-methodological trend data, and trend data rarely conform to traditional time series requirements. It is also because there has so far been little professional agreement on key drivers and variables. But as companies increasingly systematize the trend marketing process, the likelihood of creating a consumer trend model will grow.

Even though computer modelling of trends may not currently be practicable, elements of the process can be utilized to predict trend developments. Accumulating and extrapolating trend data can offer insights into potential future behaviours. It provides the basis of the forecasting process.

Everyday prediction

We are all expected to predict the future. Budgets can be set years ahead, campaigns prepared months ahead. To set budgets or work to them effectively, companies must be able to estimate next year's sales figures within a certain level of accuracy. When deciding on the composition, media channels or tone of an upcoming marketing campaign, markets must have an idea of how consumers will react to it. But how is this possible, when all that is known is today? This was a difficult enough question to answer decades ago, when rates of change among customers were relatively low. Now it is even harder. Today's consumer is very different from yesterday's. So with traditional barriers and boundaries disappearing, and media and purchase patterns in flux, how can you predict how your customers will behave tomorrow?

Trends offer a solution. By analysing trends across relevant customer segments, it is possible to predict future markets. Trends can be a bridge between the past and the future. By accurately predicting changes in consumer patterns, companies can tell what their customers are likely to think about and do in future. Understanding the direction of consumer trends helps them know in advance what tomorrow's consumers are likely to be buying, and what marketing methodologies and channels they are likely to be most open to. It offers an indication of what future sales might be achieved in given markets. This in turn enables companies to make more informed decisions about future strategies.

The predictive nature of trend forecasting is probably its most contro-versial aspect. Clearly, many things are hard to predict. If card turns or dice rolls were easy to predict reliably, gambling wouldn't be the multibil-lion-dollar industry it is today. If the results of sports events and awards ceremonies were known in advance, they would be much less exciting to watch. For many people, the fact that trend forecasters claim they can predict the future places the discipline in the same sphere as gambling, fortune telling or guesswork. But this is wrong. Unlike games of chance, trends behave in a systematic manner. They conform to long-established behaviour patterns, drivers and cycles. So it *is* possible to predict consumer trends with at least a level of accuracy. Predicting how a particular consumer behaviour pattern will develop is not like trying to predict which playing card will appear next. It is more like predicting the outcome of a scientific experiment in which all of the elements are known. Certain events, processes and behaviours can be forecast with reliability, and they can help in estimating the movements of others.

Every one of us across the globe is a forecaster. We are just not always aware that we are doing it. Every morning we predict that the sun will rise in the east, that it will travel across the sky, that some hours later it will set in the west and that a few hours after that it will rise in the east again. This is the sun cycle, and it allows us to plan our days. Because we know the nature of the sun cycle, we can even predict when certain parts of it will occur. If it is dawn now, we can predict it will be sunset in a certain number of hours, depending on the time of year and where in the world we are located. We believe so strongly in the sun cycle that we say we 'know' that the sun will set later in the day. We are not even conscious that we are making a prediction.

There are hundreds of other predictions we make on a similarly subliminal level. They are based on our understanding and experience of specific causes and effects. If I put my foot on the accelerator pedal, my car will go faster. If I jump out of a window I will fall to the ground. Predicting trends is based on a similar theory. A thing that has happened before is likely to happen again. Some things are likely to cause certain other things to happen. Understanding some of these intrinsically in our day-to-day lives provides us with an *ad hoc* prediction system that allows us to live our lives, but by formalizing our understanding of the connec-tions between them we can expand this into an active predictive process. Identifying and quantifying key drivers, barriers and outcomes within a systematic framework enable a much more robust level of prediction. Knowing the factors that can encourage or inhibit trends and mapping a trend against them make the progress of that trend predictable. I call this process 'trend mapping'.

TREND MAPPING

Why

> *It's about constantly re-mapping and reconnecting the trends, connecting ideas and trying to see how things are tied together.*

Craig Thayer, Managing Editor, Mintel Inspire,
Mintel International Group (USA)

> *Trends have lots of different components. It's only when you put them together that you get a useful story. It's like looking at the night sky. The stars are all there but, when you spot a constellation, suddenly you can tell a story.*

P T Black, Partner, Jigsaw International (China)

The generic development of a trend will depend on a number of attributive and environmental factors (Figure 20.1). Mapping it against them will reveal its potential growth pattern. These factors can act as drivers or barriers to trend growth. Some factors can be stronger drivers or barriers than others. They fall into three main categories. As detailed above, active adoption drivers are the qualities that make it easy or difficult for consumers to

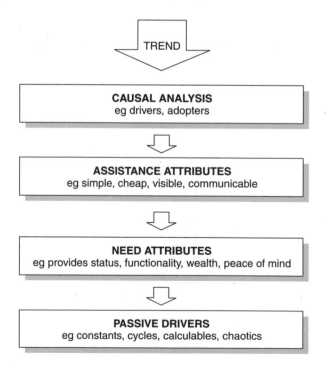

Figure 20.1 Trend mapping

adopt a trend, or that appeal to basic consumer needs. They include simplicity, visibility, practicality, value for money, safety and status. Passive adoption factors are composed of the 4 Cs: constants, cycles, calculables and chaotics. Thirdly, adopter typology drivers are the factors that will appeal to particular adopter types.

Once a trend has been identified, the question is not the probability of that trend occurring but its potential breadth, size and durability. That corresponds to the three Ws: the 'who', 'where' and 'when' of the trend. For instance, is a particular trend likely to affect young people only? Or will it, perhaps, affect young people initially but affect older people in time? Will it peak with the early mainstream or appeal to the laggards too? Where will it spread? Will it affect consumers in, say, just the food sector, or might it spread into health, holidays and even finance? Will it affect people only in one territory, or might it become a global phenomenon? How quickly will it grow, and how long will it continue? How rapidly will it move from the early adopters to the late mainstream? Will it take six months to peak or six years? The trend mapping process is an attempt to predict the generic development pattern of a trend. Only by identifying whom a trend will affect, when it will affect them and how strong its effect will be can you determine if and how it will be relevant to you and your company.

What

The first step in the interpretation of any trend is causative analysis. Once you identify a trend, you should first try to establish what caused it. This is the starting point for understanding its potential development. It can provide clues that aid in the rest of the trend mapping process.

As detailed above, trend initiators fall into one of the four PEST categories. A trend will have occurred for political, social, economic or technological reasons (see Chapter 9). You should try to establish which one of these it is. This will help you determine the emphasis to put on adoption factors. For instance, if a trend occurred for economic reasons, then adoption factors such as price should be weighted up. If it came about for social reasons, then social and emotional factors such as status will be more important.

The Wising Up trend, for instance, was caused by a mix of factors. With society changing so much, it is increasingly less clear how to behave in this 'new world'. Consumers have been introduced to whole new areas they need to understand, or at least have an opinion on: from wheat beers to wine, interior design to ballroom dancing. As technology has a greater impact on their lives, those who know how to operate that technology will have an advantage, encouraging a trend for Geek Chic among today's youth. The technological expansion of information sources has increased generic demand for, and enjoyment of, knowledge: from Sudoku to pub quizzes. In the current economic climate, the death of 'a job for life' and the rise of contract work mean that consumers need an increasing number of varying skill sets to survive. In this case economic, social and technological drivers will all be important.

Once you have established what caused a trend, you should explore the early stages of its development. You need to identify who first adopted it. You should establish in what sector or market it has seen the strongest growth. This will give you more clues as to how it might develop in future. If it has proved popular in one industry, then there is a good chance it will grow in related or similar industries. For instance, a trend that has been adopted in the food sector is likely to manifest itself in the drinks sector too. The initial adopter markets can also offer insights. If a trend was adopted first by young consumers and then by slightly older consumers, there is a good chance it will be adopted in future by even older consumers. This has proven true across a range of trends, from personal technology to entertainment products.

How

The next step is to determine the strength, depth and adoption speed of the trend. This corresponds to the three Ws: with whom, when and where a trend will develop. Whom will it affect, in terms of adopter types and demographic segments? When will it have an impact, and how long will it last? Where will it develop, as regards both industries and territories? It is possible to use a broadly similar process to answer each question, with some important differences that I will discuss below. The key to the process is to map the trend against active and passive adoption factors, to evaluate its potential.

You can take a numeric or non-numeric approach to trend prediction. For the former, you will need to give each factor a numerical value. For instance, you could give each weak driver a value of +1 and strong driver a value of +2. A strong barrier would then receive –2 and a weaker barrier –1. The probable rates of adoption can then be calculated using spreadsheets or a computer model. For a non-numeric approach, you simply employ the trend mapping process to build up a broad picture of drivers, which can then be used as the basis of an innovation workshop or scenario planning session (see Chapter 22).

In either case, the first task is to make a checklist of what the key adoption drivers and barriers to the progress of the trend might be. I have detailed most of these above (see Chapters 18 and 19), but there may be others specific to your industry or your individual business question.

You should then proceed to map each trend against active adoption factors. Beginning with assistance attributes, you need to consider if the trend is visible or easily communicable. For instance, did it originate in a visible industry such as fashion or personal technology? Is it media-friendly or celebrity-endorsed? What are the financial factors around it? Is it high- or low-cost, either to adopt or to trial? Are there other cost implications of adoption? Are there any negative implications of adoption, such as the cost of failure or the threat of fraud? How practical and simple is it to adopt the innovation? How compatible is it with current practices, beliefs or value systems? Next, you should map it against need attributes. What does it offer consumers that might encourage or discourage adoption? Might it improve consumers' lives in some practical manner, such as time saving or convenience? Might it be seen to improve quality of life? Might it fulfil any emotional needs? Might it improve consumers' status among key peer groups?

Next you should map the trend against passive adopters, to determine if the environment the trend is being launched into is likely to encourage or discourage growth. What are the relevant constants? Does it tie in with any eternals or inevitables? Does the present day compare to any case studies or periods in recent social history? If so, did any similar trends develop strongly then? Are there any calculables that could provide usable insights? For instance, what contemporary demographic trends would drive it if they maintained current growth rates? And are there other trends currently in play that might act as a springboard for the trend in focus, just as cell phone adoption encouraged MP3 player adoption? Finally, have any chaotics occurred recently that might affect consumer attitudes or behaviours in a positive or negative way? For instance, have there been any exhibitions, TV shows or films recently whose popularity could indicate that the trend is set for growth?

Who

The first question to answer is which adopter types might embrace a trend. This is the key to determining that trend's potential size and market impact. The more adopter types it could appeal to, the broader its potential impact. If it is only likely to appeal to innovators and early adopters, then it can be classified as little more than a fad and ignored by all but the most cutting-edge industries or companies. But if evidence suggests it could appeal to later adopting categories such as late mainstream or laggards, then a majority of companies will need to respond.

There are two complementary ways to determine adopter appeal. Firstly, you should map the trend against the adoption drivers for each type (see

Chapter 17). For instance, if the trend is to appeal to early adopters, it should come across as innovative, different to what is currently done or fulfilling an unmet need. If laggards are to adopt it, it should appear to be a continuous trend, or at least have links to the past, and to be relatively risk-free. Such factors need not be mutually exclusive. The Arty Crafts trend for instance was clearly traditional, but it could also be considered innovative, because it was an ironic reaction against prevailing technology-focused mainstream trends.

You should also establish which type or types have already adopted the trend. The further down the adopter cycle it has gone, the more likely it is to reach the end. It may be that you identified a trend early, and it is still at innovator or early adopter level, in which case this will not help. But if you identified it late, and it has already been adopted by the early mainstream, you know that it can at least appeal to some of the mainstream, so it may do to others. This process should be dynamic. You should monitor a trend as it passes through the adoption curve, to see how far through the diffusion process it reaches.

Identifying which consumer segments are likely to adopt the trend requires an understanding of segmented consumer behaviours. You need to determine which adopter factors will drive adoption by which consumer segments. Some factors are relevant only to particular consumer segments. Others are more relevant to some segments than they are to others. For instance, safety issues are typically stronger drivers for parents, and status-based factors for younger consumers. Traditional factors will be more important to first-generation immigrants but less so to second-generation ones. Functionality and nostalgia factors will affect most Grey Consumers, whichever generation they are from, but entertainment and novelty will be more important to Baby Boomers than to the older war generation. The latter will typically be more affected by factors such as loyalty and traditional morality. The more factors a trend has that are important to that segment, the more likely they are to adopt it. Entertaining and novel trends will probably be adopted by Boomers and loyal and traditional ones by the war generation.

When

> *Most of our new products are developed 18–24 months in advance. You can't take a snapshot of today to understand the market, because when you launch it will be a different world and your data will be outdated. Trends like superfruits are outdated now. I want trends that give me an idea of how the market will be in two years.*

Bruno Montejorge, Senior Brand Manager, Kraft (Brazil)

It's not about marketing today. It's about marketing tomorrow.

Annie Freel, Head of Knowledge, McCain Foods

Knowing when a trend will reach the mainstream is a vital element when using trends to determine company strategy (see Chapter 22). Predicting that a trend will affect a market earlier than it actually does, and producing products, services and marketing campaigns to appeal to that trend before it has actually been adopted by your customers, is a recipe for disaster. But if you predict a trend too late, you risk your competitors exploiting it before you do and gaining market share at your expense.

The speed with which a trend develops will depend on the strength of the adoption drivers and barriers. In broad terms, the stronger the former and the lighter the latter, the faster a trend is likely to grow. Trends also typically move more quickly in some industries and among some consumer cohorts than others. Trends move faster in industries driven more by personal taste than price. They also move faster in more observable industries. The less you can observe a product or service, the longer it will take for trends to move in it. Trends in more observable industries such as clothes, cosmetics, hairstyles and music spread more quickly than those in non-observable ones such as home furnishings, fitness equipment or banking.

Trends typically move faster in lower-priced categories. This is because consumers can afford to buy these products more often and upgrade more regularly. Customers will purchase clothing more often than they will cars, cell phones more often than they will mortgages. This is true even within major sectors. Trends in accessories, for instance, move faster than those in high-end fashion. A cycle can also prove useful for forecasting the temporal development of a trend. If you can identify where on a known cycle or curve a trend is, you can predict where it is likely to be in a number of months or years.

The other temporal factor to consider is durability. It is vital to establish how long a trend is likely to last. If you are preparing a three-year strategy, you can utilize a trend that looks set to last three to five years, but not one that will last only two. This is one of the hardest elements of a trend to gauge. The most effective way to predict it is to map adoption speed against positive long-term environments. To determine how long the trend for social networks will last, for instance, you should compare their high adoption speeds against both their strong continued community and efficiency benefits and their minimal but growing time poverty and privacy detriments.

Where

> *If you're in the technological world you know you need a much, much longer horizon, but for food an awful lot of it is just about evolving tastes. There is rarely anything in food consumption patterns that is really revolutionary.*

Michele Giles, Head of Insight, Premier Foods

> *Instead of people eating in their cars, as they do in the US, in Brazil it is more about people eating on the bus. So size, shape and packaging of products is affected. Products that are easy to put in a car work in the US, but in Brazil you need products you can put in a backpack.*

Bruno Montejorge, Senior Brand Manager, Kraft (Brazil)

The final step is to try to determine which sectors and territories might be most open to a trend. With the former, you will typically be trying to identify if the trend will affect your own sector. To do this, you will need to identify which drivers and adopters most affect your sector. For instance, will a price-based trend typically have more impact on your sector than a status-based one might? Or if an estimable is essential for the growth of a particular trend, is that estimable influential upon your sector?

To understand which locations a trend will grow most strongly in, you will need to map the trend drivers against the key cultural and environmental elements of each territory or block of territories. Status-based trends such as Trading Up, for instance, are likely to grow more quickly in emerging nations than self-actualization trends. Discontinuous trends will be adopted more quickly in territories with liberal cultures than those with conservative ones.

Following the trend mapping process will provide robust data on probable future behaviour and attitude patterns. The next step is to implement the data into your business strategy. This requires an understanding of which trends could be relevant to your company and then determining how best to utilize them in the business process.

Summary: Part 5

- Trends are created by innovators and influentials.

- Trends move in a regular pattern from early adopters to laggards.

- Trend marketers should adopt the most relevant aspects of diffusion theory.

- Attributes of a trend and the environment it is launched into affect adoption rates.

- Visible, communicable, simple, cheap, trusted trends grow faster.

- The closer a trend conforms to past trends the faster it will be adopted.

- Trends that satisfy traditional consumer needs grow faster.

- Trends can be influenced by constants, cycles, calculables and chaotics.

- It is possible to determine how a trend will develop if key factors are known.

- The development of a trend can be predicted by mapping it against key drivers.

Part 6

Implementation

21

Convincing the company

PRESENTATION NEEDS

A consultancy might think they have delivered a great insight because they have come up with a 'great truth'. But if it can't be commercialized or operationalized, then what's the point of it?

Alex Owens, Director of Brand Development and Consumer Insight,
Capital One

The purpose of trend marketing is not simply to predict what trends will take place in the future. It has a much more practical purpose than that. The real purpose of trend marketing is to help companies make decisions as to their own most effective strategies for the future. The following definition of market research is equally appropriate to trend forecasting: 'a means of providing management with market and marketing information… to reduce uncertainty when marketing strategy is being planned'.[1]

Trends are only as useful as the strategic use to which they can be put. The trend marketing process has to root itself firmly in the business process. It needs to be based around a practical aim that relates directly to key business issues and questions. A trend on its own is valueless, but combining trend knowledge and business needs can help identify the most effective future-proofed marketing strategies. Trend interpretation is based upon causal analysis, but trend implementation is based on impact analysis: calculating how a company can benefit from a trend.

Implementation is equal parts analysis and persuasion. It requires rigorous, formalized analysis to determine the implications of a trend for business practice. Convincing others of the necessity of changing company policy based around that trend takes persuasion. Without the latter, the former will be wasted effort.

PRESENTATION DRIVERS

Evidence

> *It's one thing having a rigorous process, having solid insights behind it, but the success and failure of NPD and innovation strategy is often down to the passion that individuals have, and their resilience in driving it through the company. You have to push and struggle and shout in order to get new policies through a company, because there always seem to be more reasons why you shouldn't launch something than why you should.*

Gavin Emsden, Food and Beverage Insights Director, Nestlé

Convincing others of the validity or significance of a trend is one of the most difficult parts of the implementation process. It can be a long and difficult task. It can sometimes take as much determination and patience as it does technique. The way in which trends are presented can have a huge effect on if and how they are utilized. The difficulty of the task will depend on the audience you are trying to convince, the type of trend you are describing and the strategy you are attempting to implement. The larger your company and the bigger your budgets, the more robust your trend data need to be. Small businesses can sometimes risk basing strategy on a very strong hunch, but a company deciding upon a million-dollar global strategy will require strong empirical evidence.

Evidence for a trend will typically need to be presented at two key points during the implementation process: at the beginning of any strategy determination process, to convince those involved in the process that the trend is important enough for them to base a strategy around it; and once that strategy has been determined, to convince those who were not part of the initial process that the strategy is based on valid insights.

In both instances you will need to employ a three-step evidentiary process. First you have to convince people that the trend you have identified really exists. This will require the presentation of statistics or examples that back up your trend. The next step is to convince them of the need to change company policy accordingly. This is best done by highlighting the negative impact of ignoring the trend and the positive impact of basing future strategies upon it. Finally you have to persuade people of the particular course of action you and your team recommend. This will require an understanding of the different individual and departmental needs and processes.

Trends

For some people trends can feel a little foreign, but everyone will have some trends that they understand much better than others. The key is finding the trends they can understand, the ones that 'click' with them.

Craig Thayer, Managing Editor, Mintel Inspire, Mintel International Group (USA)

It's easier to sell in behavioural trends, because they're more tangible. You can see behaviour and measure it. Attitude is quite challenging to sell in.

Hanna Chalmers, Head of Research and Insight, Universal Music Group

The way you present your evidence will depend to some extent on the type of trend you are discussing. Trend typologies affect both the form and the weight of evidence required. For instance, behavioural trends are easier to quantify than attitudinal trends, so audiences will typically expect to see statistical evidence for them. Attitudinal trends are by definition more qualitative than quantitative in their manifestations. Evidence for them can typically be more observation- or story-based. Style or design trends will require more illustration than topic- or activity-based ones do.

Some trends are easier to accept than others, so will require less evidence. There are similarities here with trend adoption. As with innovations, continuous and part-continuous trends are typically easier to accept (see Chapter 18). It will require little evidence to convince someone that there will be continued growth in a currently popular activity such as shopping or television viewing. Part-continuous trends will require a little more evidence, but much less than discontinuous ones. It will be easier for someone to understand how e-commerce or social networking might develop, for instance. E-commerce is simply a variant of standard commerce, and online social networking a variant of face-to-face social interaction. The environment for each may be new, but behaviours within them are similar to their offline versions. The levels of evidence required to convince colleagues of expected growth patterns in these sectors will therefore be relatively low.

It is harder to convince people of a discontinuous trend. Such trends are often counter-intuitive, so will typically require a greater input of hard data evidence. The Conserva-Teen trend is a discontinuous trend. Marketers have typically come to accept that a teenager is hedonistic and rebellious. It is hard to convince them that this may be less true in future. When I first noticed the trend for Conserva-Teens, I had problems convincing some clients of it. Simply telling them that I had observed consumers becoming less hedonistic was not enough. So I looked for the most robust quantifiable data I could find, and used those in my presentations. Statistics that showed consistent year-on-year reductions in youth purchase of alcohol or drugs were hard to argue with, no matter how counter-intuitive they might be.

Audiences

Different clients want different things. Some clients want reams of numbers; others just need one great example.

Sue Elms, EVP Global Media Practice, Millward Brown

When it comes to talking to creative people about trends, you can't dictate or 'teach'. It's more about inspiring people. You have to offer them the trends as stimulus. So I tend to say 'Here are the ideas and the recommendations, but you should use this as stimulus; feel free to go with your gut and your instinct. This should enhance your understanding and help inform your decision.' If you couch trends in those terms it becomes more palatable.

Hanna Chalmers, Head of Research and Insight, Universal Music Group

Whenever you are trying to convince an audience of something, you need to understand their point of view and language. Whenever I am asked to give a trends presentation, one of my very first questions is what sort of people will be in the audience. That determines the type of evidence I use. I need to find evidence that the particular individuals I am speaking to will believe. Different people are convinced by different types of evidence. For instance, it is important to have a good mix of financial and cultural evidence because your audience is likely to be split into those who trust one and those who trust the other. Once you have determined who your audience is, you can present your evidence accordingly.

Audiences can be segmented in different ways. One way is to identify whether they are factual or creative people. Factual people are more likely to be convinced by hard data such as statistics. But this is less effective with creative people. They are more likely to be convinced by soft data: anecdotes, stories, strong evocative images and so on. Factual people will typically be found in administrative and figures-based roles: finance, legal, sales, planning. Creative people will typically be found in creative roles such as editorial or advertising. This is not always true, of course, but it is a good rule of thumb. I have certainly found it useful to employ both types of data when addressing media companies where there are representatives from advertising and editorial departments, or advertising agencies where planners and creatives are both present.

As with any presentation, it can also be beneficial to distinguish between the ways in which individual audience members take in and process information. Typically, auditory types will be more convinced by statistical data, visual types by strong imagery and kinaesthetic types by stories and real-life examples. Mixing all those evidence types will prove the most effective way to reach a varied audience.

Territories

Some local markets can sometimes be a bit parochial. They'll say 'That might be happening with you, but it's not happening here.' The best way to respond is to allow them to customize the campaign based around the local manifestation of a trend. You can go 'Here's the overall trend, but tell me how it's manifesting itself in your territory.'

Jo Rigby, Research Director EMEA, Omnicom Media Group

Culture's very important, especially when it comes to the creative. You really should try to execute different things in different countries to cope with different societies and cultural differences. For instance, mothers in Thailand hate the idea of using sex to sell products, but they love celebrities, so you might have a nice piece of creative that uses sex to sell and it'll bomb completely there, but put a celebrity in it instead and they'll love it.

Sheila Byfield, Leader, Business Planning, Mindshare

For multi-market companies, it is not enough to convince those in your own territory. You need to convince overseas affiliates as well. But strategies will not be applied and received uniformly in each territory. As detailed previously, trends develop differently in different countries (see Chapter 10). Likewise employees in different countries will react differently to trend data. Attitudinal variations will govern how affiliates will respond to trend data. Employees in some countries are more likely to be wary of new ideas. Others will respond well to certain types of trends but not to others.

Behavioural differences will govern how the trends themselves will develop in that country. Some of the trends that a strategy is based upon may manifest themselves differently there. They may even not manifest themselves at all. The trend for locally sourced food is becoming a major trend in the UK, but is of less importance in France and Italy, where consumers have always bought much of their food locally. The recycling trend is proving strong in the UK too, where food is heavily packaged, but it is of less interest in Spain, where food is still often market bought. Organic food is of little interest to consumers in those developing countries where pesticides are too expensive and most food is 'naturally' organic. Companies should where possible include some input from overseas territories within the strategic determination process. International territories should also be given some freedom to customize agreed trends-based strategies.

PRESENTATION TYPOLOGIES

I send a monthly report out to people within the company, to our international territories and to our agencies, telling them what I have picked up in the news, anything interesting or unusual that might be relevant, what we've uncovered in our research, what research we're about to do that they might want an input on. It's important to share trends in a non-technical but involving way.

Annie Freel, Head of Knowledge, McCain Foods

We issue what we call manifestation reports every three to six months. These show the manifestations of trends from around the world in different business categories: things that are unusual or that people might not know about. We send them to all departments worldwide. The purpose of the reports is to inspire and excite marketing and sales around the trends that we're working on.

Denise Drummond-Dunn, Vice President Consumer Excellence, Nestlé (Switzerland)

There are no generic right or wrong ways to present trend evidence. The way you present depends on your audience, the types of trends you are talking about and your budgets. You can present trend data as a written report or verbally, with photos, illustrations and video footage or just plain text (Figure 21.1). You can present on one trend or on several. You can present on a single sector or demographic, or across a range of them. You can report on trends occasionally or regularly.

Verbal reports will typically be presented using some form of visual stimulus, such as PowerPoint slide shows or video footage. They can range from short stimulus talks to longer and more detailed trend breakdowns. If a presentation is based on a written report, it is best if the author presents the findings. If for any reason that is not possible, the project manager should summarize the key points of the report. A combination of written and verbal reportage is typically the most effective. If a presentation is given that is not based on a commissioned report, then the speaker should provide some form of 'leave-behind'. This can be used as a reminder of key issues or for determining action points.

Some companies prefer to commission and present reports only when the need arises. If a trends team identify a new and relevant trend, they will want to research and report on that trend. This can happen if they hear of a new trend they think might be relevant or when they are preparing to put

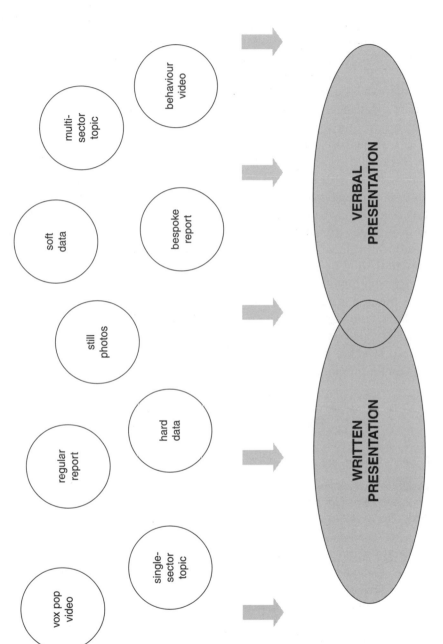

Figure 21.1 Trend presentations

together a new marketing strategy. It can also happen in media agencies when pitching for or winning a client in a sector they have less experience of. Others like to present more regularly. The regular distribution of trend data can be an effective way to help drive trends through a company. This can take the form of a physical newsletter, an e-mail bulletin or an updated intranet site. This is typically sent weekly, monthly or quarterly depending on the format, and the resources of the insight team. It will typically feature news reports, statistics, quotes and brief case studies of companies doing something interesting around a trend. It can feature trends from within the industry or from across sectors, from the home territory or globally.

I have presented a range of different report types in my career. Each time I have worked with the client to find the most effective method for its purposes and circumstances. With Siemens, for instance, I worked with a marketing consultancy to produce two types of research reports. The first was generic monthly trends reports that featured insights on specific sectors they considered relevant. These included their own industry as well as industries that they believed would provide early evidence of relevant trends, such as automotive and fashion. We also produced occasional one-off reports themed around particular sectors or concepts. These included music, fashion, community and so on. This proved a highly effective combination for Siemens, but each client's needs are different. Some clients have found one-off verbal reports most effective. Others have preferred to receive a regular omnibus report. Still others have preferred videos.

PRESENTATION TIPS

Data

> *Determining a few potential applications from your observations can make it much more real for people. It's about bringing the high-level trends down to earth. There is a sort of middle ground where you can touch both the blue sky and the earth.*

Craig Thayer, Managing Editor, Mintel Inspire, Mintel International Group (USA)

> *I first have an abstract story about what the trend is about: how it moves people, what people want to get out of it, where it came from or whatever. But then what I like to do is show early examples of things that other businesses are already doing, or concepts that students are working on in the area.*

Brechje Vissers, Manager Colour Marketing and Innovation, PPG Industries (ex-Senior Trend Consultant, Philips) (Netherlands)

People are naturally wary of change, so you will need to work hard to convince them that the trends you describe are real. A report needs to be robust, but it must also be interesting enough to take and hold a reader's attention. To appeal to the widest audience, trend reports should include a variety of evidence types. They should mix empirical data with stories and evocative real-life examples. Where possible they should also include examples of how a trend has been used to improve revenue streams or market growth. If the trend is so new that no one has exploited it yet, examples should be included of how it *might* be used.

Trends can be complex in both their structure and their manifestation. For this reason, simplicity and directness are essential. You need to determine your key points, and then illustrate them with your most arresting data. Any examples and statistics should therefore be high-impact. A huge percentage increase in a behaviour that rarely changes can make an audience sit up. So can news of any particularly unusual new activity, such as a brand new form of commerce, leisure or communication. A more normal behaviour that is manifesting itself among an unlikely demographic can also draw attention. Audiences sat up when I spoke about early adopter teens running 'guerrilla knitting' sessions. Presenters should always try to ensure that the majority of their data relate to the everyday experiences of their audience. News that Baby Boomer consumers are going to more rock concerts is likely to resonate with an audience of Baby Boomer marketing executives who might have been to a rock concert recently. Data should also be relevant to the mainstream consumer market. If high-income early adopters are doing something unusual, that may be colourful. But news that mainstream Grey Consumers are doing the same thing may have more impact.

It is important to consider names too. The unusual names trend analysts give to particular trends can sometimes be a source of amusement or scepticism, but they actually have a practical purpose. How you name trends can actually have an effect on how convincing they are to individuals. An evocative or arresting name enables easy recognition and recall. In the same way that trends with strong communicability are adopted more quickly by consumers, so trend names with strong communicability will be adopted more quickly by business and media contacts. The interest around a trend such as Metrosexuality is in part due to the name it was given. Names need to sum up the trend clearly and simply. They should also be easy to recall. This can be achieved by making a pun on a well-known term or by using alliteration or rhyme. You can choose to create your own names or utilize those adopted by other trend forecasters, depending on which you think an audience is likely to respond best to. As a rule of thumb I tend to use my own names, but I will utilize others' names if I know my clients are aware of them, as would be the case with now-accepted terms such as Conscious Consumption or Metrosexuality itself.

Visuals

At Millward Brown a lot of effort goes into training people how to deliver insights more compellingly. We've got a creative director, whose job is to make our presentations more exciting, to stop us using PowerPoint and instead use sketches and diaries and so on. You need to have a lot of confidence to speak without a big deck of PowerPoint slides, but actually those can be the best presentations.

Sue Elms, EVP Global Media Practice, Millward Brown

It is an overused cliché that a picture paints a thousand words, but it can certainly be true of a trends presentation. The more visually interesting a presentation is, the greater impact it will have on your audience. Images can capture an audience's imagination. They can also make a point. Visuals should be either striking or evocative.

They can be utilized within a written report, embedded in a PowerPoint presentation or pasted on to card as a form of 'mood board'. Such boards have been used successfully in the fashion and design industries for years. Using unusual visual props can enhance a presentation. Sue Elms of Millward Brown once created a pack of tarot-style cards to illustrate research on new consumer segmentation patterns. Each card represented a different new segment, with a visual representation of it on the front and appropriate statistical data on the back. It proved to be both arresting and effective.

I like to utilize primary observational visuals in my reports where relevant. Stills or video footage of one or more consumers actually engaged in a new activity can have high impact. So too can interviews with relevant consumers. It is one thing for a consultant to describe how an activity is occurring. It is quite another to see footage of it, or to hear how and why consumers themselves are doing it. Shopping mall vox pops and footage of focus groups have proved particularly valuable in exploring new media behaviour motivations for magazine publishing clients and technology clients. Footage of out-of-home activities and *in situ* vox pops have proved useful for drinks and entertainment companies in determining new leisure behaviours.

NOTE

1. Robin J Birn, *The International Handbook of Market Research Techniques*, Kogan Page, 2002

22

Determining strategy

IMPLICATION DETERMINATION

We have a new ideas forum every few weeks. We have a series of stages that we go through. The first is fairly informal, fairly free-form... loosely asking questions to try and fine-tune what an idea or a trend is and why it would be useful. Then, if we find a trend that works for us, we try to determine if we can just develop a new product to fit that trend or if we need to properly evaluate it. The second stage is to come up with a well formulated idea that addresses a certain number of questions, such as... who would we sell it to, what would it cost, what margin would it make over a period of time... And at that stage there might be a more formal process around commissioning a particular piece of research or carrying out a paid-for feasibility study. The third stage is a full business case.

Andy Shaw, Product Development Director, BT Agile Media, British Telecom

Once we've mined as much data as we can, we'll get a project team together. We'll lock ourselves away and then try and interpret it, try and break it down into a structure, and determine what are the macro trends, the overarching themes, and then what are the supporting trends, and how does that break down to different user audience groups.

Mark Broughton, Research Insights and Knowledge Manager, Global Product Development, Alliance Boots

Persuading others of the validity of a trend is vital to the implementation of trends-based policy, but to determine what that policy should be a company needs to understand the specific implications of a trend for its future. This requires a robust analysis process. You can use different methodologies to determine trend implications. These can be run within the confines of a single department or on a company-wide basis. Long-term strategy determination will typically involve a mix of both approaches. The frequency of implication determination will depend on company structure, policy and culture. It can be done annually, quarterly or every month.

COMMUNAL DETERMINATION

Community matters

> *The trend implementation process is better as a debate than a monologue. When we get together to talk about trends we invite people from across all relevant departments and from our advertising and design agencies. It helps having a cross-business view, so we each don't get too focused on one thing.*

Annie Freel, Head of Knowledge, McCain Foods

> *You need to involve any key players from marketing, sales, technology and finance early on. You need to bring them with you rather than presenting the finished product as a fait accompli, which is when it becomes very hard. The thing is to get their engagement early on, so they can feel a sense of ownership. If they have concerns and reservations these can be flagged up and either addressed early on before they become too big an issue or used to determine that the project is actually not worth taking forward.*

Gavin Emsden, Food and Beverage Insights Director, Nestlé

Each implication determination method takes a different form, but each involves a high level of interaction. This is achieved in two ways: by including a variety of participants and by establishing a creative atmosphere. The most effective way to determine strategy is through communal effort. The determination process should include people with a mix of attitudes and experiences, from across a variety of disciplines and functions. Strategic determination is a complex procedure. It will have an impact across each department, product and service. It requires knowledge of a range of different cross-department issues and policy. For such a process, several heads are better than one. Creating strategy based on new consumer trends can also be contentious. Trends-based strategy is by its nature dependent on variables and unknowns. It can also challenge traditional company policy. Getting such strategy accepted within the company can therefore be difficult. The more key decision makers who are involved in the determination process, the more likely it is to be accepted.

Picking participants

If we're doing brainstorming on a piece of business, the group we put together will come from different types of client teams and different types of people. We do a lot of cross-fertilization. You need the marketing person and the creative person. Sometimes you bring in planners from other brands to add an input of 'cool' or of 'mainstream'. You need to have people you consider change drivers but you also need a 'safe pair of hands', because the former can deal with big ideas and the latter with the detail.

Sheila Byfield, Leader, Business Planning, Mindshare

The trick is to determine the optimum number of people who need to be involved at each stage of the determination process: too few and you will not gain either enough input or enough leverage, or too many and the process can slow down. Trend data should be presented by one or more individuals from the trends team. The team will have been closely involved in the identification and interpretation of the trend, so will typically have both the knowledge and the passion to best articulate it. If you have the budgets, it can be worth including some form of external input. This can range from a short stimulus presentation to a more detailed report. This serves two purposes. It avoids allegations of corporate or departmental bias. It also shows that someone outside the company believes in the trend. In addition to this, there should be representatives present from each key stakeholder department.

If the strategy is company-wide, the session should include the heads of each department. If it is limited to marketing or NPD, then representatives from each function should be present. Marketing strategy sessions should include delegates from marketing, advertising, marketing communications and sales functions. Sessions focusing on a particular trend should include individuals relevant to it. Sessions on youth trends should include some of the relevant younger members of the company. Those focusing on new technology should include the recognized company 'geeks'. It is also worth inviting outside agencies relevant to the topic under review. An advertising or PR agency should be present for marketing strategy sessions. Once the participants are assembled, it is vital to ensure that all, irrespective of seniority, are given the opportunity to input their own ideas and respond to those of others.

Creating creativity

> *You need to create an innovative atmosphere. You need to foster different behaviours and mess about with people's energy levels through a variety of tricks and techniques: anything from introducing forms of music to the food that you might eat in the meeting, to the dress code, to energy games that you might play. These all help change your head a little bit and make you more creative. It's all about creating a different set of stimuli, because if you're putting the same stuff in that you would normally do in other kinds of corporate activities then you're going to get very traditional, corporate outputs.*

Ewan Adams, Head of Openmind, Mindshare (USA)

> *You have to find a way of communicating with everybody that's there, so you have to cover the range of ways people learn. Therefore a workshop needs to include music and videos and exercises, hands-on experience, as well as statistics and fun numbers. Obviously we have brochures and things like that, but we also bring trends to life through posters or videos that highlight what the day-to-day life of the consumer of the future might be like.*

Denise Drummond-Dunn, Vice President Consumer Excellence,
Nestlé (Switzerland)

The best strategy determination forums are typically based around brainstorming. The principles of brainstorming were formulated in the late 1930s by New York advertising executive Alex F Osborn. He created four rules for a brainstorming session. Participants must agree to defer judgement on each idea. They must develop several ideas in a session, not just a few 'good' ones. They must strive for unusual ideas. And they should try to build on each idea over several sessions before final evaluation. All of these rules should be applied during determination forums.

To enable the greatest number of participants to come up with the greatest number of implications or ideas around a trend requires the creation of an innovative atmosphere. Those running a session should explore any new or traditional techniques that might stimulate creativity. Some of the techniques used to create innovative company cultures can also be used. Senior executives should be seen to encourage suggestions, 'failure' should be applauded, and so on (see Chapter 6). It can sometimes be worth employing specialist creative facilitation agencies to organize the sessions.

FORMAL DETERMINATION

Choosing methodologies

A trend can be the inspiration for an idea or it can be something that you check an idea against. Sometimes it's about a fabric of trends that become the backdrop for everything you're doing. Whenever you have a communications idea, you check it against the trends to see if it's tapping into any of them. But it can work the other way around. With Carat's 'Scenic Days Out' campaign for the Renault Scenic, the communications team came to us and said 'We need an engagement idea', so we gave them some appropriate lifestyle trends.

Sue Elms, EVP Global Media Practice, Millward Brown
(ex-Managing Director, Carat Insight)

Trends can inspire as well as validate… Some of the biggest ideas come from 'leap-frog inspiration' that actually gets ahead of today's consumer playback and triggers new trends.

Tom Pickles, Senior Director, Global Menu Solutions, McDonald's (USA)

Companies can take a company-centric or trend-centric approach to determining trend implications. In the former they will take current company policy or a key business question and map a shortlist of relevant trends against it. For instance, a food manufacturer might be considering expanding into new product or consumer markets, or shifting marketing budgets into sponsorship or search marketing. Before it does so, it will want to see if such strategies will play out as trends relevant to its market growth, such as Traditionalizing or Hectic Eclectic. The best way to do this is to run a trends audit on the company.

Companies that take a trend-centric approach will study a shortlist of individual trends to determine the opportunities or threats that each presents. For instance, by studying all the key micro trends in its own sector, or a single macro trend such as the New Old, an automotive manufacturer could establish what the best areas might be for new product development, or whether current marketing channels will continue to reach key markets. This can be done using innovation workshops or, if time and budgets allow, scenario planning.

Trend audits

When dealing with creative people, it's vital that you constantly get them to think differently. [Trend-focused] sessions are a good way to stimulate people to think about change.

Wayne Garvie, Director of Production and Content, BBC

It's almost like an eye test. You begin by saying 'What can you tell me about the situation currently?' Then you give them the trend information and make them use that to consider the problem. Then ask them 'What do you now see?' And they'll not only see the problem more clearly but they'll also see the solution.

Alex Owens, Director of Brand Development and Consumer Insight, Capital One

Clients often ask me to take a look at their companies and tell them how 'on trend' their strategies are. To do this, I have devised a process known as a trend audit. This is a way of determining how future-proofed a campaign, department or brand is. It can be done whether you are working on a short-term tactical campaign or looking at the long-term strategy of a department or brand. The audit is a three-step process. First you identify the most relevant trends. The number of trends you audit against depends on the budget available, but I typically audit against five macro trends. Next you run SWOT analysis on current policy as regards those trends. Finally you use this information to recommend which elements of policy should continue, which should cease, and what new policy should be added.

Running trend SWOT analysis determines a company's strengths and weaknesses as regards a trend and what opportunities and threats the trend might pose for it. It is particularly useful because it forces companies to explore both the positive and the negative aspects of a trend as it affects them, and helps inspire specific actions and solutions. Understanding whether you are strong or weak as regards the trend will determine if the trend is a positive or a negative one for you. If you are weak in it, then the trend will be negative or a 'barrier' trend. Your job will then be to try to find ways to counter its effects. The next step is to determine what threat the trend might pose. Is it going to affect your business in some negative way? Might it potentially reduce your sales? Might it drive your current customer base to another brand? If the answer to all these questions is no, then you can ignore the trend. But if it is yes, you need to explore whether there is anything positive you can do to improve your company's positioning with regard to the trend. If you are strong in regard to it then it will be a positive or 'booster' trend for you. You will therefore want to find ways to exploit it to your advantage, to locate or grow new markets and revenue streams, determining what opportunities the trend can offer.

A food manufacturer, for instance, might want to determine how future-proofed its current product range is. It will first identify which trends are relevant to its customer base. It might decide that macro trends such as Convenience Story, Traditionalizing, Local Heroes and Trading Up are all relevant, in which case it would map their product range against each. Does it have products that conform to today's mobile lifestyles? Are enough of them traditionally designed or manufactured? Are they locally produced? Does it have a premium range? It will also want to map them against relevant micro, sector and demographic trends, so it would consider packaging and taste trends, trends in key customer groups such as tweens or parents, and so on. If it is satisfied that its product range conforms to each key trend, then it can comfortably continue with current policy, but if there are particular products that go against a large number of trends, then it might consider dropping them. If it finds that none of its products conform to an important trend, it might consider developing a brand new product that does. One trend audit I was involved in for the BBC many years ago helped identify how on-trend its then new *Strictly Come Dancing* format was.

Innovation workshops

I use consumer insights as the starting point for workshops, where people from different departments sit together and think about these trends and then come up with ideas themselves. We do it every year and develop a roadmap of short-, mid- and long-term ideas. I vary the format each year, and I try to take some issues that one of the departments, say the marketing department, has at the time. So last time there was a lot on the retail level that was changing, so I focused on trends related to retail and we came up with ideas around that.

Brechje Vissers, Manager Colour Marketing and Innovation, PPG Industries (ex-Senior Trend Consultant, Philips) (Netherlands)

We run what I call 'think days'. We sit down with future-facing topics and work out which we should be dealing with now: which do we think are relevant to us, and which do we think that we can't capitalize on? I set everyone 'homework' beforehand, which consists of a series of trend-related questions. In the meeting, we give each person five minutes to present their response to each question: why it matters, what impact it might have, what other questions we need to answer, and so on. Then, when we've gone through all the topics, we rank them in order of relevance to the company.

Annie Freel, Head of Knowledge, McCain Foods

Innovation workshops are based upon a variety of brainstorming techniques. They provide an opportunity for diverse stakeholders to discuss and hypothesize on trend implications. Key areas for debate include the validity, relevance and potential effect of each trend. Outcomes range from identifying talking points to comprehensive strategy determination, dependent on goals set and personnel present. Most companies that utilize trends run some variation of these as a basis for trend-based innovation and strategy determination.

Innovation workshops can take a variety of forms, dependent on the aims, structure and resources of the company involved. They need some formal structure but, as their purpose is to enhance innovation, it must not be too prescriptive. They should begin with the presentation of a trends report. This can be delivered to attendees before the session or presented in person at the commencement of it. Participants will then spend time debating the veracity and relevance of the trend or trends presented. They will then brainstorm any potential opportunities or threats to company strategy presented by the trend. If, say, a holiday firm was taking a trend-centric approach to the future, it would develop a shortlist of potentially relevant trends and then run an innovation workshop based around them. It might consider trends such as Wising Up, Extreme Pleasure, Come Together and Switching Off. What might these mean for its industry and its company? Might consumers be looking for more cultural holidays, or more adventurous ones? Might consumers want to take holidays in larger groups? Could the trend for mini-breaks wane as consumers demand fewer longer holidays again? It would also want to consider which micro, sector and demographic trends might be relevant and then consider the implications of these. Might Baby Boomers want to relive the backpacking days of their youth? Might the Experimental Travel trend cross over from early adopters to the mainstream? The session will typically end with a summing up of progress and a call to action. This latter can be the implementation of strategies agreed in the meeting or the commissioning of further workshops or consumer research (see Chapter 24).

Scenario planning

A more advanced form of the innovation workshop format is scenario planning, in which informed debate on corporate strategy is stimulated by a presentation of possible futures. Although it is impossible to state for sure exactly what will happen in the future, it is feasible to produce some ideas of what might happen. Exploring how and why each of these future 'scenarios' might occur, and what their possible outcomes and consequences might be, enables a company to better determine and evaluate corporate strategy. A version of the process was introduced by the military during the Second World War and then developed by Herman Kahn for commercial use in the 1960s. The term 'scenarios' was suggested to Kahn by Hollywood screenwriter Leo Rosten. It is the original film industry term for what are now called screenplays. In the early 1970s, planner Pierre Wack and his team at Royal Dutch Shell further developed the practice into its current format.

There are two types of scenario planning. Strict scenario planning is less to do with prediction than with innovation. It is not about determining which of the possible futures put forward is the most likely. Its aim is simply to help companies clarify their thinking about key issues, provoke innovation and non-traditional thinking, and enable them to make more informed decisions. Predictive scenario planning does the same, but in addition attempts to determine which of the possible futures is the most likely and therefore which of a series of potential strategies might be most effective. In both types, the scenario planner will spend time ahead of the sessions creating realistic stories corresponding to the required scenarios. These create a single fictional storyline that begins in the present and is developed typically several years into the future.

Scenario planners are free to utilize any scenarios they like, but each company will have certain scenarios that are more or less appropriate to their situation. These should be rooted in a world familiar to the participants, and the combination of scenarios should between them present a broad spectrum of possible futures. Regularly used scenarios include: the static scenario, in which circumstances remain the same; the positive scenario, in which things get better; the negative scenario, in which things get worse; the revolution scenario, where something positively or negatively transformational happens; and the new-balance-of-power scenario, in which relative purchasing patterns in two linked sectors change. A magazine publisher might want to debate what could happen if sales of magazines went up or down, if consumers stopped buying magazines altogether or if consumers started reading them on mobile e-readers. A cell phone handset manufacturer might want to consider what would happen if rates of purchase rose or fell, if cell phones became unfashionable with early adopters or if strong links were found between cell phone usage and cancer.

Scenario planners will typically begin each session by explaining the scenario concept and process. They will then present each scenario in turn, trying to bring the stories to life and engage the participants as much as possible. After each scenario is presented, the participants will debate the effect such a future might have upon the company if present strategies were to be pursued. They will then brainstorm alternative strategies that might be better suited to the scenario. The final task will be to determine if a single strategy could be implemented that will leave the company effectively prepared whichever scenario actually occurs.

23

What's in it for me?

PICKING YOUR PURPOSE

You've got to think about what you're actually looking for, what you're trying to solve, what is your hypothesis. For me the hypothesis is the reason why you're doing something.

Alex Owens, Director of Brand Development and Consumer Insight,
Capital One

Rather than wrestling with finding the correct interpretation of all the factors out there in the marketplace, start with a few key hypotheses of what you think might be happening in the marketplace. Then determine if those theories are really coming to life, ie if evidence is surfacing in real-world metrics such as per capita shift, coverage levels in the media and so on.

Tom Pickles, Senior Director, Global Menu Solutions, McDonald's (USA)

Running trend evaluation programmes is the summation of the trend marketing process. The next two chapters take you through the practicalities of running such programmes. It is the time to turn trend analysis into practical business strategy.

Trend-centric and company-centric evaluation use different formats, but share a similar analytical approach. First establish a business question. Next assemble the trends most relevant to that question. Then analyse them to determine what effect they might have and what your company needs to do in response to them. To establish your business question you first need to look at the specifics of your business, to determine exactly what problem you are seeking to solve. This can be tactical or strategic. Tactical problems can come from a range of departments. Do you have specific marketing or sales problems you need to solve? Do you need to estimate sales figures or budgets for next year? Are you trying to determine your strongest PR opportunities? Strategic questions typically cut across departments. Are you looking for cost-saving opportunities? Are you trying to locate new markets? What new products, services, product ranges or brand extensions should you launch next year?

PICKING PARAMETERS

Segmenting sectors

Some trends will affect our business more than others, so we come up with a shortlist of trends that we think are important to the business and we work them up for ideation.

Michele Giles, Head of Insight, Premier Foods

There are some sectors that we know are more relevant to us, or more inspirational or more forward-looking, than others. The fashion industry, the technological industry, communications industry, the service industry and architecture are the ones that we ensure are always covered, and then we look at some of the other ones where we've found interesting things before.

Denise Drummond-Dunn, Vice President Consumer Excellence, Nestlé (Switzerland)

Once you have determined your business question, the next step is to decide which trends might best answer it. These will then form either the agenda for an innovation workshop or scenario planning session, or the key factors to map against in a trends audit. Determining which trends might be relevant to your purposes is an important process. Today there is so much information available on trends that it is hard to know where to start. One concern I hear regularly from clients is that they are 'drowning' in data. With so many trends affecting so many different markets, you need to focus only on the most relevant trends. To determine the optimum strategic response to a trend, you need to establish the three Ws as they pertain to your particular business. Which of your current or potential customers will the trend affect? When and where will it most affect them? Which sectors should you look for trends in? To do this requires a similar approach to that used to determine the generic development of a trend (see Chapter 20).

Trends in some sectors will be more relevant to your company than others. You clearly need to study trends in your own industry. This should not be difficult. It is likely that you already do this to a lesser or greater extent. It is almost a process of osmosis. But you should ensure that you do so in a methodical manner and without industry bias. It is all too easy to take certain industry 'norms' for granted. Yet sometimes these can act as blinkers, hampering your ability to spot an unexpected trend.

You should also study trends in those industries most closely associated with, and most influential upon, your own. Some sectors have an obvious relevance. Some industries share similar purchase drivers. Entertainment is one example. Consumers purchase cinema tickets, DVDs, CDs and video games for similar reasons. Those in, say, the film industry should therefore consider trends in television, music and video gaming. Some sectors share similar business and distribution structures. This is true of the recorded music and book publishing industries. They should each be aware of trends in the other. Some industries are affected by other industries on a very practical level. Trends in the finance and housing industry will affect trends across many manufacturing industries because they affect levels of disposable income. Trends in housing will also affect trends in interiors. One way for a company to determine which sectors are most relevant is by studying some of the trends that have affected their industry in the last decade, to see which other industries they appeared in before they reached their own.

Certain industries also tend to be greater trend incubators than others. These typically fall into three categories. Some have a stronger day-to-day impact on consumers. Some have a higher trend turnover. Some are more observable. You should try to observe the key trend incubators in each section if resources allow. Those industries with the greatest day-to-day impact are typically the ones that most affect consumers' circumstances or their moods. The former include finance, which affects consumers' spending power, and technology, which affects the way they live their lives, from transport to communication. The latter typically include the entertainment, fashion and leisure industries. Certain industries launch more trends than others. These early adopter industries include the more fashion- or youth-oriented sectors, like fashion, personal technology, media, music and cosmetics. They contrast with laggard industries: the slowest-moving, most traditional or least fashion-led sectors. These include the financial services, food and automotive sectors. Some industries have a high observational profile. They may manufacture products that are displayed out of home, such as clothing, cars or personal technology. They may be based in observable environments like retail or leisure. The higher observational profile an industry has, the more impact it is likely to have on consumers, so the more trends it will produce.

Choosing consumers

Trend marketers need to scrutinize any trends currently affecting their present or traditional target market, but they also need to consider trends affecting consumer cohorts outside that market. They should study those currently influencing their target market. As consumer trust of brands and marketing declines, for instance, consumers' children or partners will have an increasing impact on purchase decisions. Trend marketers will also need to study those who are not currently their target market but who might become so owing to current trends. Smart marketers in the automotive and technology industries who spotted the Boundary Blurring trend in the 1990s would have known to study trends not just in the youth and male markets but in the female and Grey markets too.

Trend marketers also need to consider which trend adopter typologies to focus on. Smaller companies or companies in fast-moving industries need to act on trends early, so should study innovators and early adopters. Larger companies or those in more slow-moving industries should focus on the early mainstream. Until trends reach this cohort, they will typically not be developed enough to appeal to the prospective market or to offer robust enough data to determine strategy safely.

Location, location

The next question is which territories to study trends in. Even those companies that are based in just one territory need to be aware of other territories. Those that do not have a global reach can still be affected by global trends (see Chapter 10). Studying every market in detail is a costly and logistically difficult process. It is only feasible for global companies with trend teams in each market or for those that employ global trend consultancies. All other companies will need to pick and choose the markets they study. Deciding how many markets to target will again depend on factors such as company size. Single-market companies will need to place observational focus on their home market, but should try to gain some understanding of key trends in the most relevant markets. Global companies should study a broad range of different markets.

There are two key types of territories to study: target territories and influencer territories. Target territories are those you currently aim your products or services at. You are likely to know these markets well. As with studying trends in your own industry, however, you must be careful to avoid complacency or over-traditionalism. Influencer territories fall into two categories. Some are trend leaders within their own industry. Others are trend leaders across a range of sectors.

To establish which are the most important territories for your particular industry, you should study industry media and consult industry experts, but there are certain generalizations that can be followed when it comes to identifying influencer territories. Personal technology trends have traditionally originated in the United States or Asia. France, Italy and London have traditionally had the greatest impact on fashion trends. Most film trends have emanated from Los Angeles. Many social and housing trends have emanated from the Netherlands or Scandinavia. But, as rates of change increase, a greater number of territories are influencing trends, and many traditional trend incubators are being superseded. Stockholm, Tokyo and São Paulo have become strong trend incubators in recent years. Other cities have seen their influence wane, such as Paris, Milan and Detroit. Areas such as Williamsburg in New York, Shoreditch in London and Harajuku in Tokyo have launched several trends, especially within the leisure and design sectors. Forecasters today also should ensure they study the key emerging nations such as Brazil, Russia, India and China as well as Western nations. South America has had a major impact on design recently. Mumbai and Hong Kong have become increasingly important influencers of film trends. The BRIC territories are certain to have a greater impact on trends in the 21st century than they did in the previous one.

Trend timing

It's important to identify trends early so you have a chance to respond in time.

Hanna Chalmers, Head of Research and Insight, Universal Music Group

If we can understand the big trends early enough and understand how they will affect our consumers in the next three years that will give us the time to develop and launch something towards the market at the right time.

Michele Giles, Head of Insight, Premier Foods

It is vital not to act on a trend until it has reached an appropriate development point. The optimum moment to act on a trend is well enough in advance to have time to prepare your strategy but not so early as to pre-empt consumer demand. One of the most significant lessons I learned when I first started trend forecasting was the importance of timing. My initial impression was that all that mattered was identifying a trend before others did. I would get very excited about emerging trends and assumed that companies should act on them immediately. I thought the earlier you acted on a trend, the better. But this is not true. Acting on a trend too early can be just as dangerous as doing so too late. If you base a two-year strategy on a trend that does not reach your target market for three years, you could experience major sales losses.

The moment you act on a trend is determined by the nature of your company, your industry and the trend itself. Smaller and challenger companies need to pick up on trends early. There is a greater incentive in taking risks, and you need to be nimble to gain market share. Larger companies or those in slower-moving markets should be wary of picking up on a trend too early. Larger companies and brand leaders have more at stake. Markets are larger and campaigns more costly. Companies that target late mainstream consumers should not base medium- or long-term strategy on trends that are only just emerging. When a large company spots an early emerging trend, it may be necessary for it simply to monitor the trend's progress until it grows large enough to be relevant to the company's customers.

If purchase decisions in your industry are based on changing consumer tastes rather than just costs or reliability, your customers are likely to be affected by trends earlier. This means you need to pick up on those trends earlier. Companies in faster-moving industries also need to pick up on trends earlier; otherwise the trend may have passed before they have had the time to exploit it.

24

Theory into practice

THE IMPLEMENTATION PROCESS

Reactions and responses

> *Spotting trends is just the beginning. It's how you execute the strategy based around the trend that matters. It's not just the data; it's the insight.*

Sue Elms, EVP Global Media Practice, Millward Brown

> *The tricky bit is how to get my category or brand entwined with the trend in a way that works for the category, the consumer and the brand. How can I pull something out that will really resonate with the consumer and give us something we can have success with?*

Gavin Emsden, Food and Beverage Insights Director, Nestlé

Once you have established which trends are most relevant, you need to determine what your company needs to do in response to them. Here trends can be used to help determine long-term corporate strategy or to shape shorter-term policy such as the channels and tone of marketing campaigns or the development of new product lines.

It is probably most effective to break such a consideration down into the 4Ps: product, place, promotion and price. For each new trend, you should consider how it might affect the demand for particular products or services, their design and packaging, which new ones might prove popular in future, and how the trend might affect the most effective promotion of products both above and below the line. The popularity of different retail environments will fluctuate dependent on individual trends. New consumer trends will also affect the relative importance of price.

Boosters and barriers

The first step is to determine which of the trends you have chosen are boosters and which are barriers for your company (Figure 24.1). Booster trends are those positive trends that offer opportunities for a particular company or industry. They typically involve the growing popularity of the products or services they provide or of a sector they are part of. This can be a brand new interest from a new market or a renewed interest from an old market. It can also include the growth of a market that a product or service appeals to. The Traditionalizing trend has been a booster for heritage-based brands from Aga to Heinz. The Conscious Consumer trend was a booster to healthy and ecologically friendly brands. Barrier trends are the negative trends that could potentially harm a company or industry. Healthy Living was a barrier trend to fast-food companies and forced them to provide healthier alternatives to their traditional products. The trend among young people to use their mobile phone as a timepiece is proving a barrier trend for the watch industry.

It is vital that marketers analyse a trend carefully. Some trends might appear to be barriers but are actually boosters. For instance, when American consumers started turning off large saloon cars in the early 1960s it was a barrier for the US automotive industry, but it proved a booster trend for Volkswagen, which saw huge sales of the Beetle: the car 'for those who like to think small'. The Convenience Story trend was a booster for cell phone and MP3 player manufacturers but a barrier for fixed-line telecoms providers and hi-fi manufacturers.

BOOSTER TREND

New trend stimulates demand for brand
New market grows that likes brand
Traditional market for brand grows

BARRIER TREND

Old market now dislikes brand
New market grows that dislikes brand
New trend negates brand usage
New trend reduces brand revenue

Figure 24.1 Boosters versus barriers

Companies should consider both booster and barrier trends. Boosters offer the greatest opportunities for growth, but barriers can offer threats of equal proportions. Companies need to adapt their strategy in response to both types of trend. When they identify a strong booster trend they should look for potential opportunities across the 4 Ps. Supermarkets have used the opportunity presented by the Convenience Story trend to offer a range of different products, from toys to financial services. Apple used it to launch the iPod and iPhone. Upon discovering a strong barrier trend, however, you will need to identify optimum ways to avoid its negative effects. Several fast-food companies responded to the Healthy Living trend by producing healthier alternatives. Magazine publishers have tried to reverse the threat of internet publishing by producing their own stand-alone online publications.

Dos and don'ts

A common error is to get too caught up in market trends and forget the basics. In the movie Big *there's a terrific scene where they're in a conference room and the marketing person's showing the pie chart with how big the robotic market is. And they develop a product that is robotic, but the problem is that the kids don't like it because it just isn't fun. And we see that all the time. Just because there's a developing market doesn't mean that any product you roll out for that market is going to work.*

Dave Capper, President Lifestyle, Music and Media, Hasbro (USA)

Care needs to be taken to ensure that trends are relevant to your brand and your audience. Blindly following or tapping into trends can make you look like a follower or a 'me too', which erodes credibility.

Amanda Meers, Group Account Director, Jigsaw Strategic Research (Australia)

DO

Remember traditional marketing issues

DO NOT

Mistake a fad for a trend
Mistake a micro trend for a macro trend
Add trend data as an afterthought
Use irrelevant trend data

Figure 24.2 Dos and do nots

When determining trends-based policy, companies need to ensure they avoid some potential pitfalls (Figure 24.2). Just because you utilize a trend does not mean you can afford to lose sight of established marketing theory. Trends should not supersede marketing knowledge; they should enhance it. When contemplating marketing strategy, companies will still need to consider issues such as market reach, return on investment, share of voice, OTS rates and so on.

Trends must also be utilized at the correct level. Companies can suffer for assigning either too much or too little weight to a trend. The former can occur when a company confuses a fad for a trend. The latter can occur if a company mistakes a micro trend for the full manifestation of a trend when it is simply the beginning of a macro trend. This can be avoided by careful analysis.

Trend data need to be introduced into strategic planning discussions at an early stage. Trends should be considered when shaping the entire campaign, from communications channels to creative tone. Too often companies 'shoehorn' a trend into an otherwise traditional campaign. This does not take genuine advantage of the trend. It can also appear unattractive to consumers. A trend such as the New Old, for instance, should inform decision making in new product development, marketing communications, distribution and so on. Do current products need to be adapted to appeal to this demographic? Are there opportunities to launch new products targeted at them? What are the best media and distribution channels to reach them? Do creative executions need to be targeted at them specifically or will they respond to current ones? Might it necessitate changes to company structure or brand identity?

RESPONDING TO TRENDS

Product

I described some of the ways companies have successfully responded to trends earlier (see chapters 3 and 4). Although each company's needs and opportunities will be different, some generalizations can be made. When it comes to product issues such as demand, barrier trends alert companies to the dangers of shrinking markets whereas booster trends offer opportunities to target new markets. Trends can act as one or the other dependent on the brand. Trends such as Conscious Consumption or Authenticity might turn customers off certain products or brands but turn them on to others. If a barrier trend looks set to shrink your market, you will need to find ways to adapt your offering to better appeal to it (Figure 24.3). This might include

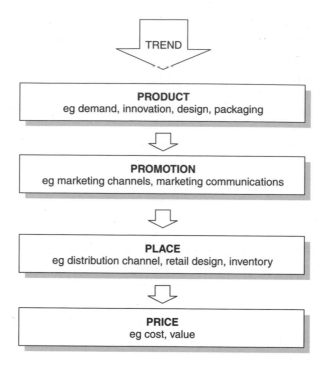

Figure 24.3 Implementation (the 4 Ps)

emphasizing qualities such as healthiness or authenticity. Alternatively a booster trend might point you in the direction of a whole new market. You may have avoided a market in the past because that cohort disliked or had no interest in your sector, brand, product or services. It might have been hard to reach, or too small a group to justify targeting it. But if its behaviours or attitudes change owing to the emergence of a new trend, it could become a much more attractive target. You should study each trend to see if it offers market opportunities.

One way to avoid a shrinking market for current products is to create new products that consumers will prefer. Again, this is relatively straightforward. Products that fulfil the new needs inherent in a trend will become more popular as that trend grows. When the Wellness trend hit the soft drinks sector, companies whose products were initially considered unhealthy were able to regain market share by manufacturing or distributing healthier ones.

As for product and packaging design, this can also be affected by both attitudinal and behavioural trends. A product needs to fit into consumers' new behaviours and lifestyles. It also needs to encourage feelings in them that they associate with popular new attitudes. Trends around mobility or convenience typically drive demand for smaller products, but materialist or cocooning trends will encourage the purchase of larger products, from books to televisions. Old-fashioned or authentic packaging becomes more popular during traditionalist or provenance trends, but more stylish or cutting-edge packaging succeeds when status or risk-taking trends are on the rise.

Promotion

As the rate of media and behavioural change has grown, an understanding of trends has become an essential part of the marketing planning process. Trends can affect all aspects of promotion, above and below the line. They can affect media, channel, tone and placement choice. Some trend implications will be obvious. Identifying a trend among customers for increasing e-commerce will necessitate a greater marketing spend online. Other implications may be less obvious. If consumers are spending more time in social networks, the role of friendship and trust will change. They may respond better to word-of-mouth and advocacy campaigns. They might also respond to a more communal brand message. Trends such as Are You Experienced and Come Together are also opening up new opportunities for below-the-line marketing. As consumers spend more time communally out of home and less time watching broadcast media, experiential marketing and sponsorship are becoming more important. Consumers' growing communality is encouraging word of mouth and advocacy. The stronger such trends are among a target market segment, the more important such methodologies will become in targeting them.

Trends can prove a highly valuable tool for public relations campaigns too. Evidence of a good new trend can provide a company with strong national media coverage. Given the nature of their business, companies in some fields can sometimes find it hard to gain mainstream media coverage for their brands. By identifying and aligning themselves with new trends, they can gain not only usable strategic insights for internal use, but a strong media story as well. The first step is to identify a relevant new trend. This needs to be something that the company in question can associate itself with and that has yet to gain mainstream media coverage. Next, a primary quantitative study is run to provide robust new evidence for the trend. Finally, a media-friendly report is produced that the PR company can use to gain media coverage. The trends-based marketing communications campaigns I have worked on for companies such as HSBC, Standard Life and Friends Provident have all been able to deliver coverage across national and regional print and broadcast media.

Place

Trends can affect the sorts of environments consumers purchase in. They can alter preferences as regards channel, size, design, location, provenance, inventory and so on. The Boundary Blurring trend has seen consumers losing some of their loyalty to traditional retail channels. Physical shopping is today such a popular pastime that some form of it will remain. Consumers still enjoy the social, interactive and browsing opportunities it offers. But as trends such as Money Talks and Convenience Story grow, they will increasingly seek alternative channels. The most obvious recent example of this has been the trend for greater e-commerce, which I have detailed elsewhere. But other examples include a growing demand for mobile or m-commerce: the purchase of products via a cell phone. This has been driven by the Mobility Ubiquity trend. It has proved popular in Asia, and there is an increasing demand in Europe and the United States too. The same trend has also encouraged a growth in the scope of vending machines. As noted in Chapter 3, in Japan and parts of Europe and the United Sates these now offer iPods, DVDs and cell phones as well as the traditional food and drink. Meanwhile the Traditionalizing and Local Hero trends are driving some Western consumers back to independent local retailers.

Price

Pricing questions will also be affected by trends. As their economic situation fluctuates, consumers typically move from value-driven trends to values-driven ones and back. In the former, price is usually the key driver of purchase but, in the latter, issues such as authenticity and provenance become stronger. What constitutes value can also evolve owing to trends. At a time of economic decline, consumers become increasingly concerned over the future, and drivers such as reliability and longevity can come to outweigh cheapness. Alternatively, as more emotive trends grow, the ability of a product to offer emotional value becomes more important. For instance, the perceived value of products that provide closeness to or memories of family or friends can grow.

THE NEXT STEPS

Research

At the early stage it's just a question of saying 'Here's the territory we're looking at. Here are the products that are out there currently. We think there's space here. This could be the next big opportunity for us.' But as we go through the process we need to provide more facts, more quantifiable research. We might do a study to see if we can make the numbers stack up or to see if we have the technology to manufacture it. Once we've brainstormed various thoughts and concepts, we'll probably do some qualitative work to get a sense of how it's resonating with our consumers, and if something seems to be working we'll fine-tune it using quantitative research.

Gavin Emsden, Food and Beverage Insights Director, Nestlé

Once we've identified a relevant trend, we might then go and do a deep dive into that area and say 'Right, let's explore that qualitatively to understand the likelihood of that trend happening, what needs to happen in the environment for that to actually happen, and how do we then respond to it and in what sort of time frame.'

Mark Broughton, Research Insights and Knowledge Manager, Global Product Development, Alliance Boots

During the course of each implication determination session, participants will debate the inferences for company policy of one or more trends. At the end, an action will be recommended based on the analysis of those trends. This will take one of three forms: to do nothing; to find out more about a trend and its potential relationship to the company; or actually to put new trends-based policy into effect.

If it is agreed that the trend is not relevant or important enough to necessitate the alteration of company policy, then the trend marketer will seek out other more relevant or important trends to study. If it is decided that further research is required before a policy change can be agreed, then it is the trend marketer's role to ensure the research is carried out, and the results discussed and acted upon at a further session (Figure 24.4). No matter how careful and robust the analysis, the nature of any future-focused process means that there will always be at least some element of uncertainty around the findings, and some potential for the unexpected.

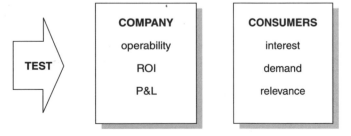

Figure 24.4 Reasons for research

Sometimes this is so slight as to be acceptable. At other times, the company might decide supplementary research is required to reduce risk levels still further.

The purpose of such research will be to provide insights into the operability, development and potential profitability of any new policy. A trend may be growing strongly in another sector but a company might want to run research to determine the potential in its own sector, or it might want to determine exactly how a trend will appeal to its core customer base. Such research will provide the company with the final confidence to put its theories into practice. Such research can be consumer or business based, or a combination of the two. If participants believe that their customers will be interested in the products of the new policy, but it is unclear how it will work within the current company structure, then business-based research will be needed. It will be necessary to work with the productions, sales or finance departments to determine how feasible or profitable it might be. Alternatively, if it is clear that the new policy will be both feasible and profitable, but it is not clear how customers will react to it, then focus groups or quantitative polling should be run to test potential response. After the required research has been carried out, the trend marketer should organize a further analysis session to debate the results and determine how to proceed.

Action

After the workshop and the development of the roadmap I keep in touch with the participants. So, for instance, I want to get sign-off on three specific ideas to be taken up in business planning for the next year, so I will talk to the R&D director to see what kind of specific goals we can set and I'll work it out in a document that I get them to approve.

Brechje Vissers, Manager Colour Marketing and Innovation, PPG Industries (ex-Senior Trend Consultant, Philips) (Netherlands)

We have intranet sites where all the trend information is available, both current data and archived reports, and we publish a book every year that is distributed internally that captures all the key aspects of what we think happens in the next few years: all the trends that are relevant to Nokia. It's a translation of all the material gathered over the year from all over the world and from all the different agencies.

Liisa Puolakka, Head of Brand Identity, Nokia

If participants agree that a trends-based revision of policy is necessary immediately without further research, it will be up to the trend marketer to ensure all relevant departments have enough information on the trend to carry out their part in it. This can include relevant trend reports, statistical factsheets, mood boards and other stimulus material. The trend marketer should also centralize relevant contact lists and act as both a driver and a facilitator of trends-based change. The trend marketer should maintain contact with each department throughout the implementation process, offering support and updating them on any developments to the trend.

Summary: Part 6

- Trends are useful only if they can be implemented into company strategy.

- Implementation is equal parts persuasion and analysis.

- Evidence presented for a trend should be a mixture of hard and soft data.

- Trends can be used to inspire or future-proof strategies.

- Strategy is best developed communally via trend audits or innovation workshops.

- Companies need to determine which trends are most relevant to them.

- Trends can be boosters or barriers to current company strategy.

- Trends can beneficially influence company strategy across the 4 Ps.

- Further research may be necessary once a trend has been analysed.

- Trend-based strategic decisions need to be followed up by relevant actions.

Afterword: Tomorrow today

The world of trends can appear ambiguous and complex, but the way trends develop and are adopted follows a clear path. Understanding how this process works enables companies to predict and then exploit trends to gain hugely profitable results.

Consumer behaviour lies at the heart of global commerce. When such behaviour changes it can have a huge positive or negative impact on brands, companies and even entire sectors. Understanding up front how, when and where such change will occur can provide huge benefits right across the business process, but such information does not just appear. It requires a systematic process of identification, interpretation and implementation. This can be done in-house or using external consultants, but to effectively implement it requires internal preparation. It also requires an understanding of the many different forms that trends can take, the different size, tone and weight of impact they can have and the different sectors, territories and demographics they can affect.

Trends can be identified using a variety of different methodologies: primary or secondary, observational or theoretical, statistical or informal. Once identified, trends must be analysed to determine how they will develop. Adoption and growth rates are driven by a trend's attributes and the environment it is being launched into. The development of a trend can be predicted by mapping it against key drivers. Trends that satisfy traditional consumer needs grow fastest. So too do those that are visible, communicable, simple, cheap and trusted. The final step in the process is to implement trend data into company strategy. To do this requires equal parts persuasion and analysis, and an understanding of which trends are most relevant. Communal forums such as trend audits and innovation workshops can then be used to determine new company strategy.

> *More companies are utilizing trend data than ever. Even sectors where they've not looked at trends before are looking at them now.*

Craig Thayer, Managing Editor, Mintel Inspire, Mintel International Group

So what can be predicted for the future of future prediction? The drive to understand tomorrow's consumer is certainly gaining momentum. Consumer trends are an increasingly important part of marketing strategy across industry. More and more companies are using them. Many that had not used them previously are doing so now. Many of those that took an *ad hoc* approach before are becoming increasingly systematized. This looks set to continue. Trends are likely to become embedded earlier and deeper in the marketing function. More robust and relevant data will be included in the analysis. Technology too looks set to improve the practice. As trend analysis becomes more systematic and technology improves, marketers will find ways to utilize computer modelling more within the process. The trend marketing process is a dynamic one. As researchers run more research and gain more knowledge of consumers and trends, they will develop further methodologies. I hope this book provides a forum for debate on ways to take the trend analysis process forward, and I welcome feedback. It will be fascinating to monitor how the process develops in the future.

However the trend marketing process develops, one thing is certain. Consumers themselves show no sign of staying still. Every week brings news of new developments in one sector or another. Some have the potential to boost your business and provide huge financial opportunities. Others will threaten current practices and markets, and will need to be swiftly countered. Hopefully this book has provided you with the breadth of knowledge and a set of tools to deal with both kinds of development much more effectively. The future is there for you to exploit. Good luck!

Appendix: Trend marketing in action

This appendix is designed to offer a practical illustration of trend marketing in action. It shows how I identified, interpreted and determined the implementation potential of three different macro trends. The trends I have chosen are Traditionalizing, Come Together and the New Old. Between them they offer examples of most identification and interpretation methodologies. I am not just describing how to identify trends that 'might' happen. These are trends that *have* happened. They have already had a huge impact on industry, and as they evolve their influence is far from over. As macro trends, they are relevant to a wide range of industries, and each is composed of several different micro, sector, national and demographic trends, so any exploration of them will provide examples of those typologies too. Traditionalizing at first appeared to be a micro trend but soon evolved into a macro trend encompassing retro, heritage and provenance. Come Together was the trend that drove the multimillion-dollar social networking industry. The New Old is a single-segment trend that is already having a massive impact across sectors.

For each, I first define the trend. Then I list the evidence found and the different methodologies and sources used to identify it. Next I explain how I interpreted the trend, predicting development patterns by mapping it against key trend factors. For reasons of simplicity, I keep the identification and interpretation stages separate in the text, but this rarely happens in practice. There is typically overlap between the identification and interpretation stages: after identifying some examples of a trend, you will initiate interpretation of it to determine if it is worth continuing to monitor. Finally I detail how I was able to make a number of commercial inferences about the trend. Some of these have since been taken up. Others are yet to be exploited by those forward-thinking companies that also spotted the trend.

The examples are not definitive. They are only three trends and, even within these, there has not been room to include every instance, but I hope they offer a practical illustration of the processes offered in the book and that they perhaps stimulate ideas about how and where else the trends might manifest themselves or might be exploited.

TRADITIONALIZING

Definition

The Traditionalizing trend is seeing consumers in the emerged nations looking to the traditions, skills, products and behaviours of the past for their inspiration. The trend is being driven as much by the young and cutting-edge as by the old and conformist. It began as a renewed interest in traditional crafts such as knitting, but it grew to encompass heritage and provenance, retro and simplicity.

Identification

Much of the evidence for this trend was observational. I got my first clue about Traditionalizing from an expert interview. As part of a global trends project, I was interviewing Debbie Stoller, the 30-something editor of alternative women's lifestyle magazine *Bust* in New York in 1999. During the course of an interesting discussion, she mentioned that she was writing a book on knitting. This was the first time anyone younger than 50 had mentioned knitting to me, so I made a note of it. A few months later, I spoke to a fashion expert who told me that several of the models backstage at Paris Fashion Week had been knitting between shows. Not long after I received a memo from one of my scouts telling me of a group of 20-something early adopters called 'the Cast-Off Knitting Club for Boys and Girls'. They were holding 'guerrilla knitting' sessions on public transport: sitting and knitting on buses or subway train carriages. Individually these examples were minor and suggested a fad, but taken together they implied there might be a bigger trend. I decided to run some reverse identification on the topic. I started looking at specialist leisure and craft magazines. It turned out that wool sales were actually on the rise. Scout observation at retail also showed a new type of consumer frequenting wool and handicraft departments. Visits to trade fairs showed a growing interest in other traditional crafts, from crochet to scrapbooking. One of the most popular products in interior design magazines was Scandinavian designer Tord Boontje's Garland light, which combined an old craft style with cutting-edge technology. The spirit of craft fairs and garage and lawn sales began being evoked. Tombolas and bring-and-buy stalls were appearing at 'cool' launch events in Soho. Events like Emily and Julie's Extraordinary Jumble Sale and the Art Car Boot Fair, which featured stalls run by prominent modern artists like Gavin Turk, were appearing regularly in London's East End. Scouts told me how similar events were starting to take place elsewhere too. In Bristol, the boutique Here held a village fête at which artists sold their work from stalls. Knit-ins were being organized in Edinburgh and Edwardian costume nights in Manchester. Meanwhile Debbie Stoller's book on guerrilla knitting, called *Stitch and Bitch*, was becoming a cult favourite.

There was certainly at least a micro trend here. I christened it Arty Crafts: a pun on Arts and Crafts yet with a twist that indicated it was an edgy take on tradition. But as I began to interpret it I realized how broad the trend could become. Further observation offered evidence that the trend was not just limited to crafts. It was actually a general look back to the past. Fashion magazines and cutting-edge boutiques had recently started featuring the Retro Chic trend. Men's magazines starting running features on how poker and ten-pin bowling were regaining their 'cool'. At concerts and in clubs I started seeing early adopter musicians combining modern sounds and traditional English folk music to create music they called variously 'nu folk', 'acid folk', 'anti-folk' or 'folktronica'. The latter combined the authenticity of folk singers like Bob Dylan and Nick Drake with the 'chill-out' groove of Electronica. Meanwhile, despite digital downloads driving down physical CD sales, studying industry statistics showed that Britain was actually seeing a resurgence in the vinyl format in the UK. Sales rose fivefold in the first five years of the decade.[1] New FMCG products began using older ingredients. Castile soap was being added to some washing powders and personal care products. In Italy manufacturer Dixan was even using wood in its Active Ash line. Scanning non-news media offered further evidence for the trend. On television, history, nostalgia and family shows were increasingly popular.

Eventually the trend would reach the mainstream. Scouring the pop charts, we saw nu folk go mainstream, with the success of artists such as Jack Johnson, James Blunt and Dido. Topshop ran 'knit-ins' and Selfridges a Couture Car Boot Sale. Manufacturer Rowan launched a new wool brand, R2, targeted at younger, more cutting-edge consumers. Traditional board games like Monopoly and Cluedo began returning to the pages and stalls of toy-industry magazines and trade fairs and racked up sales across demographics. Retro books such as *The Dangerous Book for Boys* proved popular. Perhaps most importantly, an increasing interest in tradition and heritage combined with health and social concerns to encourage a greater interest in provenance, which had an enormous impact on the food industry. Today fashion and interiors magazines regularly feature retro styles on their covers. The listings publications are full of old bands reforming for sold-out concerts. Retro-styled shows such as *High School Musical* fill the schedules. Supermarket shelves bulge with 'traditional' products and packaging.

Interpretation

Once I had identified the Arty Craft trend, I mapped it against key trend factors to determine its potential impact and longevity. Early adopters were those postmodern iconoclasts who saw it as a reaction against then prevalent technology-focused lifestyles. There were also some who saw the combination of old with new as being something new in itself. But the trend would not remain restricted to early adopters. The idea of tradition is actually a strong driver for laggard adoption of a trend, and the trend would also spread to those laggards for whom craft was a more 'natural' fit: the old and the traditional. The two different reasons for adoption suggested there might actually be two distinct strains of the trend. On the one hand there was an ironic, occasionally humorous enjoyment of 'old-fashioned' pastimes. On the other it gave those more traditional consumers who enjoyed crafts for their own sake the confidence to return to take them up again. But there were some segments it would not appeal to: those who enjoyed the novel for its own sake and those who enjoyed it for the status its adoption brought. Crafts were today more associated with women so the trend might prove less popular with men.

Causal analysis showed the trend had strong roots, and suggested it could be bigger than I first thought. Global political instability in the late 1990s and early 2000s had created a sense of constant low-grade fear among consumers. Many were feeling confused by increased technological and social change rates. In such circumstances, consumers will often look back to past times and pastimes that in retrospect appear safer and simpler. Historicals showed that the end of a century is also typically a time of taking stock. Clearly the end of a millennium would be an even greater one. This drove me to conclude that the trend had the potential to become much more than just about crafts. The traditional aspect of the trend might itself be the trend. The more evidence I gathered, the clearer it became that a macro trend was growing. I christened it Traditionalizing.

Others factors too suggested growth potential. One of the cycles that consumer attitudes run through is the modern/traditional cycle: an interest in the modern is superseded by one in the traditional and so on. That looked set to happen here. A huge amount of technological change had occurred in recent years, which had excited consumers in the modern and the futuristic but, as with all cycles, that would naturally swing back. Calculables such as a continuance of economic decline and political instability would further encourage it. The trend also had several strong assistance and need attributes. By its nature the past is continuous and trusted. Older products and services are typically simpler than modern ones. The trend would be easily understood and readily communicable. It was visual. Many of its manifestations were out of home. Early adopters could 'dress up' in traditional costume. It was also media-friendly. Editorial on the past is easy to produce, and evocative and popular with readers and viewers. Traditional products were typically considered safe and healthy at a time when technology, from GM foods to cell phones, was being seen as increasingly toxic. This fulfilled needs such as peace of mind and self-status among parents.

The Traditionalizing trend looked set to appeal to even more consumers than the Arty Crafts trend. It would attract those parents concerned over the effects that modern products, from food to toys, were having on their children. It would appeal to men more than the crafts trend did. It would also be picked up by the new Conserva-Teen segment: those young people who were becoming interested in more traditional values.

Evidence for the trend was appearing across a wide range of sectors, but were there any industries it might not affect? I determined to test those sectors such as personal technology and the automotive sector that might seem the most immune to a traditionalist trend. Trade fairs were a good source of data. At the global automotive shows, there were an increasing number of retro designs. The hot rod and muscle car styles of the 1950s proved particularly popular. Many major companies started revisiting car designs from the 1960s and 1970s. Ford revived the Mustang, Chevrolet the Camaro and DaimlerChrysler the Challenger. Meanwhile at consumer shows for the home and interiors industry I started seeing examples of products designed to traditionalize technology. For instance, one company was launching a wooden sideboard with a flat-screen TV that sank down inside at the push of a button. Studying international interiors magazines I discovered further evidence of such 'traditional' technology. Companies such as Sweden's Swedx and Italy's Zaverio were manufacturing wooden computers and computer accessories. Japanese homewares store Muji was selling cardboard hi-fi speakers. US trend reports told me how manufacturer Microdia had launched Fruity Flash Keys, flash drives that are scented with different fruit flavours, and Connectland had produced an oil-burner plug-in. This all pointed to a massively cross-industry trend. If even such technology-focused industries were being affected, then few if any sectors could afford to ignore it.

In terms of where the trend would grow, early evidence was restricted to the United States, Europe and Japan. To determine if it might spread elsewhere, I studied cycles and need levels in the emerging nations. Most of these had not yet reached the Maslovian level at which consumers react against the modern. They had also not yet moved far enough through the modern/traditional attitudinal cycle. In the short term at least, the trend looked likely to be limited to the developed world.

I was interested to see how the trend might evolve as it grew. To determine this I looked for calculables. Whilst interpreting the trend I came across government data that showed some evidence of a return to traditional social conventions. Marriage numbers had been in decline since the 1960s, but in 2001 the trend reversed.[2] The divorce rate too started to fall.[3] These data prompted me to consider an even wider interpretation of the Traditionalizing trend. Could it actually be the beginning of a return to more traditional *attitudes*? Could the traditions of the family and social convention be returning? Scanning secondary polling provided further evidence of this. Government figures showed that British families were now eating together more often.[4] Concerned over absentee parenting, parents were starting to take more time off work to be with their children. Almost half of British mothers were now working flexitime, compared to just 17 per cent in 2002, and the number of new fathers now working flexitime had risen by almost 300 per cent, from 11 per cent in 2002 to 31 per cent in 2005.[5] New government laws adopted by divorce courts meant that both sides involved in the divorce would be required to cover their own legal costs, leading to a likely reduction in the number of couples who seek a divorce. Meanwhile the Conserva-Teen trend was encouraging traditional values in a younger consumer segment.

But how long would the trend last? It showed no signs of declining in the medium term. Trend drivers were strong, and adoption had reached the mainstream consumer. But there were factors around it that suggested it would certainly not last in the long term, and the nature of a cyclical trend means that attitudes will eventually swing back again. Traditional products and services can lack the excitement of the new. They are also typically slow. This was part of their appeal as a reaction to the forward rush of the modern, but ultimately could become frustrating to those brought up in an age of speed. Traditionally manufactured products are also often more expensive than others, negating their appeal in an economic downturn.

Implementation

Having identified and interpreted the trend, the next step was to consider how it could be beneficially implemented into business strategies.

Interpretation had shown that the trend was likely to affect consumers across every industry and would appeal to the late mainstream and even laggards. This meant that every company would need to respond to it in some way.

So what implications might there be for marketing policy across the 4 Ps? Certainly the trend would be a booster for manufacturers of traditional products. Long-established brands and brands using traditional materials or designs would be likely to see markets grow. New products that appealed to traditional attitudes would prove popular. I remember being very excited at a BBC innovation workshop when *Strictly Come Dancing* (also known as *Dancing with the Stars*), then a new show yet to be broadcast, was first mentioned. Since then the show has several times attracted audiences of 12 million and been successfully exported to 30 other countries. In contrast, those currently producing 'modern' products would need to investigate how they could traditionalize them. Older materials would need to be considered, heritage emphasized and packaging designs altered.

When it came to promotion, a greater emphasis on history was encouraging consumers to care more about heritage. Provenance and 'authenticity' were clearly going to become hugely important sales drivers. In order to take advantage of this, companies would need to take a more heritage-focused approach. Many subsequently have (see Chapter 3). For instance, luxury brands such as Chanel, Lacoste, Du Pont and even cutting-edge Dior have since run campaigns based around their founders and their history. FMCG manufacturers from Heinz to Premier Foods now utilize traditional packaging and advertising creatives. High-end car manufacturers like Mercedes and BMW, and luxury jewellery and watch brands such as Richemont and Cartier are utilizing experiential heritage marketing to build and sustain brand loyalty.

A move towards more traditionalized technology suggested brands might need to emphasize the softer side of their technology products or the humanity of their technology services in their marketing communications. Orange led the trend with its 'Blackout' campaign, which showed how 'good things' can happen when users turn off their phones. Other cell phone companies now regularly emphasize how their products and services enable easier communication with friendship groups.

If consumers decided to return to simpler, more traditional values, this would be likely to affect their attitudes to marketing too. Communications strategies that emphasized the simplicity and morality of traditional family values might become more effective. The traditionalist 'Oxo approach' might have more effect in future than the edgy 'PlayStation approach'. Many brands have now returned to a more traditional family-focused creative approach.

The trend might have an effect on retail environments too. Tradition was not likely to eclipse trends like convenience and functionality – they were too well established – so the trend would not be enough to see bricks-and-mortar retail reassert itself against e-commerce, but consumers might prefer a more traditional 'feel' to their retail environments. The traditionalism of small independent local retailers might also prove more popular, with farmers' markets and delicatessens both seeing growth. In terms of price, issues such as long-term value could become more important, and more consumers might consider paying a premium for well-crafted products and the use of traditional materials.

COME TOGETHER

Definition

There has been a trend towards community in recent years: a shift from the 'I' of the 1980s and 1990s to the 'we' of today. It is an increasingly active trend, something that consumers are creating not just accepting. I call it Come Together, after the song the Beatles released back in the community-loving 1960s. It was the driver for localism and online social networking.

Identification

The very first indication I had of the Come Together trend was actually the informal observation of a mainstream event. The funeral of Princess Diana in 1997 was spontaneously attended by huge numbers of mainstream Britons. Although attendance at such events had been popular in the first half of the 20th century, it had fallen off in recent years and had not been encouraged by the royal family. I had not set up The Next Big Thing by then, but the event lingered with me and, when I came upon early evidence of the trend, it was one of the factors that encouraged me to investigate it further.

The first statistical evidence of the trend came while scanning secondary polling data on youth attitudes. Time series data from omnibus surveys showed that Britain's 15–18s were proving less individualistic than their forebears. According to one poll, just 59 per cent considered it important to 'be individual not just one of a crowd'.[6] The most important thing they made time for was 'hanging out with friends or partner'.[7] Other polling data showed me that consumers were increasingly seeking the company of others across a range of sectors. They were joining together in formal and informal communities and enjoying more communal activities. Attendance at music concerts and festivals was growing. So too was membership of communal associations such as book clubs. Eighty-seven per cent of Britons were now members of something.[8] Listing publications showed evidence of a growth in the number of street festivals and other communal events. Historical re-enactment and live action role-playing (LARP) societies were on the rise. Teenage magazine problem pages were featuring 'friendship problems' more regularly. Environmental websites showed that car sharing was on the rise, and government figures that gang membership was growing.

Cutting-edge consumers were not immune to the trend. Informal observation in nightclubs showed the growth of collective activities such as themed dressing up. Local cultural fanzines in cities such as Sheffield and Manchester were beginning to take a greater pride in their neighbourhoods. There was also a fad for 'flash mobs', in which individuals collect at a prearranged point at a prearranged time, either to do something specific or simply to 'be'. Although this latter was short-lived, it gave another clue that something was growing.

To determine if such a trend was limited to the UK, I began testing for it in other territories. I studied statistics on global communal leisure activities and found concert attendance was growing elsewhere. Concert-ticket sales in North America increased from $1.7 billion in 2000 to over $3.1 billion in 2005.[9] Since 1999, Germans have been spending more on attending live music events than on CDs, and music festivals were flowering.[10] A global research report showed that half the adult population of France was now a member of at least one association, with some 60,000 new clubs launching each year.[11] All over Europe the role of friends was enjoying a boost. A majority were now claiming that friendship was more important than career or money.[12] The Roper World Report values indices of friendship rose. 'Friends and relatives' were now a more popular source of information than television in 10 out of 15 European countries. Three-quarters of over-40s in Spain and almost two-thirds of those in Italy were today influenced by friends', family's or colleagues' opinions when deciding what film to watch.[13]

The trend was not limited to out-of-home activities. Even in the early 2000s it was becoming clear that, despite fears of screen-focused isolation, the evolution of the internet was actually towards community. Most topic-based websites had begun as information sites, but as consumers grouped together on them they wanted a means of communicating with each other, creating a demand for forums and bulletin boards. As time went on, many sites became more focused on the community element than on the informational. Subsequently, of course, this would lead to the social networking phenomenon.

Talking to games experts I was alerted to the growth in online gaming. In particular I became interested in massive multi-player online role-playing games (MMORPGs) such as World of Warcraft. For years gaming was typically a solo activity, but MMORPGs were as much about social interaction with others as about personal enjoyment, and they were becoming hugely popular. There were 11.5 million people now playing World of Warcraft,[14] including approximately 4 million in China alone. Business and methodological news media provided evidence that communal activities such as networking and collaboration were affecting business practice. There was a growth in concepts like 'co-opetition', in which potential rivals create mutually beneficial joint ventures, and open source, in which companies create products that others in their community can add to and utilize free. Consumers were also grouping together to enable better time- and cost-efficient purchase choice. C2C recommendation sites such as IGoUGo had begun to appear, where consumers recommended good holidays, restaurants and other products or warned against bad ones. The trend and its enablement through technology were also encouraging consumer protest: what one forecasting website amusingly referred to as 'consumer-generated *dis*content'.

As part of a campaign for a financial services company, I ran a primary research campaign around this time on the growing influence of neighbourhoods on house purchase patterns. This provided further evidence of the trend. One focus group participant alerted me to the fact that friends were increasingly buying homes collectively, a trend later confirmed by several estate agents. In-field quantitative polling with first-time house buyers provided evidence of an increasing interest in the local community. Over a third of first-time buyers now considered 'community spirit' to be one of their three key reasons for moving to a particular location, ahead of good schools, transport facilities, bars and clubs and a good cultural scene. Companies worldwide would later take advantage of the trend. Working on a global trends project for media agency OMD, I was in communication with OMD Croatia. They told me of a successful campaign being run by Konzum, a popular retail chain present in most Croatian neighbourhoods, to renovate children's playgrounds in communities around the country. Reverse identification and liaison with global partners later offered similar international examples.

The growing importance of the local community was also starting to have a huge impact on the food industry. An early warning about the potential impact of 'food miles' from a food expert enabled me to investigate the topic a long time before it reached the mainstream. Subsequently, locally sourced food has become one of the biggest growth areas in the industry.

Meanwhile, online social networking proved to be another hugely important spin-off of the trend. In the early days of the trend there were few social networking sites. MySpace was not founded until 2003 and Facebook until the following year. When they did start to appear, it was clear from any analysis of them within the context of the trend that they had an enormous potential for growth. It was very exciting to first encounter pioneering site Friendster. Since then of course numbers have rocketed. MySpace now has over 100 million members globally and Facebook over 150 million. Bebo has over 40 million members worldwide and Habbo Hotel almost 10 million. Total global revenues from the social networking industry are now estimated at approximately $6.5 billion.

Interpretation

So what initiated the trend? Consumers had enjoyed the independence and levels of choice that individualism had offered them in the 1980s and 1990s, but several factors drove them towards community. As with Traditionalizing, one of the trend initiators was consumer fear brought about by rapid technological and social change and political unrest. Another was a growing sense of detachment and even loneliness caused by an increasing reliance on technological interaction.

Unusually, early adopters of the trend came from across all demographics. There were few if any demographic barriers to growth. The oldest members of society grew up with a highly developed sense of community, which was at its height during the Second World War. But the friendship groups created as surrogate families by 'latchkey kids' and the communality of the rave scene also created a strong community spirit among Generation X. The trend appealed across socio-economic segments too. In fact it was likely to be particularly strong among LNWIs: a sense of community has been a traditional feature of the working class in many countries.

Other factors suggested the trend would grow. The desire to feel part of a community is a universal consumer need. In terms of assistance attributes, communality does not need to be an expensive behaviour. It is typically simple and continuous, and it increases social status. Chaotics had an important impact too. The terrorist attacks on New York, Madrid and London and the tsunami made many consumers re-evaluate their life priorities. Relationships with friends and family became increasingly important. Polling data from the time showed that a quarter of Britons believed the terrorist attacks on London made them more aware of the importance of family. Meanwhile the show *Big Brother* introduced community to television screens. The programme, and the other reality shows that followed, encouraged consumers not only to take an interest in interactions within a community but also to talk about it with others. Elements of the trend had their own drivers. Online social networking itself offered consumers several perceived benefits, including the ability to communicate more effectively with others, meet new people, and improve social status through profile creation and friendship numbers. Technology gains could be predicted to improve the usability and scope of networking sites. C2C recommendation sites enabled consumers to save time and money.

The trend was clearly set to grow, and to spread across cohorts and industries, but it would not last indefinitely. Historically and cyclically periods of community are followed by periods of individuality. Once today's socio-economic fears subside and their confidence returns, consumers would slowly return to more independent attitudes.

So how would social networking itself develop? The growth potential of online social networking was certainly not in doubt. The phenomenon had enough assistance and needs attributes to remain hugely important. But, as sites grow, they could lose two of their need attributes. Consumers want to meet new friends, and to feel safe and in control as they do so. These qualities encouraged initial network adoption, but neither is easy to achieve in an environment as large as today's social networks have become. This suggested that a trend for more niche networks, or virtual villages, might develop. There has already been movement in this direction. MySpace Boudoir in France, a fashion spin-off of the popular networking site, and Lovefilm and CarSpace from the United States, networking sites for film buffs and car enthusiasts respectively, have all seen growth. Services enabling groups of users to set up their own small social networking sites have even started appearing. Ning, set up in 2004, now has half a million different social networks running from its site.[15]

One of the drivers of community is in-person interaction. Because of this, *online* networking might ultimately seem limiting. This has encouraged the growth of networking sites that enable users to organize communities and plan events in the 'real world'. The biggest of these, Meetup.com, now claims to have over 3 million members, organized into groups formed around every imaginable topic, from scrapbooking to wrestling. As with general networking, the trend also looks likely to nichify. Sport is one sector likely to grow. Social networking and commerce site Craigslist experienced a tenfold increase in the yearly postings in its sports and activities sections from 2001 to 2005. Specialist sites such as ExerciseFriends.com allow members to search for like-minded exercise companions whom they can play sports with. Just a year after launch it had become the fifth most popular sports website in the world.[16] An even more specialist sports site is Meshtennis, which helps members to find partners specifically for local tennis games.

The trend looked unlikely to be limited by geographical borders. I had already seen evidence of the trend growing across Europe and the United States, but it was unlikely to be restricted to these territories. Community is a social need and as such is relatively low in the Maslovian hierarchy. Most nations have now reached this stage, at least in their urban centres. The initiators of the trend, rapidity of change and political unrest, are present across the globe. It was clear that individual parts of the trend would also grow. Online gamers now enjoy playing with partners across continents. Online social networking by its nature would not be bound by geography. Users anywhere can be connected to those not just in that nation but in any other, as long as they have access to a private or public computer terminal. Only issues such as politics and privacy might limit its growth in some nations such as China and Iran.

Implementation

The trend had some immediate business implications. It would certainly prove a booster across many sectors. Companies would have increasing success with products designed for use with friends, or that encouraged interaction with other people. Sales of interactive multi-player games have since increased, from pop quiz boardgames to Wii Sports. So too have sales of food products and technology designed for in-home and out-of-home get-togethers, from barbecues to home bars. As noted, locally sourced products were likely to become popular.

As friends and family became more important, brands would need to mirror such relationships, with a 'brand as friend' approach. Magazine and book publishers would increasingly benefit from offering their readers advice. Brand websites too could offer unbiased assistance. Microsoft's online magazine *Home* now offers customers advice on computer issues, and the website of the pharmacist Boots offers advice on a range of health matters.

It was also clear that, the more communal their customers become, the more brands would need to find ways to enter into or work with those communities. To combat consumer protest, companies would need to utilize brand advocates. Starbucks has since launched an online social networking community, MyStarbucksIdea.com, where customers can make suggestions which get voted on and the most popular of which Starbucks puts into action. Aga now runs special evenings in Russia, where those who currently own an Aga offer advice to potential purchasers. Mosh Nokia allows consumers to download and trial new Nokia products as they are being developed.

As the importance of word of mouth grows, brands will find it harder to influence their customers directly, but it appeared that social networks might provide a solution. They are likely to be a booster trend for most marketers. They provide opportunities for brands to develop relationship and word-of-mouth marketing: vital at a time when many consumers are actively avoiding above-the-line advertising.

As new media outlets freed the previously 'captive audience' in the 1980s, so the cost-effectiveness of mass marketing declined, but online communities could become the captive audience of the future, offering massive cost-effective opportunities for target marketing. Online applications or 'widgets' provide one way into such networks. OMD promoted Pfizer's Champix anti-smoking aid in the Netherlands by producing widgets that participants could integrate on their personal profile pages to help garner the support of friends and family. Another suggested route was for companies to create their own branded communities. Wrigley's Interfresh Fusion gum was launched in Europe with its own social networking site, MyPartyFusion.com, a mixture of chat, dating and gaming, where young people organize and attend virtual parties. Dutch national newspaper *Trouw* has created a social networking platform for Green enthusiasts on its website.

If social networks were to become more specialized, that too would offer further marketing opportunities. They could be used to connect marketers with users who have similar interests, in an environment that they enjoy being a part of and interacting with. Brands would benefit from creating or partnering with sites based around something unique to that brand. Honda, for instance, has become involved with specialist networking site CarSpace.

Using virtual identification in such sites would also offer opportunities for cost-effective CRM and research. As community retail such as farmers' markets and bring-and-buy sales grew, multiple retailers would look for ways to mimic that feel in their stores. Multiples would also benefit from a more active involvement in local communities, as Konzum have in Eastern Europe. In the UK, Tesco has contributed to community schemes, offered employment to the local homeless and even changed store fronts and fascias to fit in with the local environment. As C2C recommendation sites grow, companies will increasingly need to focus on value and service over price.

THE NEW OLD

Definition

Populations in most EMEA markets are getting older. Across the EU the proportion of people aged over 50 is rising dramatically. Half of the populations of Italy and Britain, for instance, will be over 50 by 2030.[17] Grey (55-

plus years) and greying (45–54 years) markets will become increasingly important, and not just by weight of numbers. Today's typically healthy and home-owning 45–80 age group also looks set to be tomorrow's most afflu-ent and highest-spending consumer segment. But today's Grey and Greying markets are very different to yesterday's. With the ageing of the ever-youth-ful Baby Boomer market, a New Old are emerging. What constitutes older behaviours is changing. These consumers are not settling down into a quiet old age, but maintaining the hobbies and hedonism of their youth.

Identification

The New Old is a trend limited to older consumers. Early adopters in this age cohort are typically less likely to exhibit their behaviours in traditional informal observational environments, so identification of the trend typi-cally relied more on secondary or formal primary research than informal observation. I learned a great deal by studying relevant polling data from research company, government and corporate sources. I was also lucky enough to work on several qualitative campaigns for music and finance companies that included interaction with older consumers. Focus group after focus group showed me how different today's Grey or Greying consumers were, and enabled me to learn of and explore their attitudes and behaviours first-hand.

However, as with many trends, the inspiration to investigate it first came from an informal observation. Attending a Meat Loaf concert at the Birmingham NEC Arena some years ago, I was struck by the composition of the audience. It was not just that they were older, which was unsurprising given that his famous *Bat out of Hell* album came out in the 1970s, but that they were quite 'alternative' in their dress and their attitudes. They were in their 40s or even 50s but they were dressed the way they would have been when the album was released: tight-fitting rock T-shirts and denim or leather jackets. I was intrigued. Who were they? Did they dress like this during the day, or did they keep these clothes at the back of the wardrobe, behind their usual suits and sweaters? And if they still enjoyed this youthful pursuit, did they still enjoy others?

It was this image I had in my mind when I read a research report from a music industry magazine a few years later that said 40-somethings now bought more albums than teenagers.[18] I determined to learn more about this demographic. If they still loved rock and roll, what about the other two tenets of traditional youth hedonism: sex and drugs? Were older consumers retaining their hedonistic ways even here? Further investigation suggested that many were. Polls showed that, for instance, 85 per cent of Britons aged over 50 'make an effort to look fit and attractive for their age'. Internet dating sites were proving increasingly popular. Health media showed that prescriptions for Viagra-style drugs were doubling year on year.[19] When it came to sexually transmitted diseases, the highest rates of increase were actually to be found among 45- to 64-year-olds, up on average over 200 per cent![20] Government statistics showed that drug taking and drinking among the New Old had not fallen as much as one might expect as they had aged. In fact, in Britain, over-55s were five times as likely to drink daily as 18- to 34-year-olds.[21]

I decided to investigate further and decided that their hedonism was not the only behaviour they were displaying that was more traditionally associated with youth demographics. They were still spending, at an age when consumers have traditionally shifted towards saving. Over-50s were spending £205 billion per year, and those still in employment outspent under-50s by over 20 per cent.[22] Credit card debt was at its highest amongst the 53–59s.[23] What they were still spending on was surprising too. 'Adolescent' entertainment products across the board, from DVD box sets to video games, were proving increasingly popular with older consumers. So too were youthful fashions, rather than the more conservative styles they might be expected to adopt. One poll showed that a quarter of women over 45 like to 'keep up with latest fashions and trends' and over a third 'often read fashion features in magazines'. They were also enjoying and exploring personal technology more than might be expected of consumers their age. Over a third of all European 55–64s accessed the internet at least once a week.[24] The 55-plus has now overtaken 35- to 44-year-olds as the biggest online demographic in the UK.[25] Other products related to their youthful interests were also proving popular. The 1960s and 1970s saw the first flowering of the green movement and the rise of Eastern spirituality. Spending in these areas has risen exponentially among them as they have aged and their disposable income increased. Many are now even returning to the backpacking holidays of their youth, creating a whole new typology of Grey travellers.

Interpretation

The New Old trend is taking place among a single cohort, the Baby Boomers, born from 1946 to 1964. With such a large cohort, the effects will differ across it. The trend will have some effect on everyone born between those years, but it will have more impact on some than others. It will be stronger among those Boomers who grew up in the heady 1960s rather than the 'hangover' of the 1970s. It will also be stronger among those who most conform to such 1960s qualities as iconoclasm, liberalism and hedonism. Traditionalists who grew up in those years but did not share such values will behave more as the previous war generation did as it aged. Life stage is becoming increasingly less important than life*style* when segmenting markets today.

So what caused the trend? When running causal analysis on single-cohort trends, it is essential to study the environmental factors affecting the cohort's early development. These affect their attitudes and behaviours not just when they are growing up but as they age as well. The majority of New Old attitudes and behaviours were shaped in the Boomers' youth. As detailed in Part 5, the Baby Boom was a chaotic, caused by the Second World War, and subsequently an inevitable. The unique environment in which they grew up informed lifelong Boomer attitudes and behaviours. Their parents were predominantly conservative. The Boomers' hedonism and iconoclasm were to some extent a reaction against this. The young also saw their opinions making a difference. The products they liked became popular. The protests they went on achieved many of their goals. This led to increased feelings of empowerment and even self-importance. Those who grow up in a time of wealth tend to feel financially secure and adopt a 'live for today' attitude. It is for this reason that Boomers have typically been spenders rather than savers. Their education gave them greater knowledge, confidence and expectations. Their high opinion of youthfulness means they are particularly open to products that offer to extend their youth. When it comes to purchase and consumption behaviours, their upbringing means they typically admire novelty, believe they deserve 'the best', and have a strong sense of financial justice. The remarkable popular culture explosion encouraged an enjoyment of popular culture that has remained with them. Used to freedom in their youth, they still expect it in their old age. They also became used to change, so have found it easier to adapt to new concepts, products, technologies and trends than their parents have.

So how would the trend develop? Again, the drivers were strong. Many New Old behaviours, from dating to playing music, fulfil universal needs. Youthfulness increases status among New Old peers. The trend is media-friendly. Many of the most influential figures in the media themselves are part of the New Old. The majority of readers of most newspapers and print magazines are too. The trend is also popular with many high-profile youthful Boomer influentials, from rock stars like Mick Jagger to actors like Jack Nicholson. The enormous size of the cohort was a predictable, ensuring the trend would have an equally large impact.

Health statistics were another calculable offering evidence that youthful behaviours would continue. One reason the New Old still behave in this way is because they *can*. They are typically fitter and healthier than previous generations were at their age. In Britain the over-50s today take part in the same amount of sport as 25-year-olds did in 1957.[26] Chronic disability amongst the 65-plus age group in the United States has fallen by almost a quarter since 1995. Almost half of all marathon runners in the United States are aged over 45, up 26 per cent since 1980.[27] However, there is one important inevitable. They will not be able to escape the effects of the ageing process. And as Boomers age they will become increasingly physically less able to behave youthfully.

The trend will not grow globally, however. It was caused by specific socio-economic influences affecting the Boomers as they were growing up, but such trends did not exist in every country. They were typically limited to the United States and Western Europe. Those growing up in Russia or China at the same time were subject to very different socio-economic influences. For this reason, the trend is not relevant to most emerging or BRIC territories.

Implementation

It was clear that there were two industry segments that needed to respond most quickly to the New Old trend. Those that manufacture products or offer services that Boomers have traditionally enjoyed, such as the entertainment and leisure industries, would still be able to sell to them, but would need to adapt their products as their market aged, and those sectors targeted at older consumers but that offer products or services that appeal to 'Old Old' or war generation values would need to adapt to New Old values if they were to survive.

When it came to the 4 Ps, the New Old trend offered boosters and barriers. If relative amounts spent on leisure by under- and over-50s remained constant, they would account for half of *all* leisure spending by 2050.[28] This level of spending would clearly boost many industries. With the New Old still interested in youthful pursuits, they would continue to spend on 'adolescent' entertainment products and services. One magazine publisher in the UK coined the term '£50 Bloke' to refer to a middle-aged professional who will happily spend £50 on CDs and DVDs or video games during a single unplanned browsing trip to an entertainment store. This will benefit industries such as leisure, entertainment and fashion.

But the trend may be a barrier to some sectors. Boomers' 'live for today' attitude means they have typically not felt the need to save. Even as they reach their 50s and 60s, the time at which many consumers traditionally begin saving, they are still not doing so, either to support their old age or in order to leave something to their children. Three-quarters of upcoming British retirees are intending to spend their savings rather than leave them to their children. In order to encourage them to save, financial services companies will need to create financial packages that appeal more to the New Old mentality. These could be more fluid perhaps, or combine saving with spending. Elsewhere, with this cohort valuing freedom so highly, subscription- and rental-based brands will need to offer more flexible terms.

Growing up at a time when youthfulness was celebrated, the New Old will want to hang on to not just their youthful attitudes but their youthful appearance too if they can. Unsurprisingly, seniors are now the fastest-growing cosmetics sector in Europe and the United States. They spend almost $10 billion on cosmetics each year.[29] Anti-ageing products were the fastest-growing sub-sector within the cosmetics market from 2001 to 2006, up almost 100 per cent to reach sales of over $12 billion.[30] It is not just the cosmetics industry that will benefit. So too will gym owners and fitness equipment companies, manufacturers of healthy and probiotic foods, cosmetic surgeons and sportswear and sporting goods manufacturers.

But not all the manifestations of ageing can be hidden or combated. The New Old's faltering eyesight, slower movements and falling levels of dexterity will affect the design requirements of those products previously limited to younger consumers. On several occasions I have tested products such as CDs and mobile phones with older consumers only to find them unable to read the type or the screen because these were designed for younger eyes. Although the New Old are generally fitter than previous generations, they may have even greater problems in some areas than their forebears. Prolonged exposure to loud music over the years will increase hearing loss. In fact, hearing aids are at a premium today: the average waiting time for one in the UK is now almost a year. Ageing is also something new to them. They have been late to accept it, considering themselves young even when middle-aged, so brands will benefit from helping accommodate them to it.

It is not just product developers that need to consider the New Old, but marketers and planners too. For them the issue will be more about New Old *attitudes*. Growing up at a time of non-conformism, the New Old typically still see themselves as rebels, even though many lead relatively conservative lives. Typically well educated, they respond well to a scientific or data-based approach. L'Oréal has made the now 67-year-old, rebellious Baby Boomer heroine Jane Fonda the face of its anti-ageing range. Dove's Pro-Age campaign created a positive message out of the ageing process. Italian manufacturer Barilla promotes its probiotic food range Alixir at events where nutritionists, writers and even DJs talk about the theme of 'living better'.

As the New Old's influence grows there will be more opportunities to target them more effectively. There are an increasing number of media outlets focused on the demographic, from retro sports channel ESPN Classic to Netherlands public broadcasting channel Max, which provides programming tailored specifically to today's 50-plus audience. There has also been a rise in the number of social networking websites targeted at the over-50s market, such as Wanobe.com, SagaZone.co.uk and Eons.com. Marketers across all sectors will be able to use these outlets for targeted marketing campaigns, and smart media companies will be able to add their own outlets to the list. As the Silver Surfer trend grows, the fastest growth in e-commerce today is among the over-55s, and it is estimated that nearly a quarter of European over-55s will be shopping online by 2010.[31] E-commerce will therefore become an increasingly important distribution channel for Grey products.

NOTES

1. British Phonographic Institute, 2006
2. Office of National Statistics, 2005
3. Office of National Statistics, 2006
4. Food Standards Authority, 2005
5. Department of Trade and Industry, 2006
6. IRDSI, December 2001
7. ROAR, 2001
8. British Social Attitudes Survey, 1999
9. *The Economist*, 2007
10. Association of German Concert Agencies (IDKV), 2006
11. Insee, 2007
12. Future Foundation, 2007
13. nVision, 2007
14. Blizzard Entertainment, 2008
15. Ning Blog, 2008
16. Business Wire, 2005
17. Eurostat, 2007
18. British Phonographic Institute, 2004
19. Isis Research, 2003
20. British Association for Sexual Health and HIV, 2005
21. Mental Health Foundation, 2006
22. Datamonitor, 2006
23. Consumer Credit Counselling Service, 2006
24. nVision, 2006
25. Hitwise, 2007
26. Help the Aged, 2007
27. *Time*, 2006
28. Eurostat, 2007
29. Euromonitor, 2007
30. Euromonitor, 2007
31. Future Foundation, 2007

Index

NB: page numbers in *italic* indicate figures

Don't let anyone tell you that the world is flat

www.koganpage.com

Fresh thinking for business today